Business information:
Systems and strategies

Business information: Systems and strategies

Carol Cashmore

Principal Lecturer
City of London Polytechnic

with Richard Lyall

Senior Lecturer
City of London Polytechnic

PRENTICE HALL

NEW YORK   LONDON   TORONTO   SYDNEY   TOKYO   SINGAPORE

First published 1991 by
Prentice Hall International (UK) Ltd
Campus 400, Maylands Avenue
Hemel Hempstead
Hertfordshire HP2 7EZ
A division of
Simon & Schuster International Group

Typeset in 10 on 12 pt Plantin
by MHL Typesetting Ltd, Coventry

Printed and bound in Great Britain by
Redwood Books, Trowbridge, Wiltshire.

Library of Congress Cataloging-in-Publication Data

Cashmore, Carol.
  Business information: systems and strategies / by
Carol Cashmore with Richard Lyall
    p.   cm.
  Includes bibliographical references and index.
  ISBN 0-13-552720-1
  1. Management–Data processing. 2. Management
information systems, I. Lyall, Richard. II. Title.
  HD30.2.C39 1991
  658.4′038′011 – dc20

British Library Cataloguing in Publication Data

Cashmore, Carol
  Business information.
  1. Management. Information systems
  I. Title II. Lyall, Richard
  658.4038

  ISBN 0-13-552720-1
  ISBN 0-13-552712-0 pbk

5 95

Contents

3 The flow of data and information   39

4 The right information system for the organization   52

Part Two Techniques and technologies for providing information

5 Fast cycle systems   73

Preface

Business information systems have been transformed in recent years by rapidly improving technology. Today there is a growing realization that managing information and information technology is far more important than has been perceived in the past. It is so important that information and information systems are considered by many to be major business assets, perhaps even the most important asset. Yet, because they are invisible — unlike traditional business assets such as equipment and buildings — organizations have been slow to realize their importance. Organizations have even been driven out of business because of their failure to recognize this fact.

Planning for information and information systems is a major business activity: all managers — not just technical managers as was the case in the past — must be involved in assessing and determining future needs. If new technology is used only to do faster what has always been done before — namely 'number crunching' — most of the potential benefits of improved technology will not be realized. Because of the added importance and scope that recent technological advances have given to business information systems top management must be actively involved in planning for changes in the organization's information systems. For example, the information system can and should be used as a strategic weapon to gain competitive advantage.

This book reflects the recent change in opinion on the nature of business information systems and is written for business students from the point of view of a manager rather than of the data processing or information systems department. Therefore, there are no chapters on computer hardware, software, system design, etc. Instead the book attempts to show how good business information systems, whether they use technological advances or not, can lead, for example, to better decision making, quicker attention to the customer's needs and a reduction in stocks and costs.

The book also attempts to take the mystique out of an information system and subordinate it to the information needs of the business. Technology is a fine servant but there is a danger that if it is not mastered organizations will be swamped under the ever growing weight of partially digested data. In the words of Peter Drucker:

> Advanced data-processing technology isn't necessary to create an information-based organization...the British built just such an organization in India when 'information technology' meant the quill pen and barefoot runners were the telecommunications system.[1]

But as technology becomes more prevalent all managers have to select, analyze and diagnose — that is choose and obtain the information they require — even more intensively. If they do not they risk being swamped by the data generated.

The book emphasizes the importance of information rather than the system that provides it. A system, that is the equipment and infrastructure, is worthless if it does not provide information which the organization requires. Part One is devoted to what information is, or should be, required by the management of a particular business before any consideration is made of the type of system required and its possible components.

Part Two looks at the different information techniques and technologies which are currently available for providing information. The introduction to this part emphasizes the importance of the information or communication infrastructure. This is because it is the base upon which data and information flow from their source, the collection point, to the user, the decision maker. This theme is picked up again in Part Three which considers how to formulate and implement information strategy. This includes a detailed study of security and controls and of the behaviourial problems that might arise.

Although aimed primarily at the business student, the book is also written with non-technical managers in mind who might wish to update their knowledge. It therefore adopts an easy-to-read style and avoids technical or specialist words wherever possible. In addition many of the points made in the text are illustrated with examples or cases taken from the business world.

Note

1. Peter Drucker, 'The coming of the new organization' *Harvard Business Review*, Jan./Feb. 1988.

Part One

Information

Part One

Interpretation

Business information and information systems

1

SCOPE AND CONTENTS

This chapter starts by considering the power of information and its value as an invisible asset. Next the proliferation of information in recent years is mentioned before defining business information and information systems for the purposes of this book. The difference between data and information is outlined. Then information systems are considered: their purpose, importance and financial value. Lastly the influence that information systems may have in influencing the strategies and the structure of an organization is briefly discussed.

1.1 The power and value of information

Information, whether true or false, can have a major impact on events. In 1988 a report went out on the news lines that another nuclear disaster had taken place in the USSR similar to that of Chernobyl. Instantly the world's stock markets reacted and the gold price moved considerably. It was discovered a day later that the report was not true, it was in fact a test message. Similarly, rumours such as the death of the president of the USA have had a major impact on the stock markets for a few hours until they have been proved to be false. If an individual has a piece of information to which others are not privy, or receives information in advance of others, it may be used to advantage. In the previous example the information could be used to make money by determining which way the stock market would move and acting accordingly. An organization should use information in a similar manner to react more quickly than its competitors to a particular fact or circumstance. The organization which makes a strategic move first, if the move is correct, will improve and strengthen its position relative to its competitors.

Information is therefore a powerful and valuable asset. It must be actively sought, guarded and conserved. From an organization's point of view information is just as much an asset as its buildings and equipment. The resources of an organization have traditionally been recognized to be land and buildings, staff, money, materials and machines. These are all visible assets which are difficult to overlook. In contrast it is easy to ignore the invisible asset, information. Today it is recognized to be just as important as any other business asset; indeed some people regard it as being more important. Hiroyuki Itami, Professor of Management at Hitotsubashi University, adheres to this view and is of the opinion that real **competitive advantage** comes not from the visible assets but from the invisible assets which may collectively be described as information or information flows.[1] This opinion is derived from the assumption that all the visible resources may be bought or copied fairly quickly but the accumulation of corporate information takes many years.

Information bestows power and advantage upon its possessor, but these are realized only if the owner *uses* the information. It is not enough just to possess it. As with all assets ownership is not important, it is the use to which the asset is put which is important. This is true regardless of whether the asset is a piece of manufacturing equipment or information about customers' needs and desires concerning products.

1.2 The information torrent

The head of military intelligence in the USSR, Colonel-General Vladlen Mikhailov, said in an interview recently:

> We are interested in all new developments in the West. The same as your intelligence is interested in ours. Of course, the details differ with each side. But the methods that were used in the past, stealing things and bringing them over, are never used now. ... Now our lives are so full of information that you can find out almost anything without getting deeply involved in secrets. We take lots of magazines; we send people openly to exhibitions, conferences and airshows.[2]

Whether we are members of military intelligence, managers of a company or just ordinary citizens we are bombarded by information from all directions. Any specific piece of information which is required is nowadays fairly easy to come by. This was not the case in the past. For instance, nowadays books are much more plentiful than ever before. 'Information' books such as *The Good Food Guide* or *Where to Stay in the Loire Valley* abound and every abstruse minute area of knowledge seems to have at least one book devoted to it. As a consequence of this deluge of information in the workplace, some individuals feel that just keeping up to date with it is a lifetime's work let alone using it to any advantage. Many others, though, appear to welcome the torrent and collect information avidly. Whether this assists them in carrying out their job effectively is open to question as much of this information may be of little real use and may not make them more efficient managers. Robert Heller summed up this type of manager rather well, if somewhat harshly:

> Managers are to information as alcoholics are to booze. They consume enormous amounts, constantly crave more, but have great difficulty in digesting their existing intake.

On the whole the availability of information is generally considered a good thing but this is not always so: some jobs have become more difficult because information is now so widespread that it is available to the world at large. People who gain their living by accumulating information or knowledge and then using it to their financial advantage may well find now that this knowledge is readily available to all. Consider, for instance, a professional gambler who makes a living by betting on the horses. Years ago the gambler would painstakingly gather information by watching races, gallops and noting every run on every type of going. Today specialist publishers such as Timeform, produce annuals giving details of every horse including information such as the going and distances which suit it plus a form rating. Timeform also provide cards for most meetings with up to date information on all the runners. So anyone investing a small sum of money can have access to almost the same information as the professional gambler. Whether they *use* it to such effect is another matter. However, it makes the professional gambler's job a much harder one.

But what is information? Is the torrent of 'information' that daily bombards the average individual via the papers or television really information? The recent instance of BSE, mad cow disease, illustrates this question well. The British public were showered with vast quantities of what purported to be information. In fact it was not information but rather a series of speculations and hypotheses drawn from incomplete data. The interpretation of data is fraught with difficulties and what is known as the *post hoc ergo propter hoc* syndrome (the fallacious belief that when one event follows another, the first must be the cause of the second) is liable to take place if an individual with few interpretational skills analyzes sets of data. One instance of this would be the conclusion that watching television causes lung cancer since lung cancer has been found to be more prevalent among those individuals who watch television for long periods than in those who do not. The reasoning is, of course, invalid. Often, too, published data are not **primary data** but second or third hand. Thus secondary sets of data with quite different interpretation may be published which were originally drawn from the same source. This occurred during the energy crisis in the UK in 1973 when at least fifteen sets of data from apparently different sources were published: on examination they were derived from only four primary sources.

1.3 What is business information?

Business information embraces all information flows both within the organization and between the organization and external parties — customers, suppliers, the general public, government, etc. Business information, therefore, may be considered to be any item of fact, rumour or speculation which may be accumulated by the organization and used by an individual, whether employee or manager, to make decisions which will improve his or her performance and thus improve the performance of the organization. It also includes outward flowing information about the organization to, for instance, a potential customer so that he can make an informed purchasing decision.

Good business information is without doubt one of the most important assets that an organization may possess. It is, however, an intangible or invisible asset, that is one which an accountant or valuer cannot easily place a price upon. Hiroyuki Itami put forward a simple thesis,[1] namely, that all invisible assets are based on one kind of information flow or another. He identified types of information and information channels (listed below) and divided them into three groups. The information channels are listed together with information as invisible assets even though the reader might consider the former to be visible assets. The reason for this is the interdependency of the two: information can scarcely be called information if it is not available or in a suitable form to be used, thus it is of little value if it does not flow through channels in a suitable form for the individual who requires it.

1. **External information** (inward flowing)
   - Accumulated customer information, e.g. customer needs and preferences.
   - Technological know-how and skills, e.g. R&D and engineering knowledge about equipment and materials.
   - Distribution channels: their existence and capacity to obtain information.
   - Customer networks: their existence and capacity to obtain information.

2. **Corporate information** (outward flowing)
   - Reputation
   - Advertising know-how   } all required to create positive infor-
   - Marketing know-how   } mation in the minds of customers about
   - Brand names   the company and its products

3. **Internal information**
   - Corporate culture, e.g. style, spread and effectiveness of information flow.
   - Managerial skills, e.g. interpretation and responsiveness.
   - International management, e.g. knowledge of different cultures

The three different types of information are illustrated in Figure 1.1. Traditionally far too much emphasis has been placed on internal information, in particular the collection of facts and figures concerning what has been done, how quickly and how much it cost. The average organization has only recently become aware of

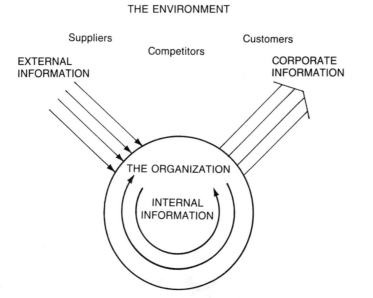

Figure 1.1 The flow of business information.

the immense value of information flows to and from the customer and the world at large, and the potential of these flows in achieving competitive advantage (although brand names and advertising have been used and appreciated for many years).

The following example illustrates the power of the invisible asset of information and its associated distribution channels. Reuters is in the information business, it supplies news and financial information to customers around the world. Virtually all Reuters' assets are information assets (such as computers and networks) which permit information to flow from its source to the customers. These information channels or invisible assets have become so valuable that they are threatening the existence of the traditional stock exchanges. Previously stock exchanges had a national monopoly but this is being broken as organizations such as Reuters, which previously supplied information on stocks only, begin to set up their own dealing systems. Many organizations now appear to prefer to trade off-exchange through Reuters — thus highlighting the power to be gained from invisible assets.

1.4 What is an information system?

In order for information to flow from its source to an individual who can use it, some sort of system, physical or otherwise, is required to collect, store and then to move the information within the organization. This book will consider a variety of systems which relate to different parts of an organization and provide information for different levels of managers and employees. The word 'system' should also be considered in a broad sense, and may be looked on as being any channel or chain of channels, visible or not, through which information can flow and in which it can be stored either permanently or temporarily. Thus information channels may consist of a mixture of equipment, people and procedures.

Too often we think of an information system as being a series of computer systems linked to **databases** holding stored information. This is far from being the case. People may be regarded as information systems or channels: as individuals go about their daily lives they collect snippets of information from a wide range of sources, most of which is stored in the brain, but some is stored in a personal filofax or diary. As they move around they carry the information with them before disseminating it or putting it to use themselves. A salesperson behaves in the same way when visiting customers or potential customers. He or she collects data about them which is stored until it is needed at a later date either to complete a sale or to make a further sale. If the salesperson feeds the data into a personal computer and it is then stored on the organization's database until the salesperson or a colleague wishes to retrieve it, two information systems have thus merged or been linked to form a larger one.

It is this linking of individual information systems that produces a corporate information system. A good corporate information system is not necessarily built by spending considerable sums of money. This is because it takes time and effort to build a system and the system consists of more than just physical assets. It is in fact built up over the years by the collective skills of the individuals in the organization and as such is a precious asset that cannot easily be replaced. Hence Hiroyuki Itami's view on the competitive advantage of invisible assets.

An information system therefore is comprised not only of hardware or formal predetermined channels but also of informal, transient and invisible channels. The hardware or formal channels consist of such things as paper, filing cabinets, computers and telecommunication lines and these provide a fairly rigid or permanent framework. On the other hand, an ever-changing flexible framework is provided by individuals meeting and talking to one another.

However diverse different types of information system may appear to be they are all made up of four elements:

- Collection of data: facts, figures or rumours.
- Storage of data: whether on a computer, folders in a filing cabinet or in one's head.
- Manipulation of data: arranging, collating, aggregating and interpreting it.
- Presentation of information: providing the potential user with information in the most suitable form such as the spoken word, pages of figures or pictures.

1.5 Data and information

The raw material of an information system is data. If it is to survive in a useful way the information system must continually be fed the required data. Data comprise facts and figures which have been collected from a variety of sources, both from within the company and outside. They are not information until they have been arranged in a suitable manner for a particular individual to comprehend and extract meaning. Information, therefore, is data that have been assembled in a suitable form to provide an individual with knowledge in a specific way on a specific subject so that the individual may make decisions. Or as Peter Drucker so succinctly put it: 'information is data endowed with relevance and purpose'. It is important to note that different individuals may need the same data arranged in quite different ways to give them information. These relationships are shown in Figure 1.2.

Information which does not contribute to the aim of the business is a costly irrelevance, therefore data should be carefully examined for relevance before it is collected. It is far too easy, as technology improves, for an organization to expand the amount of information it provides managers without considering whether *all* this information is necessary.

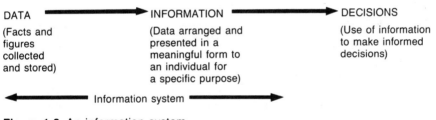

DATA   ⟶   INFORMATION   ⟶   DECISIONS

(Facts and figures collected and stored)   (Data arranged and presented in a meaningful form to an individual for a specific purpose)   (Use of information to make informed decisions)

Information system

Figure 1.2 An information system.

1.6 The purposes of an information system

A corporate information system is made up of different subsystems which have different functions and purposes. There are many different subsystems but they all attempt to fulfil one of the following purposes:

- To collect and store data which are capable of being turned into useful information which *may* be required by the organization at a later date.
- To provide, in a suitable form, the **operational information** required

by employees to perform their jobs to the best of their abilities and to ensure the smooth day-to-day running of the organization.

■ To provide, in a suitable form, **strategic information** to managers so that they can make the best possible decisions about the future of the organization.

■ To extend the **value chain** of the business. By this it is meant that the organization's information system should link with external information systems, in particular to those of suppliers and customers, thus creating benefit and providing further information. For example, a manufacturer of a product would find it very useful to analyze final customer purchases through a particular type of retail outlet.

The relationship between the four purposes or functions is illustrated in Figure 1.3. This illustration attempts to show in a simplified form the different functions of information, the way in which these functions interrelate and ultimately assist in the making of different decisions.

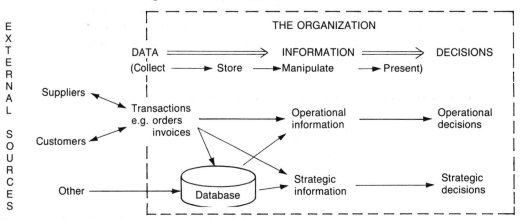

Figure 1.3 An information system showing linkages and flows.

In the past there was much emphasis on the collecting and storing of data relating to business transactions and on the provision of operational information. This was because when the functions were carried out manually it required a large percentage of the organization's staff to record the data and turn them into a suitable form for operational control. So much time was spent getting data that they assumed an importance they did not really merit. In a relatively static world, as the business world was in the past, the future requires little planning, thus the emphasis falls on the day-to-day running and control of activities. The use of information systems in management decision making *for strategic purposes* has not been emphasized until recently. If several organizations are in competition, the one which has the best information (that is current and relevant) should be in the position to make the best decisions and thus formulate winning strategies and achieve competitive advantage. Further potential exists for most organizations to develop and improve the provision of information in the strategic decision making area. Similarly, considerable potential benefits are still to be realized by extending the value chain by linking different businesses together. This aspect is still in its infancy and many organizations have yet to become aware of the potential benefits.

1.7 The importance of information systems

If an organization is to have a successful long-term future its primary aim must be to meet the needs of its customers in a more satisfactory and profitable manner than its competitors. Any expenditure or activity within the organization can only be justified in terms of this primary aim. It follows, therefore, that any expenditure on information systems must generate some benefit that is perceived as such by the customer, or must reduce the cost of providing the service or product to the customer. Thus the installation of an information system just to store more data which will provide more informaton is of little use. The information obtained must actually be used to give the customer a superior service or product. This may mean, for example, a better quality service or product, a cheaper one or a faster delivery time. Networked information systems and **expert systems** (discussed in detail in later chapters) have great potential and can play a major part in achieving this objective. The following illustrations will explain this more clearly.

At the operational level, a network could be set up by an organization which provides a maintenance service for office equipment such as a photocopier. When customers telephone in to report a breakdown they may be connected to a national central office instead of being connected to their local office as would previously have been the case. The telephone operator at the central office is able to select the nearest repairer free to do the job. The repairer is then able to get details about the customer and the equipment from a computer terminal. This gives a case history from which the repairer is able to diagnose possible problems and identify the spare parts which might be required and which ought, therefore, to be taken to the site. Thus the customer will get a faster and more efficient service as the repairer is unlikely to have to make two journeys — one to see the equipment and diagnose the problem and a second, after acquiring a spare part, to fit it.

An **expert system**, which is a system containing specific knowledge, could also be used in a repair business. Equipment specifications change regularly and repairers are often called out to deal with a model or product they have never seen before and, therefore, have no knowledge of. With a terminal in the van giving access to an expert system the repairer is able to acquire the knowledge and diagnostic information he needs to carry out the repair. This will speed up the job considerably and make sure that the product is repaired properly the first time round.

1.8 The right information at the right price

A system, whether traditional or 'high tech', is of little use if it does not provide the information that is required. It may provide a considerable amount of information, but if it does not provide the one or two pieces that are vital for the organization, or if it does not provide the information in a useful form, then it is of little use. Two major internal problems that an organization faces are:

- Costing accurately its various services or products.
- Assessing the profitability of servicing individual customers.

The organization needs this information so that in doing battle with its competitors it is not left servicing only the unprofitable customers, or producing a poor mix of services or products which consists mainly of those that other organizations consider insufficiently profitable. This information is vital for a business, but too often it has not been properly available to managers when making strategic decisions.

Technology, of course, comes at a price. Any system must provide a benefit — additional, more reliable or more timely information that has a specific use. It is difficult enough to estimate the costs of running and maintaining the system, but it is much more difficult to put a value on the long-term benefits. Who can accurately assess the long-term benefits of altering product mix or customer mix? What new products, markets or benefits might it lead to in the future? As a result of this difficulty some systems are accepted with blind faith and other perfectly good ones are turned down, usually by accountants, because they cannot be financially justified as they do not have a demonstrably quick payback. A manager should have the ability to feel instinctively whether a project is the right one for his organization without relying unduly on figures or making acts of faith.

1.9 The influence of an information system on business structure and strategy

If an information system is to be successful it must be suitable for the organization. In the past it was felt that systems should play a passive role, fit unobtrusively into the business, generate data and provide information in standard ways that had come to be accepted over the decades. Unfortunately the information provided by these systems was not always the information the organization really needed. Nowadays, however, the relevance of the information provided is improving and technology has made information systems very powerful. So powerful in fact that whole business strategies can be formulated around them. The information system in some instances governs the structure of the business and follows immediately in the decision chain after determining a potential business strategy. This chain is illustrated in Figure 1.4.

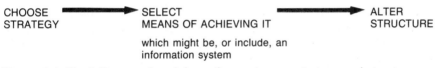

Figure 1.4 The influence of an information system on strategy and structure.

Sometimes the change in structure brought about by the information system may be very small-scale. Thus the installation of an accounting package in a small business may make the employment of a part-time book-keeper no longer necessary. A larger-scale structural change caused by the information system might be the removal of the need to employ a group of people working directly on the product or service. Alternatively, if the information system is linked to suppliers' information systems the structure of the purchasing department will change considerably. The information system could even remove the need for a whole layer of management. In these examples the information system has altered the structure simply by removing jobs. However, this is quite a rare occurrence in practice; instead it is much more likely that an information system will cause a change in the nature of the organization thus affecting the composition of the organization structure. Examples of this type of influence are given in Chapter 4.

The examples in the previous paragraph illustrate changes brought about by an information system in the internal structure of an organization only. However, in some cases, the information system has the power to alter the structure of a whole industry. A small number of systems have sufficient impact to increase or decrease the number of suppliers, customers or competitors, or they may even alter the type and nature of service or product provided. The strategy followed by Reuters in developing specific information channels (which was described briefly in section 1.3) is one example of the impact of an information system on an industry. Another is that of the large retail chain stores which have become involved in the financial services business which until recently was the prerogative of the banks. This came about initially by the retail stores issuing in-store credit cards to their customers which entailed building a database containing information about the card-holders. Using this database, companies have been able to extend considerably the financial services they supply. Marks & Spencer, for example, which issued its first chargecard only a few years ago has already extended its services into insurance and unit trusts. Thus the information system led to a dramatic change in the products and services provided. This has had the effect of changing the structure of part of the retail industry and leading it into a line of business which had previously been considered totally unrelated.

If any final proof of the power and influence of an information system is needed, consider the influence of television — the most powerful of all the information media. It is powerful in that it can communicate instantly and it communicates with two of our senses — sight and hearing — rather than just the one (as is normal with most other media). It also reaches many more people than any other information medium. Proof of its influence was demonstrated clearly in Romania when fighting took place around the television station: both sides realized the importance of controlling the medium in order to convey their views of events to the people. Satellite broadcasting has extended the influence of television and spread the views of an individual or group around the globe — thus expanding the knowledge and horizons of individuals in some countries. Exactly the same phenomenon has occurred within the business world where a better information system can make the consumer more aware of different product options as well as giving the company a better understanding of the consumer, its competitors and the economy.

NOTES

1. Eduardo Punset and Gerry Sweeney (eds), *Information Resources and Corporate Development* (Pinter Publishers, 1989).
2. From an interview with Carey Schofield for a book on Soviet armed forces.

FURTHER READING

Punset, Eduardo and Gerry Sweeney (eds), *Information Resources and Corporate Development* (Pinter Publishers, 1989), especially for the chapter on the invisible asset by Hiroyuki Itami.

EXERCISES

1. Consider the type of information system that a modern railway company might use to provide information on the flow of traffic along a single track line in a remote part of its network. Contrast this with the system used in the UK a hundred years

ago which necessitated the guard collecting a baton before the train was permitted to pass through the single track section. The baton was left at the other end of the single track line for the next train to collect. What merits do you see in each system?

2. Determine the single most important piece of information that you would like to know for certain about the future in order to achieve your aim in the following circumstances. You wish to:
   (a) Pass your examinations.
   (b) Be promoted at work.
   (c) Make £1m in the next year.
   (d) Write a best-selling novel.

2 What information does management require?

SCOPE AND CONTENTS

A: From decisions to data. This section deals with the poor provision of information that is common in most organizations. It takes the view that the decisions that managers need to make should be the starting point for determining the information needs of management. It outlines the identification of critical success factors in order to establish what decisions are made and what information is needed to make the decisions. Once the information need is clarified it is possible to determine the data that should be collected. Finally the importance of both timing and the mode of presentation in making the information valuable is considered. In this context executive systems are discussed.

B: Information needs. The information needed by management is divided into two main categories: information for strategic decisions and information for operating decisions. The different needs and problems of each are considered. The budgeting system is examined in detail as a system for providing a basis for operating decisions and its inadequacies discussed.

C: Illustrative example: the costing system. The costing system's uses are outlined and its success in providing information which is needed is examined. Four different informational needs from the costing system are considered: published accounts, operational control, product cost measurement and customer account profitability.

A: FROM DECISIONS TO DATA

2.1 Data should not dictate the information provided

In many organizations no informed decision is made concerning the information which should be provided to managers. This failure leaves the 'paper-processing tail wagging the information dog'.[1] When little attention is paid to the real information needs of a manager the systems which record the day-to-day transactions of the business, such as payroll, invoicing and stock, determine what information is provided. These paper-processing systems generate data which are turned into information for management — therefore information is a by-product of the day-to-day transaction systems. Transaction systems generate vast amounts of data which in turn can generate vast amounts of 'information' and normally this 'information' is circulated to all managers who may be considered to be slightly interested in it. The information being circulated is not usually real or useful information to an individual manager as it has not been designed to meet that individual's specific needs. One senior executive ascertained that he received no less than ninety-seven reports in the course of a month. Almost all of these were originated by someone else who felt that he should be receiving this 'vital information'. Presumably it would take most of the month to read and digest the ninety-seven reports; and if this were done little time would be left for running the business.

Permitting the paper-processing (transaction) systems and other managers to determine the information supplied results in most managers finding that:

- They receive much too much information.
- Information is not tailor-made to their individual needs.
- Information is not presented in the most suitable form for them.
- Information is not provided when it is needed.

Thus too often management are not in control of their personal information system and as a result they have to make do with poor quality information. In recent years, however, many middle managers have taken matters into their own hands and have started to collect and store their own information. This is because the growth in use of PCs (personal computers) has given them a better understanding of what information could be provided and the wherewithal to provide it. Where the required information is not being provided adequately from a central source, such as the information centre, managers have started to provide it for themselves. This they can do on their own PCs by setting up their own small databases to supplement that of the organization thus producing their own reports in, what is to them, an easily usable form. From the point of view of the company this is not always to be encouraged because it is wasteful of the organization's resources and can give rise to security problems. In addition it enables managers to keep information to themselves in order to create an information blockage, or power base, so as to gain importance and kudos for themselves.

2.2 Management decisions dictate the data collected

Top managers do not, on the whole, have the keyboard skills nor the time required to collect relevant data and build their own reports. It is vital, therefore, that the right information to meet their needs is supplied — and this requires that the correct steps are taken to identify those needs. In section 1.5 it was said that data are the raw material of information and that information is the raw material for decision making. This process was illustrated in Figure 1.2. It might thus be thought that information is dependent on the data available. To a certain extent this is true, as it will always prove impossible, in practical and cost—benefit terms, to supply every piece of data that could possibly relate to a particular business decision. However, *the data should not, and must not, determine the information supplied*. Rather the decisions to be made must determine what information is supplied and in turn the information to be supplied must determine the data to be collected. Often the transaction systems are allowed to dictate the provision of and be the sole supplier of information. If this is the case then decisions which require other data, for example external data relating to economic forecasts and competitors' moves, cannot properly be made. The information system *must* provide what is needed for decision making rather than management having to make do with information provided from an unsuitable system. This requires identifying what information each individual manager needs.

2.3 Decision making analysis

'What information do you require?' is a very simple question to ask, and also to answer, one might have thought. This is not so. It is in fact quite a difficult question to answer and the answer may well be misinterpreted by the questioner, thus further aggravating the situation. The questioner will normally be the provider of the information — he may be an information systems manager, a management accountant or, indeed, anyone else whose job it is to provide information.

One way to ascertain the information that a manager requires is to use a decision making analysis technique (DMAT). This requires the decision maker to determine as far as possible the future decisions that he will make. From the decisions one can in turn determine the information necessary to make them. This method predicates that information is the raw material for decision making. Therefore, the starting point when determining what information is needed is to see what decisions are made by individual managers. The information required in its turn dictates the data that must be collected. It is not adequate just to collect convenient data and turn it into what may seem to someone else to be appropriate information for a particular manager to receive. The information needs of each manager may vary depending on the job and temperament of each individual. The only way, therefore, to ascertain the information needs of individuals is to ask them specifically what they require using DMAT.

2.4 Critical success factors

One of the most popular DMATs is the **critical success factor** method. This requires a manager to assess what factors are critical to successful fulfilment of his job. It has the added benefit to the manager that focussing on the key aspects of his job may clarify his role and make him more effective. The critical success factor method was first developed at the Massachusetts Institute of Technology in the late 1970s and can be applied both to the performance of an individual manager or to an organization as a whole. In any organization, between three and six factors can usually be identified as crucial to the performance of the organization. The factors might include a good distribution system, the ability to listen and respond to the customer, a successful research team and consistently effective advertising. The idea of critical success factors may be applied to the organization as a whole (see section 11.5) but for the present we are interested in critical success factors as they apply to individual managers. Just as an organization has its own particular success factors so does an individual manager. These are the areas of activity which must receive constant and careful attention if a manager is to be successful.

To determine the information needs of a manager by using the critical factor method requires the information provider to act as an analyst and to carry out several interviews or sessions with the manager. This process was described in 1979 by John Rockart (the director of the Center for Information Systems Research, Massachusetts Institute of Technology) as taking place in the following way.[1] In the first session the manager's goals should be recorded and the critical success factors that underlie these goals should be discussed. The interrelationship of the goals and critical success factors should then be discussed in order to clarify the position and possibly to combine or eliminate some of the latter. Then an initial attempt should be made to determine the specific pieces of information or measures needed to achieve the goals and their underlying critical success factors. The second session should review the results of the first after the analyst has had a chance to work on them and should then go on to consider the specific measures and possible reports in detail. A third session might be necessary in some instances. The total interview time should be between three and six hours. It is also necessary during the interviews to consider when and how frequently the measures and reports are needed. This is discussed further in section 2.5.

After studying the critical success factors, the analyst should then study the existing reports received by the manager to compare the current information supplied with the information determined by the critical success factor interview. It is suggested that this should be done *after* the interview, rather than before, so that the analyst's vision is not too blinkered for the interview by some preconceived idea of what is required. Any major discrepancy between current and required information should be investigated before the new system is put into practice.

The process of 'decision making analysis' may seem to be either too simple or just a waste of effort and time. This is not so. The fact that managers are not being provided with the information they require proves that it should be done and any expenditure in this area should be amply repaid by financial gains arising from better decision making. Unfortunately, the benefits of investing time and money in information systems are usually hard to quantify. This may be one reason why insufficient time is given to ascertaining the precise information needs of managers.

2.5 Timing and presentation of information

Providing the precise information required by a manager is only half the battle. The timing and presentation of the information are also vital if it is to be of use. Perhaps in the past it was justifiable to provide infrequent information and to update it only rarely. However, with today's technology there is no excuse for not providing information as frequently as is necessary. Out of date information is of little use to a manager and its provision may be a total waste of time. The one-time UK Prime Minister Harold Macmillan, when talking about the value of official statistics in the management of the economy, once said that using them was 'like planning a train journey with last year's Bradshaw Guide'. Many managers know just how he felt.

The main criterion for deciding the frequency of the information, or even whether it is required at all, is that the benefit obtained must be greater than the extra cost incurred. Organizations are changing and operational control information, in particular, is often now supplied much more quickly than in the past. One of the main reasons for the change has been the introduction of new working habits such as the 'just-in-time' philosophy, discussed in Chapter 5. This requires up to the minute information for monitoring the workflow.

Because two managers making the same decision will not necessarily require the same information all managers should have personalised information systems. The technology for this exists today. However, far too many companies are still stuck in the rut of providing standard reports at standard times for their managers and have not yet realized the freedom that technology allows in this field. In the past it was not possible to vary the presentation greatly because it would have taken too much time and effort to present the same information in a range of ways; today it is quite possible to draw information from a database and present it in a variety of formats. Standard reports produced without regard to the training and background of their recipients are unsatisfactory in terms of presentation. For instance, not all managers like to look at a page of figures: some like the information in graphical form. For example, the heavy reliance on pages of figures is the traditional financial approach. It may be unsuitable and can easily be avoided today. A page crammed with figures may provide information very satisfactorily for an accountant but may be most unsuitable for many other managers. Top management seem to have a definite preference for visual or graphical presentation, wherever possible.

Unsatisfactory presentation of information is not just the prerogative of business. Kevin Keegan, the ex-England footballer, once commented on Don Revie, the ex-manager of England's football team, in an interview on television. He said that Revie provided each player with a complete dossier of information on the playing habits of their opposite number in the coming match. This would contain information such as how many times the opponent shot at goal with his left foot rather than his right. All of this was presented in statistical form in tables on pages and pages of paper. How useful this is to a footballer who has to go out the next day and react instantly to his opponent's moves is doubtful — perhaps a video would have been better. Kevin Keegan said that the team did not use the information but they found the back of the paper very useful for keeping the score at cards while killing time prior to the match.

2.6 Executive information systems

The use of computers had until recently done little to improve the presentation of information. For lower level managers, who have been using information from computerized systems for many years, presentation is not an issue. This is because they are dealing with only a limited range of information which they use regularly. Thus the presentation is at least familiar to them even if it is bad. Top level managers on the other hand are a different matter. In many cases they have neither the time nor the will to learn to operate a non 'user-friendly' system or even one which requires a modicum of learning such as a spreadsheet. It is so much easier to open the door and shout for the information from a secretary or subordinate. However, during the 1980s executive information systems (EIS) started to become popular. They are designed to be easy and quick to use. Thus the 'dialogue' or communication between user and machine is straightforward and, therefore, satisfactory for top managers. Traditional keyboards are replaced by touch screens or infra-red keypads, and complicated commands are replaced by 'hot spots' or icons (pictorial representations). Executive information systems not only allow good communication, they also allow managers to find the information they need for themselves easily and quickly. This is done by moving down from broad headings of information to the specific details: a process known as 'drilling down'. The various choices at each stage are presented in a clear manner — possibly pictorially as files in a filing cabinet. Alternatively the system may be 'drilled down' by touching a figure on the screen to call up an underlying report. Pointing at a picture of a graph may allow the information to be displayed that way. Lockheed–Georgia, one of the first companies to devise an executive information system, made theirs so simple that a manager could be taught how to use the system in fifteen minutes.[2] Written instructions were deliberately not prepared so that the system had to be simple. In addition it was recognized that most managers would not bother to read the instructions in a manual.

Executive systems allow top managers to obtain access to the information they require whenever they want it rather than having to wait to be provided with it. This is the start of a major change in the provision of information. It might be thought that it is no longer quite so important for the specialist information provider to determine what information is required if the manager can obtain it himself, but this is wrong. The data must be available to build into information and they must be unbiased and fit for their purpose. Therefore a knowledge of what information is required for which decisions is still vital. There is, however, a danger that when top managers can gain access to information themselves they may use it for purposes for which it was not prepared and is not really fit. An example of this might be the measure return on investment, capital or assets, for which there are different definitions for different purposes. The user must be aware of this and of the specific contents of the figure obtained from the information system and for what it may be used. (This information may be obtained from a data dictionary, described in detail in section 9.7.)

Information providers of the future will need to decide whether any information *at all* should be provided regularly for top managers or whether all information should be obtained by the manager when it is needed.

B: INFORMATION NEEDS

2.7   What decisions do managers make?

The decisions that managers make may be split into two broad categories: those relating to the formation of policy and those relating to the day-to-day running of the organization. In addition a third, or middle, category is often used, namely tactical decisions. This category is treated in Chapter 12. The two categories discussed in this chapter are:

- Strategic decisions.
- Operational decisions.

It is important that the providers of information recognize this division because the different decisions require different types of information, provided at different frequencies and probably in different formats.

The first category — strategic decisions — encompasses all one-off decisions which influence the future direction and strategy of the business, such as:

- Whether to takeover a competitor.
- Whether to start a price war.

- Whether to use a delivery company rather than company-owned vehicles.
- Whether to introduce a new product line.

This type of decision is made once only. Once made, the clock can rarely be wound back to remake it. Instead the effects of the decision remain and influence the future strategy and direction of the organization.

Operational decisions, in contrast, are shorter-term, repeat decisions which relate to the planning, co-ordinating, monitoring and control of the day-to-day activities of a business. Examples are:

- How many units to make today, tomorrow, next week.
- What staff are required in which department to do what job.
- Has the organization enough cash to meet its day-to-day needs.
- How to react to a material price increase.

This type of decision is continously being made and remade during the short-term planning and control cycle.

Every manager makes some decisions which fall into each category. On the whole lower management make more operational decisions and top management make more strategic ones. This is a very approximate distinction, however, and the types of decisions made often depend rather more on the type of business and the current circumstances of the business. It is also possible to divide the two broad categories of decision further. For instance, Chapter 12 studies tactical decisions which are decisions taken to implement a particular strategy. (That distinction, however, is unnecessary in the study of information needs.)

2.8 Information needed to make strategic decisions

As strategic decisions are one-off decisions it is extremely difficult to prescribe categories of information needs. At the time of making the decision on what information to supply to a manager to meet his needs many of the decisions to be made will not be known. Therefore, to assess accurately the information requirements will be quite impossible. However, the types of decision to be made will be known even if the precise decisions themselves are not. Thus it is quite possible to make a reasonable judgement as to what information is required.

It follows that not all of the information will be available when it is needed: instead some will have to be collected as required for a particular decision. The disadvantage of collecting data at this late stage is that the decision may be delayed. This could prove disastrous. On the other hand it is much cheaper to do it on this *ad hoc* basis and it is totally impossible on cost grounds to furnish a manager with all the data and information that he is ever likely to need when making strategic decisions. Thus an expedient balance must be sought. The bulk of the organization's information, however, will be collected on a standard basis either to be issued regularly or held against a specific need. Additional information will be collected on an *ad hoc* basis to supplement the standard information.

The information which may be needed by managers for decision making will include information concerning competitors, customers and the economic situation, in addition to information about the company itself. The interaction between competitors, customers and one's own company is sometimes referred to as the strategic triangle or the strategic three Cs and may be said to be the basis for all strategic decisions.[3] This is shown diagrammatically in Figure 2.1 where the three Cs are placed in the context of the expected economic and political situation. This diagram portrays a company 'fighting' with its competitors, in a particular economic and political environment, to provide customers with products and services which the customer considers to be better than those of the rivals.

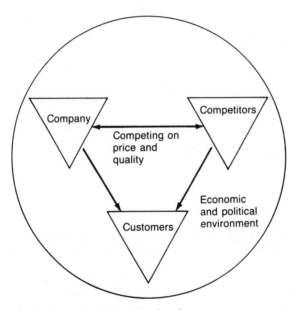

Figure 2.1 The strategic triangle.

Examples of the type of information needed by the organization for each category, or player, in the diagram are outlined below, together with the type of decision to be made. This list is not exhaustive and gives only the briefest idea of the type of information needed.

Competitors

Information   What are competitors' future plans in terms of new products, markets, etc.?

(Decisions   To determine one's own product market moves.)

Information   What is their attitude to sales volume versus profit margin?
(Decisions   Are competitors likely to cut margins and start a price war?
                How will they react if one's own company did this?)

Information   Will competitors invest to meet all possible sales or will their
                investment programme be cautious?
(Decisions   Those relating to market share, growth and one's own
                company's investment.)

Information   What are competitors'organization structures, i.e. who makes
                the decisions in specific areas?
(Decisions   How will they react to a particular event? E.g. a finance-
                dominated board of directors will react more conservatively than
                a marketing orientated one on a decision concerning a major
                business opportunity.)

Customers

The first information requirement will be a detailed analysis of existing
customers and their buying habits in order to focus on particular **segments**
of the market and to target future advertising.

Secondly, information on movements and changes in population and the effect
of these on the business's existing and potential customers is needed. For
instance, the proportion of young people in the population is decreasing in
Europe, so a company which sells clothes only to teenagers would have to
look for other customers/segments if it wished to continue to grow.

Changes in taste and habits must be monitored. For instance the Green
movement and its effect on established products. In Victorian times there
were companies selling bears' grease for the waxing of gentlemen's
moustaches — where are they now? Do they make furniture polish or
cosmetics or were they forced out of business?

Information on the cost of serving particular customers in terms of
production, delivery and service, so as to concentrate efforts on the most
profitable categories of customers.

Company

Apart from all the normal facts and figures which will already be provided
for operational control, a dispassionate study must be made of the company
to assess, among other things, the company's critical success factors (discussed
in section 2.4). For a company these are the attributes which, above all else,
give rise to a decisive competitive advantage if identified and utilised
effectively. The critical success factors might include the following:

- A brilliant research team which consistently gives the company a leading
  edge on new products.
- An extensive distribution network which puts competitors at a distinct
  disadvantage.

- A particularly rich deposit of ore which means that extraction costs are lower than those of competitors.
- A superior information network which means that more useful information is available more quickly than is the case with rivals.

To ascertain these a careful analysis of the organization must be made highlighting its particular strengths and weaknesses. The information needed to support and preserve these critical success factors must then be identified.

Economic and political environment

Information is needed to predict trends for specific countries or markets. This may include:

- Gross national product.
- Retail price index — to establish inflation trends.
- Trade deficit.
- Interest rates.
- Exchange rates.
- Commodity prices.
- Trade liberalization, e.g. the opening up of Eastern Europe.

This information will be required in order to provide a background for the decisions at international, national, regional and business sector levels so as to be in a position to answer such questions as:

- Should we be investing in new assets now, ready for an upturn in trade in eighteen months' time?
- Is our profitability going to suffer in the next year or so because of exchange rate movements since we rely heavily on the US market?
- What is the long term trend of raw material prices? What effect will that have on the product's sales, price and volume?

2.9 Information needed for operational decisions

As operational decision making involves making similar decisions over and over again it should be easy to predict the information required. Most organizations' information providers think they know precisely the information required for operational decisions. However, this is not always so. This topic is discussed in more detail in the illustrative case later in this chapter where the adequacy of the costing system for providing information for different purposes is considered.

Once knowledge of the information required has been ascertained a suitable system can be set up for acquiring and presenting it. Information for operational decisons will be required regularly, every month, week, day, hour or possibly every minute depending on the nature of the decision. Manufacturing processes, such as a plant filling bottles with a precise amount of liquid or one generating nuclear energy, will require information continuously. Information is needed for every primary activity in the business. For instance, the production and marketing functions will need information on the following:

- Production: number of units made and to be made
                number of rejects
                machine breakdowns
                machine set-up times
                labour productivity
                labour efficiency
                stock and work in progress units
                material waste
                material and labour costs

- Marketing: customer orders
               customer leads
               product mix
               product availability
               product margins
               discounts given
               promotion
               marketing costs

Some of the information in the list will be required hourly or daily in order to plan, monitor and control the production cycle and to make best use of marketing leads. Other information such as cost information may only be required monthly. As information for operational decisions is required at frequent intervals it will normally be provided by the information department in the form of standard reports.

Information for strategic decisions, on the other hand, may not be specifically provided but will probably be available on the computer database for the manager to obtain as required. Sometimes the data for strategic decisions will be turned into information ready for the manager to retrieve. On other occasions managers may prefer to dip into the data, collecting and arranging them themselves to meet their needs. This 'dipping into data', rearranging standard information and making unusual connections can be of considerable benefit in that relationships between different factors may be uncovered of which management were completely unaware.

2.10   Budgetary control subsystem

The **annual budget** with its monthly reports for control purposes has been the focus for many operational decisions. The budget usually contains predictions of every single amount that will be spent in the coming year, even down to the last biro which will be taken from the stationery store. It is planned by cost category as well as by department so that control may be exercised from either angle. With its emphasis on finance it provides good information for operational decisions relating to costs but it neglects non-financial information. Therefore, if virtually all that is provided for management is the budget and its control statements most managers will be operating under severe difficulties. It can be seen from the lists of production and marketing information needed, given in section 2.9, that few items are cost items.

Operational control is achieved when the actual results are compared with the budget. The differences are known as 'variances'. The comparison has traditionally been done monthly on statements with a standard layout for all departments. Managers are expected to scan their statements for adverse variances and then take action to correct them thus controlling future performance and expenditure or, if the variances are favourable, to capitalize on them. That this process has not been satisfactory has been known for a long time but little seems to have been done to improve it. In 1952 Chris Argyris, who had been studying employee responses to budgets, quoted the replies of some supervisors on the adequacy of the monthly statement which highlighted the adverse variances. One said:

> Let's say the budget tells me where I was off. I didn't make it. That's of interest. But it doesn't tell me the important thing of why I didn't make it or how I am going to make it next time. Oh sure, they might say all I need to do is increase production and cut waste. Well, I know that. The question is how to do it?[4]

Perhaps that reaction was expecting too much from an information system in the 1950s but companies should be trying to provide some help in that direction today. One or two US companies have tried to predict future variances to help their managers control activities. These predicted variances show the effect that current changes will have upon future results and serve to guide managers as to which are the most important items to control because they are likely to recur. In the rare cases where this system is used it seems to work well and managers look at the predicted future variances rather than the ones for the past month. However, even this would not have been a great deal of help to the complaining supervisor from the 1950s who wanted to be told *how* to put things right.

The normal monthly variance reports are generally of little help. They provide the recipient with little information of which he was not already aware. Nor do they provide the information necessary to make future decisions or take control action. The reports may even be counter productive: for example, they may have the effect of 'rubbing salt into the wound'. This could occur when a manager receives a statement with adverse variances one of which was caused when a piece of machinery broke down nearly a month ago. The manager had spent a fraught day trying to get it repaired as quickly as possible to avoid production hold-ups, and a certain amount of work had to be rerouted, etc. Now, just when he has forgotten it he is reminded of the problem for no real reason: it will not help the future of the business for the manager to receive a statement a month after the event because any possible control action was required at the time of the event.

2.11 Influence of the accountant

For too long accountants have had too much influence over what information should be provided. This has led to a concentration on cost at the expense of other aspects such as quality, performance and **downtime**. While it is important to control cost, cost control often follows from controlling other factors. It is not the price so much as the usage of a resource, wasteful or otherwise, which affects cost. Furthermore, the way the accountant splits the figures may not be helpful for other managers. For example, an accountant will provide figures for sales revenue and number of units sold because this is what he finds useful for the accounts he prepares. The marketing manager, however, needs figures showing margin per product line. If the monthly control statements are no help to the manager they will not be used and all the effort of preparation will have been wasted. It is easy to imagine a hard-pressed manager sitting at a desk feeling weighed down with daily operational problems that seem to pile up as quickly as they can be solved. At this moment the monthly accounts are delivered. It is quite plain to see that they are the monthly accounts, they are weighty, they are copied on pink paper or else they are an almost unreadable computer print-out. As they do not give the information wanted for the job, or maybe the items wanted cannot be found amid the mass of data, they are put in the waste paper bin or the bottom of the furthest filing cabinet. They get deposited there quickly and the hard-pressed manager returns to more urgent problems. This, unfortunately, happens far too often.

The inadequacy of the present state of affairs for top managers, both in the provision of information generally and the budget as an information system on which to base operational control and decisions, is summed up rather neatly in the following recent statement:

> Perhaps the greatest problem, however, is identifying and then satisfying the real information needs of executives. It's been noted that traditional management information systems are bulging with information that is irrelevant to senior people. Data from operational and transaction systems — such as the accounts — is religiously aggregated, summarized and presented. But most of it never gets read — because it is internal, divided into inappropriate time periods and often out of date. As one executive puts it, they are 'damage reports you get after you've hit the iceberg, rather than the radar signals that steer you round it'.[5]

2.12 Data do not always generate useful information

Data are collected by the various subsystems of the organization and often some processing is carried out immediately. This may just be aggregating and summarizing which can produce unhelpful information, but sometimes the data are processed further so that they gain a particular bias. The initial processing is done with the first or main user in mind but little thought is usually given to subsequent users and the biased data or information that the subsequent users have to work with may be unsatisfactory for their purpose. This problem is sometimes caused by the organization trying to squeeze too much data onto a database: in order to get the quantity required onto a computer with inadequate capacity some data are aggregated to reduce storage needs. Once the data have been aggregated they may be of little use for some information requirements.

The problem of data not generating useful information is not usually attributable to poor data but rather to the manner in which they are assembled and turned into information. Inadequate information is often unwittingly provided simply by continuing to use traditional ways, methods and systems which are out of date and unsatisfactory for all present day uses and decisions. To illustrate this the adequacy of one of the subsystems of a management information system — the costing system — is examined in the next section. A good provider of information should continually assess the standard systems which generate information for operational decisions to ensure that they still produce what is needed and that the nature of the organization has not subtly changed so that different information is required.

C: ILLUSTRATIVE EXAMPLE: INFORMATION FROM THE COSTING SUBSYSTEM

During the 1980s many writers, the most notable of whom was Robert S. Kaplan, commented on the inadequacy of the majority of cost accounting systems. The gist of his and most of the others' arguments was that costing systems had not changed at all since the 1930s — and of course the organization and its costs had changed considerably since then.

2.13   The uses of the costing subsystem

Cost information system designers have failed to recognize the different uses to which costing information is put. Kaplan identifies three different functions or uses of cost information:[6]

- To produce published accounts in keeping with statutory requirements (the Companies Acts in the UK). This necessitates valuing stock.
- Operational control: the controlling of resources and expenditure and the measurement of day to day efficiency.

- Product costs: for setting prices, determining sales mix, making decisions on brands, etc.

Perhaps a fourth function should be added:

- Segment/customer account profitability: to concentrate resources and effort in the most profitable segment or on the most profitable customers.

Even if the designer does recognize these four needs, top managers often insist on one 'official' system.[7] As a system is normally designed with its primary use uppermost in the designer's mind, it is rare to find a system which meets all needs satisfactorily. Systems are invariably set up to meet the statutory requirements of the Companies Acts and the other needs suffer as a result. A system which has been set up to produce published accounts for statutory purposes cannot adequately meet the needs of the other three functions because of the different nature of the information required. In order to achieve satisfactory operational control, information is needed daily if not hourly, whereas information for stock valuation for financial accounts is required only quarterly or annually. In order to value stock only production costs are required, but to assess the profitability of a segment or customer account all costs are needed, namely: production, marketing, distribution, design, after sales-service and administration. The four different uses of the costing system and their requirements are now considered in more detail.

2.14 The legal requirements of the Companies Acts (UK): valuation of stock

According to British law stock must be valued at production cost in a company's published balance sheet. This includes the cost of the materials that constitute the product, the cost of labour involved in making the product and a fair allocation of the remaining production or factory costs (overheads). The valuation does not include the cost of administration, research and development (R&D), or sales, marketing and distribution. The latter costs will not be differentiated properly in an information system which focuses on providing information for published accounts: instead they will be amalgamated and overlooked, and as a result they will not be analyzed and controlled adequately. Yet these are crucial costs when it comes to making decisions about product cost and customer account profitability. Furthermore, it is quite normal today for production costs to constitute only one-third of the total cost, so any costing system which concentrates on only one-third of the cost *must* be deficient.

2.15 Operational control

Operational control involves reporting to individual managers actual data which are compared with a budget so that they can assess the performance of their section and take corrective action to improve future results. The information provided must be timely — it may be adequate to provide some cost information monthly but other information is required daily or even hourly. For instance, expenditure on R&D probably does not need to be monitored more than once a month. However, if a lemonade bottling plant is out of control and is putting the wrong volume of liquid into each bottle, even an hour's delay in reporting can be costly and is scarcely adequate. Much of the control information needed by managers will be non-financial and, therefore, will not be provided under a system set up solely to meet the needs of published accounts. The additional (non-financial) information needed will include the number of breakdowns, yields, defect levels, customer complaints and percentage of delivery dates met.

If any benefit is to be gained the information supplied to managers must match their area of responsibility and must concern items over which they have control. This entails collecting data by department, cost centre or activity as well as by function (i.e. production, marketing, distribution, etc.).

2.16 Product cost measurement — production costs only

It is vital to have information on the exact cost of each product or brand so that the correct selling prices may be set, accurate quotations for work be given and correct decisions on promotion made. If costs, and therefore profitability, of products are not known then decisions to enter or leave particular markets may also be incorrect. Costs must be collected not by department, as was required for operational control, but by product.

Nearly every organization uses standard product costs. These are the anticipated or predetermined costs which will be incurred in making the product or providing the service. As with everything else they are normally designed with published accounts in mind, in order to value stock rather than to make product decisions. Hence the problem of **overhead absorption**, its accuracy and its impact on product profitability, arises. Published accounts do not require costs other than production costs to be traced to the unit of production. Therefore, costs such as design, marketing and delivery are not properly analyzed in an information system whose prime aim is merely stock valuation.

Research and development costs present a slightly different problem, namely one of timing. In UK published accounts R&D costs must be written off in the year in which they were incurred. In other words they must be written off against current products and not against the future ones which the research and develoment is to benefit. This has the effect of depressing the profit margin of the current products. A product may just break even according to the method dictated for published accounts, that is by charging current R&D to it. It may, in fact, be quite profitable when the R&D, which is not caused at all by the product under consideration, is removed. Conversely, a new product which has recently incurred considerable R&D costs may now look misleadingly profitable because it has not been charged with these costs.

2.17 Product cost measurement — direct product profit

The importance placed on the valuation of stock has led to an over-emphasis on production costs at the expense of other types of cost. Many industries have suffered from this over-emphasis. Taking the food retailing industry as an example, there are no production costs as the goods are bought from the manufacturers, stored and then transported to the shops where they are sold. Therefore, the industry incurs storage, transport and marketing costs. The traditional emphasis on production costs, and from this the calculation of gross margin (which in production companies, where costing systems were first designed, is sales revenue less direct production costs) led other types of business, including retail industries, to use this method although they had no good reason to do so. In the case of retailing companies, gross margin is the sales revenue minus the bought-in price (the cost price of the good) and does not, therefore, include any of the company's own costs. This meant that the company could incur what costs it liked without affecting the reported individual profitability of any of the goods it sold. This way of marshalling data into information is clearly misleading and a more suitable system was needed for this type of business.

The system adopted by most of the food retailing industry is quite novel and has only been used to any great extent in the last ten years. It is called direct product profit (DPP). Direct product profit is the gross margin adjusted for direct revenues and direct costs as indicated below:

Gross margin
Plus Direct revenues   (e.g. discounts for prompt payment, advertising allowances)

Minus Direct expenses
    warehouse costs   (e.g. labour, space, insurance)
    transport costs   (e.g. labour, fuel, vehicle)
    store/shop costs   (e.g. labour, shelf space costs, insurance,

The result of doing this in a specific instance is shown below:

	Gross margin %	DPP %
Spray cleaning polish	24.6	17.7
Butter	10.0	4.5
Cigarettes	12.2	13.5
Boxes of tissues	15.6	0.0

If the company had used the traditional method of gross margin it would have got its profitability assessments quite wrong: it would have thought that tissues were relatively profitable. The reason for this considerable change around in the profitability of tissues under the two methods is that they are bulky and take up a considerable amount of storage and shelf space, much more than a pack of twenty cigarettes, for instance. Therefore the tissues must generate considerably more profit to overcome the extra costs involved. The profitability of cigarettes increases under DPP because the manufacturers of the cigarettes give discounts which are not related to the product in the traditional costing system. Butter, because of the expense of refrigerated storage, decreases in profitability considerably when DPP is used.

A recent UK survey found that 78 per cent of users of DPP said it led to better decision making and understanding of product performance and identified it as a technique which enabled them to focus on developing strategies to give competitive advantage.[8] The majority of retailers using it do so for decisions on shelf space management and store layout, pricing, advertising and new products.

2.18 Segment/customer account profitability

Whatever the industry, the recent trend has been to segment the market to an ever greater extent and thus to aim at a small group of customers who have specific needs which the company can meet satisfactorily. Some customers will be more profitable than others, and obviously the organization will want to sell to the more profitable ones. Large customers should be cheaper to service since large orders mean less paperwork per £ of sales than small orders. Large production runs are cheaper with less change-over and set-up time. Distribution costs are cheaper because delivery to one site will be quicker than delivering to many. Therefore, companies tend to favour large customers who put through big orders by giving them large discounts. But is this really warranted?

On occasions companies wishing to increase profit have given greater discounts to their large order customers in the belief that they are the most profitable customers. The result has been to decrease profit, possibly because the large order customers demand quick delivery dates which disrupt production, or perhaps they require a particular specification. The following is an example of the reverse tack — increasing large order sales by discouraging small orders.[9] An engineering business decided that its small customer orders were disrupting production and were generating little profit. Therefore, to try to eliminate them they raised their prices. They raised the price several times in fact as the small order customers were not put off by the higher prices and kept on ordering, because they would face high switching costs if they went to another supplier. In addition, the existing supplier was reliable and provided a satisfactory product even at the increased price. Two years after they had begun to put up prices the company found that the small sales orders had become very profitable and were in fact the most profitable part of the business.

To determine customer profitability, Shapiro *et al* suggest that costs should be categorized as follows:[9]

Pre-sale costs:
- Time spent travelling by sales staff.
- Number of times a particular customer is visited.
- The amount of sales effort, e.g. are directors required to visit?
- Non-standard products calling for individual design and specifications.
- Time spent finding sources of materials, components and any special equipment needed.

Production costs:
- Order size, scrap rate.
- Individual design — slower production.
- Special packaging.
- Timing of order — off-peak cheaper.
- Quick delivery required — disruption of production schedules.

Distribution costs:
- Quick delivery required — extra transport costs.
- Location of customer.
- Return load possible?

Post-sale costs:
- Spare parts.
- Repair service.
- Training of customer's staff in use of equipment.
- Updating systems.

Customers generally fall into four categories as shown in Figure 2.2. The accepting customers are the most desirable as they are willing to pay a high price yet the organization can provide them with the product or service

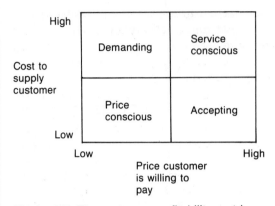

Figure 2.2 The customer profitability matrix.

cheaply. On first consideration it may seem surprising that this category
exists but further thought reveals that it is quite possible to find such
customers. The low cost of serving may simply be due to the fact that the
customer is located very close to the supplier's business. Alternatively, the
customer may be willing to pay a high price because the expenditure is too
insignificant to warrant tough price negotiations. More likely, though, the
cost of switching supplier is too great for the customer. This tends to occur
more frequently today than in the past as businesses become 'tied together'
by the same information systems. High switching costs can also occur with
highly specific engineered parts where a change of supplier may mean
redesigning the product.

The next best segment for the company to concentrate on is the service-
conscious customers. Providing these customers with the product or service
is costly but they are willing to pay a high price. The worst category are
the demanding customers, these are normally large companies who order
large quantities at one time and who use this fact aggressively to obtain
cheap prices.

It can be seen, therefore, that knowledge of the relative profitabilities
of the different types of customer is vital if the business is to achieve the
best possible profit. Obviously no company would be happy if it failed to
exploit its accepting trade or became over-burdened by demanding
customers. This knowledge can only be obtained by analyzing customers,
and in order to make this analysis possible the information system must
be capable of relating costs to customers or market segments as well as to
departments and products. A system designed primarily to satisfy statutory
accounting requirements will be inadequate for assessing customer
profitability just as it is for providing useful operational and product cost
information.

The main point to be drawn from the illustrative example's examination of the costing subsystem is that what is assumed to be 'information' may not in fact be so. This fault is not exclusive to the costing subsystem and is equally likely to apply to information provision in other subsystems. Steps should be taken to check all information provided on a regular basis, that is every other year or more frequently, as follows:

- Managers should be consulted to make sure that the 'information' provided really is information to them, i.e. it is what they require.
- 'Experts' in the relevant disciplines (such as the accountant) should also be consulted but their opinions should take second place to those of the managers (the users of the system) except on points of technical interpretation.
- Methods of sorting, collating, aggregating and interpreting data when providing information must be questioned to make sure that the 'information' provided really is information. This is working from the data end of the process, which may appear to be the wrong place, but it may shed new light on the adequacy of the information provided.
- Experimentation in the way in which data are turned into information may be successful in highlighting new relationships which are of considerable assistance to management. For example, traditional classifications of sales data could be replaced by new ones, such as segment/customer classsification. Alternatively, data may be turned into graphical information rather than numerical to improve its usefulness by making it easier to absorb.

NOTES

1. John F. Rockart, 'Chief executives define their own data needs', *Harvard Business Review* Mar./Apr. 1979.
2. George Houdeshel and Hugh J. Watson, 'The management information and decision support (MIDS) system at Lockheed—Georgia', *MIS Quarterly*, Mar. 1987.
3. Kenichi Ohmae, *The Mind of the Strategist* (Penguin, 1982).
4. Chris Argyris, *The Impact of Budgets on People*, (Cornell University, 1952).
5. Ian Meiklejohn, 'Computing matters', *Management Today*, Sept. 1989.
6. Robert S. Kaplan and H. Thomas Johnston, *Relevance Lost* (Harvard Business School Press, 1987).
7. Robert S. Kaplan, 'One costing system isn't enough', *Harvard Business Review*, Jan./Feb. 1988.
8. *Direct Product Profitability: Results of the first UK industry survey*, Institute of Grocery Distribution and Touche Ross.
9. Benson Shapiro, V. Kasturi Rangan, Rowland Moriarty and Eliot Ross, 'Manage customers for profits (not just sales)', *Harvard Business Review*, Sept./Oct. 1987.

FURTHER READING

Kaplan, Robert S. and H. Thomas Johnston, *Relevance Lost* (Harvard Business School Press, 1987). A well regarded text that analyzes costing systems and the role of management accounting.

EXERCISES

1. Suggest possible critical success factors for the following managers and outline the information and data requirements that result from these:
   (a) Marketing manager.
   (b) Sales manager.
   (c) Financial accountant.
   (d) Management accountant.
   (e) Personnel manager.

2. Consider what data should be routinely collected and obtained by an organization which wishes to analyze its markets regularly.

3. How often should data/information be supplied to individuals doing the following tasks controlling:
   (a) A metal cutting machine?
   (b) The department's costs?
   (c) Material waste?
   (d) The quality of meals provided?
   (e) The time taken to answer customers' telephone queries?
   (f) The building of a new office block?
   (g) Electricity costs?
   (h) The launch of a new consumer product?

The flow of data and information

3

SCOPE AND CONTENTS

The different ways data and information may flow from source to destination are examined. Then the structure and function of the information department are considered. How to create the best flow paths for information and the different types of information which flow through the system are then examined. Lastly examples of poor data and information management are given.

3.1 Collecting data

The first part of this chapter deals with the collection, processing, storage, transmission and presentation of data and information within an organization. Readers who are familiar with the business environment may wish to skip this part and move on to section 3.5.

The following decisions have to be made about collecting data:

1. At which point to collect them.
2. How frequently to collect them.
3. In what physical form to collect them.

Let us assume, for instance, that data on the number of items sold and their value are required for management decision purposes. These data must, therefore, be collected. Before this can be arranged it is necessary to determine exactly when a sale is considered to take place. This is important because that will be the point in the business cycle at which the data have to be collected. Does the sale take place when the goods are dispatched, when an invoice is raised, or at some other time? If the first is correct the sale may be recorded from a paper dispatch note. If the second is correct the sales invoice may be used. Alternatively, the organization may be a shop and the sale made at the till, in which case the till roll will record the sale.

The second factor to consider is how frequently managers need the information. Do they require it instantly, hourly, daily or weekly? For instance, information about production processes and tolerances will be needed at least hourly to prevent the processes becoming out of control. In some organizations once a day may be considered adequate for sales information, but most large organizations are moving towards systems which provide almost instant information. If the sales information is required only once a day, the data need not be recorded the moment a sale is made, but only daily. However, information on expenditure which is needed for control purposes may not be required more frequently than once a week.

The third factor for consideration is the physical form in which data should be collected. Data may be collected from a range of different sources which are quite different in nature. These sources include the following:

- **Paper**, including invoices, receipts, till rolls and **punched cards**.
- **Voice**, usually by telephone, direct reporting or possibly by tape-recording or by a voice recognition system.
- **Optical**, including bar codes, EPOS (electronic point of sale) terminals and OCR (optical character reading).
- **Magnetic**, including bars and stripes.
- **Instrument**, including sensors, counters, radio tags and instrument readings.

Traditionally, paper documents were used as the source from which data were obtained, but the cash register and till roll have been replaced in many shops by an **electronic point of sale** (EPOS) terminal with a wand that reads bar codes. It is the job of information management, together with the relevant functional managers, continually to consider the ways in which data are collected. This is to make sure that the collection is always done in the most efficient and cost effective way. At some point changes will need to be made if the system is to continue to be the best for the organization. For instance, most retail organizations have had to make the change from cash registers to EPOS terminals. This is likely to be a major change. It is one which has strategic implications and should be planned by the organization as part of the overall business strategy.

3.2 Processing and storing the data

Once a decision on the collection of data relating to a particular transaction has been made, the next decision to make concerns how, if at all, the data should be processed at this stage. Assuming that we are considering a retail sale, there are many possibilities for processing. The data could be given to the user 'raw', possibly on a long till roll. But this would not be information within the meaning of the word in this book and the user would have to do a considerable amount of work on it to make much sense of it. It is hardly an improvement to type the data onto sheets of paper. True, it is in a slightly more manageable form, but it is still a jumble of figures. It is necessary to aggregate or group the data in one way or another to give it meaning. This might be by sales per till per day, sales units or revenue per product group, sales units or revenue per department or section, sales margin per product group or department, or sales per hour. There are many other possibilities.

If the data are aggregated or grouped and *then* stored, the original data are lost unless a permanent paper record remains. After being aggregated and stored the data or information can only be used in a limited number of ways: they are no longer useful as raw data. It is likely that the sales data will be needed by quite a few managers who will all have different uses for it, therefore preliminary processing is almost certainly not advisable. If it is done then great care should be taken in making sure that the processing is acceptable to all users. It is, in fact, much better to store the raw data and process them at a later stage when information is required by the managers. The main problem with this is the storage capacity required.

Storage may mean bits of paper in a filing cabinet or a basement full of old documents. However, most of the data required by managers are now usually stored on a computer database whence it can be taken, processed and presented as required. (Databases are discussed in Chapter 9.) The length of time that data or information is required to be held before they are destroyed is important to the way in which they are stored. If access to visual records is, or may be, needed for many years it is likely that they will be stored on microfilm, thus saving on space and storage costs. Alternatively, image processing may be used. See section 9.9 for more details on both of these methods.

Decisions have to be made from time to time on the size of the computer database, how to partition it and where to site it. Will it be a large central database? Will it be situated near the source of the data or near the main user of the information? For how long will the data be stored? These decisions depend on when and how frequently the information will be needed, how many people need it and where they are located. This is influenced by the next stage: the transmission and communication of the information.

3.3 Transmission of data

Transmission facilities will be needed between sites and within sites. This involves building information networks internally and probably linking them into the national telecommunication system for external transmission. Traditional telephone systems were analogue and one channel was used for a single communication. Now, however, telephone communication is digital and communication from different types of equipment may be interleaved and sent at the same time through the same channel. A decision will have to be made as to the extent to which the organization should use the national network or lease lines from a telecommunication company. This decision will depend on the amount of traffic and this in turn depends on the volume and frequency of the flow of information. For instance, will the retail managers and directors want information about sales once a month, daily or instantly? It would be a poor manager who was satisfied with sales data monthly. It may be adequate on a daily basis, in which case the data could be stored in a computer in the shop and sent at night at a cheaper rate to a central processing unit. This is what Halfords do, as described in the case below. Alternatively, the information may be required instantly, in which case an on-line database will be needed together with instant transmission facilities.

3.4 Illustrative case: Halfords' Halo system[1]

Halfords, the bicycle and car accessory retail chain, have an EPOS system which gives stock control, cash control and automatic ledger balancing. The system, introduced in 1985, is called Halo. The reason for introducing the system, as in many retail companies, was to control stock and check its movement between warehouses, depots and stores. The system links the stores via a network and can produce four hundred different reports. The tills in the stores write all the transaction data to an audio cassette data recorder throughout the day. At the end of the day the data are batch uploaded from the magnetic tape onto the branch's PC. The PC breaks down the data by till, analyzes the data, reconciles the cash and produces updated files ready for transfer to the central office. These files are transferred at night, using British Telecom's midnight line facility, to a cluster of PCs. They split the information at this point into two parts: that pertaining to stock and that required for finance purposes. The stock information is required to update the warehousing system which runs on two MicroVax computers. The stock control system also generates suggested orders for branches which the store manager may override. The other part is destined for the financial and management information package which runs on a minicomputer. This includes a cash management facility and integrates financial planning with corporate reporting. The information generated is available for use on terminals at head office by 9.30 the next morning.

3.5 Presentation of information

The presentation of information was discussed in section 2.5. The normal methods of presentation to managers and employees are via the PC screen or the printed page. However, information can also be presented vocally, either by face to face communication, telephone or prerecorded message.

It is said that 70 per cent of all the information that we absorb is acquired visually rather than through the senses of touch, smell and hearing. Therefore it would seem obvious that an information system which presented information in a visual way would be more effective than one that did not. The aim of an information system, beyond presenting the required information at the required time, must be to present it in such a way that it may be readily absorbed. Anyone who has sat listening to an audio tape or to a teacher will know that it is only too easy to let the eyes stray and the mind to wander. On the other hand, watching a video in a darkened room is not wholly satisfactory as too often half the audience fall into a semi-slumber, especially when the presentation is of little interest or proceeds at the wrong pace. Information systems which allow the user both to dictate the pace at which information is provided and to select the information required help to overcome these problems.

For an information system to be effective it should, therefore, present the information mainly in visual form, but if it can also incorporate another sense, especially hearing, it will be even better at holding the attention of the user. Until computers become proficient at language this dual type of information system is likely to remain rare. They are used at present, however, in warning systems where it essential to catch the monitor's attention immediately.

3.6 The information department

The information department is responsible for the flow of data and information. This involves providing and maintaining the physical system and safeguarding the data and information under their care. It also involves the analysis of the flow of data and information so that the best and most suitable flows for the organization are in place. The information department is responsible for most, but not all, of the information provision and its related systems within the organization. The overall information system may be divided into the following areas:

- The information network or **infrastructure**.
- The provision and storage of information for the organization as a whole — organization-wide computer processing and databases.
- Specific systems/procedures/applications. These are normally for specific departments or activities and are outside the direct control of the information department.

The information department will be headed either by an information director or by an information manager. As organizations become aware of the great importance of information systems to their future well-being, so larger companies are creating the position of information director in order that due weight is given to the function. The manager or director will be in charge of a department which has expanded considerably in many organizations in recent years and is now as large as most of the other departments.

Although organization structures vary considerably from business to business, Figure 3.1 shows *one possible* structure for a large organization. It consists of three distinct sections or functions. The communications function, which is responsible for maintaining and developing the telephone systems and the network infrastructure, is obviously very important as all information flows depend on it. If the infrastructure is damaged then information cannot flow to the user. Communication networks can also be costly to set up and keep up to date. Data processing has been an established function in most organizations for many years and covers the processing of transaction data, the storage of data and information and the provision of standard reports.

The information systems department, or the information centre as it is more usually known, is the newest section of the three. Many large organizations set up information centres in the middle of the 1980s to meet the growing needs of user departments. The section offers advice to functional or user departments on types of system and their purchase. It sets organization standards for user department equipment, tests equipment and software and prepares programs as

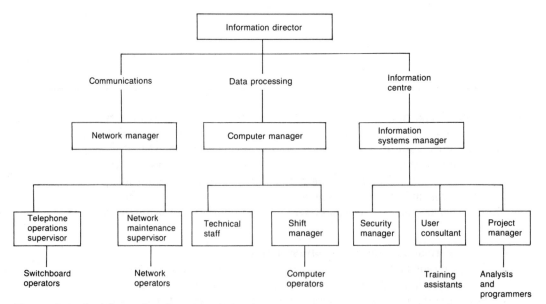

Figure 3.1 An information department structure.

required. It also provides internal training and education in new technology. The information centre may include a security manager who is responsible for the security of data and information throughout the whole organization. Security of information and equipment has recently become a more important issue than previously, largely due to the publicity given to legal cases involving **hacking** and **viruses**. However, industrial espionage is also increasing and its threat should not be taken lightly.

Overall, the information centre provides an invaluable service and it has been found that it usually recovers its initial set-up costs rapidly. Its activities would normally include:

- Acting as in-house consultants to all system users.
- Spreading the 'information culture' and supporting end-user computing.
- Avoiding unnecessary duplication of application programs and ensuring that data recorded are used to their full potential — different departments may be interested in using similar data.
- Providing in-house training.
- Ensuring the security of all data and information.
- Ensuring that adequate accuracy controls on data and information are in place.
- Avoiding problems concerning the integrity of the data. For instance, it is thought to be more likely that errors will creep into the system if the users are allowed to change and update figures. Measures have to be taken to guard against this.

3.7 Creating the best flow paths for data and information

The information department is responsible not only for the physical network and equipment but also for the flow paths of data and information. It needs to plan these carefully. It also needs to make sure that everything is done to target information correctly by directing the required information, but *only* the required information, to the individual user. The calculation of critical success factors by managers and information providers, discussed in section 2.4, will help to make sure that the managers receive the correct information in order to make their decisions. However, it is unlikely that critical success factors will be worked out for all the employees in an organization because of the time required to assess the factors properly.

In order to keep the business operational on a day-to-day basis, information other than that determined by critical success factors must also must flow. This will include information to answer questions like: Has Y company settled its account? Which accounts need to be paid? What are present stock levels? What component should department X be producing in the next hour? A whole host of employees need this type of information in order to keep the business operating satisfactorily. Assessing critical success factors is probably not the correct way to set up a basic, day-to-day information system. If it were tried it could result in no-one considering that it was critical to their job to send out invoices.

What is needed instead is a flow diagram of all the data and information flows that are required to run the business on a day-to-day basis. Data and information flows are based chiefly on activities and so a flowchart of the organization's activities is required initially. This will be a physical plan identifying the area in which each activity takes place and showing how each activity is linked to others. From this an unmanageably large diagram or model can be built up showing where the data come from, who handles them, what they do with them, how they are processed or pass through the organization and what the data are ultimately used for. This is not easy to achieve on one diagram and so it has to be broken down into sections. This can be done by having separate detailed charts or overlays. One overlay might show the activities, a second how the data move, a third where the data are stored or processed, and a fourth who uses the information. It should be noted that data flows are based on activities and not on departments. A department is a unit for administrative purposes and many activities cut across departments.

It is important that information should flow in a logical manner through the organization. Many departments and offices have probably not changed their location or even structure for many years, and the current one may no longer be the best for the activities they now perform and for the efficient flow of information. From time to time the activities of a department ought to be examined to make sure that they are still logically grouped and situated. Detailed flow plans showing the equipment and transmission channels are also needed and should be checked intermittently to make sure that they are still adequate and suitable.

These aspects should be studied carefully as a logical office layout is just as important as a logical factory layout. It would be thought crazy to site the final production process in a factory next to the first, so that the product had to pass through the final process on its way to the second, and back again. Unfortunately this does actually happen on occasions in factories. If it can happen in factories, where the flow should be obvious to all, then there is a greater chance of it occurring in offices where the flow of information is not nearly so visible.

It was stressed in the previous chapter that data are not, or should not, be collected merely for the sake of doing so. Neither should information be provided this way. The only criterion for providing information is that someone somewhere in the organization needs it to make a decision. After producing a data and information flow model, therefore, a decision flow model should be drawn up. This will show who makes what decision, where it is made and to whom is the decision imparted. Information should flow only to those who need it to make a decision, otherwise there is a danger that other managers will find their in-tray clogged with superfluous information and miss that which is vital. The decision flow is the only justification for the information and data flow model. Thus once the decision flow model has been drawn up the data and information flow model will probably need to be amended accordingly.

To summarize, the stages in creating a data flow model are:

- Physical plan.
- Flowchart of activities.
- Data and information flow model — initial.
- Decision flow model.
- Data and information flow model — amended.

3.8 Layers and types of information flow

In order to appreciate the flow of data and information through the organization it is necessary to have some concept of the different nature of the flows. Henry Mintzberg put forward five different types of flow which cover all the different linkages within the organization.[2] They are:

1. **Formal authority**. This equates to the organization chart of individuals, and to the natural divisions of an organization in what may be described as a hierarchical flow. Different organizations have different structures but they will be broadly similar to the following levels:
   International between companies
   National between business units
   Local/regional between divisions
   Site between departments
   Area between groups of workers
   The basic network structure or infrastructure must reflect these different divisions or hierarchies within the organization.
2. **Regulated flows**. The regulated flow of information is that which is required to provide the product. It includes information relating to the movement of materials, the manufacture of the product to customer order and so on. Types of information system that fall into this category include production control and scheduling, and **CIM (computer integrated manufacturing)**. Another example on the retail side is an EPOS (electronic point of sale) system which 'pulls' new goods from the warehouse to the store as a result of sales.
3. **Informal communications**. These are the spontaneous and flexible ties created by personal relationships. They may be focused around unofficial centres of power. The telephone and the fax are probably the two most widely used informal communication systems, but electronic mail is growing in popularity.
4. **Work constellation flows**. These are flows between people who work together

regularly. They will need common systems, **LANs (local area networks)** which connect them and allow them to work together.

5. ***Ad hoc* decisions**. These require the provision of *ad hoc* information which may be used to make one-off decisions. Executive systems (discussed in section 2.6) allow managers to draw the information they require from a database and thus assist in this type of decision making.

The information department must aim to make information flow as smoothly and as quickly as possible. In order to do this the right equipment must be in the right place and the links between the equipment must be correct. With five different types of information flow to be planned and all the different interconnections within an organization this is not an easy task to perform well.

To do this satisfactorily current technology and equipment must be separated from the basic data flow model. The data flow model will remain unchanged for long periods. The information that managers need will change, perhaps quite rapidly, but the data from which the information is derived will not change. The flow of data awaiting transformation into information must be maintained, preserved and improved over the years. The information infrastructure supports the data flow and consists of the telephone system and computer networks. It is the means of connecting an individual to others, regardless of which type of terminal or telephone that individual has at present. Decisions concerning the infrastructure are long-term and must therefore be planned carefully. This is especially important in an ever-changing world in order to ensure that the organization has an up to date and flexible system which meets its needs.

3.9 Poor data and information management

The data and information flow model will be the foundation upon which all systems and networks are built and so it is vital that the flows are logical and rational. Too often managers have realized that there is a problem with the flow of information through the organization and decided to solve it by installing a computerized system. After installation they are amazed that the problem still remains and that the computer has solved nothing. They should not be surprised that they ended up with a computerized mess when they started with a mess. If the data and information flows are illogical or otherwise poor then the installation of the most advanced information system in the world will not solve the underlying problem.

Good information systems do not need to be complicated or high-tech. The Japanese kanban system of using cards or coloured balls to impart information is wonderfully simple and accurate, and it does not break down. However, some information systems do need to be technically complex, but they must also be simple to use and reliable. If they are not then they will not gain the support of employees and will never be adequately used.

It must not be presumed that data management is usually good. Examples of bad management abound. One traditionally poor area in the UK is the academic library service. Even today a request sent out for a book on an inter-library loan frequently takes six or nine months to find a copy. A good electronic messaging system and carrier ought to produce the book within a few days. Alternatively, if a central database was kept of all books in UK libraries a request could be made directly to the holding library. The library information system is poor for two reasons. Firstly the system is out of date and secondly it no longer (if it ever did) operates efficiently. Its operational failure may be due either to the staff not realizing the value of the service to the customer or, more likely, the staff not considering a user in a different library to be a customer. Alternatively, the staff may be unable or unwilling to give inter-library loans the necessary attention for an adequate response time. It should be noted that if the last possibility is true then a computerized system would not greatly help.

There are other examples where modern systems have been put in place but, because they have been badly designed, they prove inadequate at managing data. For instance, a bank wishing to install an **on-line** cash management service was unable to do so despite the fact that its competitors had provided this service. The reason for this failure was that the information could not be made available even though all the data required was stored in the system. This was because the database had been poorly planned and was inflexible, so information which had not been specified in the original requirements could not be extracted. A massive reprogramming was required which took years: meanwhile the bank was at a severe competitive disadvantage. This type of situation is not uncommon and is a relic of the large rigid database systems that were installed in the 1970s. Although, as has already been said, the data flows change very little over the years, the requirements of user managers and employees do. Therefore it is important that data should be preserved in the system and be capable of extraction in any number of ways, some of which may be unforeseen at the time of installation.

Some of the worst examples of poor information infrastructure planning in the UK occur in the public sector. Here administration has become a career in its own right, divorced from the main function of the organization. It seems on some occasions that in order to protect and preserve administrative jobs the free flow of information is deliberately blocked. For instance, in some educational establishments the academic staff have no direct access to student or course records. There is a clear need for a database which records any particular student's name and address, course, examination results, prior qualifications and so on. It should also be possible to look at students enrolling and enrolled on a particular course and to compare numbers and grades over a period of years. Often these facilities do exist is some manner for the administrative staff, but access to the data is often zealously guarded on the grounds of data protection, so that those who need the information cannot obtain it. The situation could be likened to sending a new salesman to deal with an established customer without giving him any details such as purchases, equipment and discounts given.

The lack of a good information system for all stops the flow and means that the information is duplicated. It also means that more administrative staff than necessary are employed. A good information system probably does more than anything else to improve the morale of all staff, improve co-operation between departments and improve efficiency when dealing with customers.

3.10 Purchased information systems management

The skills needed to run the information department are many and some companies find that they lack the depth of skills required. For instance, the ability to link technical knowledge with management knowledge and skills is vital. Therefore any information director or manager must have a thorough grounding in management as well as having the necessary technical skills. Management skills are rarely gained simply by rising through the ranks from computer operator to programmer to analyst to designer and finally to manager. If these skills, or others, are not available within the organization they can be purchased from a specialist information systems management and equipment company. Such a company, known as a facilities management company, provides and is responsible for all information staff. Normally a fixed fee is agreed for a specific type of service including maintenance. This service may well be useful for small or medium sized businesses which have experienced difficulties in the provision of information services in the past. It may not be suitable, however, if the organization's information is particularly sensitive and tight security is required.

NOTES

1. R. Orme, 'Why Halfords wears a Halo', *Accountancy*, Jan. 1989.
2. Henry Mintzberg, *The Structuring of Organizations* (Penguin, 1979).

FURTHER READING

Clifton, H.D., *Business Data Systems*, 4th edn (Prentice Hall International, 1990). Contains chapters on data flow diagrams.

EXERCISES

1. Consider an office or department layout that you are familiar with. Draw a simple data and information flow model and suggest ways in which the layout could be improved to assist the flow.
2. Exercise 2 of Chapter 2 referred to the data which an organization should collect and obtain in order to analyze its markets. Consider how these data should be collected, stored and processed. To whom should they be presented as information?

4 The right information system for the organization

SCOPE AND CONTENTS

This chapter deals with the factors which have a bearing on the choice of the overall information system created within a particular organization. It outlines three influencing factors concerning the particular business, namely the type of industry, the stage in the industry life cycle, and the size of the organization. Four other factors are also considered: the state of technology, management style, the geographical spread of the organization, and political and economic influences. The chapter includes consideration of a product/industry life cycle and the Greiner model for an organization's development.

4.1 Why do different organizations need different systems?

There is no such thing as the perfect information system. To use a well known quotation from Carl Jung: 'The shoe that fits one person pinches another; there is no recipe for living that suits all cases.' It is impossible to expect that an information system could be developed which would suit all organizations regardless of their individual nature and information needs. A company cannot squeeze itself into someone else's information system just as the ugly sisters found that they could not squeeze their feet into Cinderella's shoes. To take the metaphor further, nobody could expect to have a pair of shoes bought for them as a child that still fitted them comfortably when they were forty. Similarly, as an organization grows and changes so must its information system if it is to remain 'a good fit'.

Therefore, an information system should be as flexible as possible in order to meet the changing needs of the business. It should be able to cope with both the maturing of the business and any relatively minor change in the nature of the business brought about by takeovers, **repositioning**, etc. The problem, of course, is that a system capable of adaptation will probably not be tailored specifically to the current needs of the business. So a compromise will possibly have to be made, and, at the very least, the system will have to be totally overhauled at various stages of the organization's development. This needs to be done in any case at the present time because of the rapid changes in information technology. Without the occasional major overhaul to update the information system's technology and techniques it would become antiquated and be unsuitable for the organization's current needs.

4.2 Factors affecting the type of information system needed

Different types of system are needed according to the particular circumstances of an organization. The factors governing the style of system to be used are:

- Type of business or industry.
- Stage in the industry life cycle.
- Size of the business.
- The current state of technology.
- Management style.
- Geographical spread of the organization and its markets.
- Political and economic influences.

4.3 Type of business or industry

Running a chain of restaurants is quite different from running a bank, a hospital or a high-tech electronics company. The managers in each will have different information needs: for instance, they may have different objectives — operating for profit or serving the community. They will certainly need different types of information to control their organizations and different performance measures. They will also have different planning needs and horizons. In addition, the need for immediacy of information may differ.

The information system must be responsive to the organization's needs. Sometimes it is paramount that information is received immediately to maintain a competitive stance — for example, a retailer may need information on sales to restock and meet future demand. If this is the case then the system must provide it immediately. If this is not done then market share will be lost and the company's strategic position weakened. If, on the other hand, information is needed in several different ways for measuring the performance of business units and products then the information system must be capable of producing the information in these various forms from the data recorded on it.

4.4   Stages in the industry life cycle

It is widely thought that every product and industry goes through the life cycle depicted in Figure 4.1. The shape and length of the curve may vary considerably but the four stages are still recognizable. A product life cycle may vary considerably in length. For instance, crazes such as skateboards have a very short product life and the maturity stage of the curve is almost non-existent. A product such as binoculars, however, has been produced in a fairly similar form for at least a century and the maturity part of the curve will appear long and quite flat. Sometimes there are unpredictable occurrences which affect the curve, such as took place in the American undershirt market in the 1930s when Clark Gable appeared in a bedroom scene of a film in which he was rather daringly, for the time, naked above the waist. The story goes that this had a great effect on young American men in that they perceived that it was unmanly to wear an undershirt. This caused a drop of 70 per cent in the sales of undershirts during the following year. So the undershirt manufacturers who imagined that their product was one that would have a long and steady life in maturity had a rather unpleasant shock. The product of course did not go into total decline but the level of sales fell considerably.

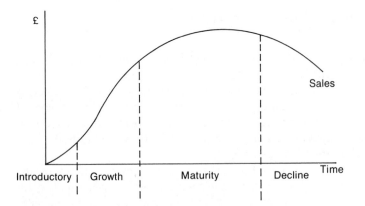

Figure 4.1 The product/industry life cycle.

An industry/business segment as opposed to a single product will normally have several cycles within the overall one. A classic example of this is nylon which was first manufactured by DuPont just before the Second World War. Unsurprisingly its first main use was in parachutes and cords. When the war ended this market reduced substantially. However, there was a bigger and better one waiting, namely ladies stockings, which up to that time had been made of silk for those few that could afford them. As maturity was being reached in this market, nylon began to be used as cord in the manufacture of tyres thus keeping the industry of nylon manufacture in the growth stage. Since then there have proved to be many uses for nylon, and each new use increases the maturity level of the industry curve. Figure 4.2 illustrates the type of curve that an industry such as the manufacture of nylon might have during its growth stage.

Figure 4.2 Hypothetical growth curve of an industry.

The stage reached in the life cycle affects the type of information system needed because management will require different types of information and use different key measures according to the stage the **business unit** has reached. Table 4.1 shows probably the four most important measures that management could use in assessing the performance of their organization's different business units. This particular model has been used by several manufacturing companies for performance assessment. The percentage weighting given to the measure shows the relative importance that the organization attaches to the measure at each stage of a business unit's life.

The growth phase of a business or industry is the market-getting stage and the most important factor, therefore, is to capture market share. Market share gained at this time should, it is usually believed, remain with the business through maturity and therefore be of benefit for many years to come. In addition it is considerably easier to increase market share when the overall market is increasing rather than when the market has stopped growing. Usually the only way a company can increase its own market share during maturity is at the expense

Table 4.1 Business unit performance measures

Key management measures	Stage		
	Growth %	Maturity %	Decline %
Return on assets	10	25	50
Cash flow	—	25	50
Investment in assets and working capital	45	25	—
Market share/growth	45	25	—
	100%	100%	100%

of another company who will not normally relinquish its share without a fight. Hence during the growth stage the information system should be geared up to assist in the logistics of making, distributing and marketing the product so as to increase volume at the desired rate. This will involve, for instance, co-ordinating activities and matching production to increasing demand.

When the whole industry reaches maturity a different set of needs emerge. The individual business is no longer achieving a reducing cost per unit by increasing volume as would have been the case during the growth stage. Therefore cost reduction must be achieved by other methods. This means that a more formal approach to monitoring and controlling costs is necessary. More emphasis should be placed on controlling events and keeping costs within a pre-set budget by using variance analysis. While the business was growing the managers would have tended to concentrate on increasing market share and breaking into new markets rather than on cost control. Once an industry reaches maturity, however, increased market share is only likely to be achieved by niche marketing — that is by subdividing the overall market into segments and concentrating marketing efforts on one or two segments in which competitors cannot easily compete. Therefore an information system which gives details of cost per market segment, e.g. by outlet, geographically or customer type, is of great importance as is one which gives details of costs for control purposes. Overall the information system at this stage will be more formal and regulated than previously, reflecting the more formal nature of the organization.

As the industry or business unit ages and goes into decline the management philosophy will be 'to get what we can while we can'. Top management's attention may often be focused elsewhere on new businesses or products which will be the profit earners of the future. As far as the declining business is concerned, it must generate adequate profit (as measured by return on assets) and cash — cash which is needed to fund the profitable businesses of the future. The business will gradually be milked of cash and therefore gradually run down. The information system will be tuned to close cash monitoring and tight cost control in order to maintain the profit level for as long as possible.

4.5 Size and organization structure

Generally speaking, the larger the organization the more formalized the information system must be. In a small business it may be largely an informal word of mouth system with simple computer programs for such things as accounting and invoicing. A large organization operating in this way would find it impossible to digest the information available and to act quickly enough upon it. To illustrate the effect of organization size on the information system, a model is described which shows the different ways in which a company may change its structure and grow throughout its life. We then show how an information system may change to accommodate the change in size and structure. The model was formulated by Larry E. Greiner who studied a number of American companies during the 1970s. (For an alternative model see Exercise 1 at the end of this chapter.)

Reproduced in Figure 4.3 is a chart which shows the five phases of growth of Greiner's model.[1] The chart, which depicts the growth of a company from birth to the largest existing company, shows five distinct stages of evolution and the crises involved in maturing. Overcoming each crisis calls for major structural changes within the organization if it is to proceed to the next growth stage. In a different era and in an entirely different economic environment the stages would be quite different — thus the model must be considered in its setting and not taken as applicable in all circumstances.

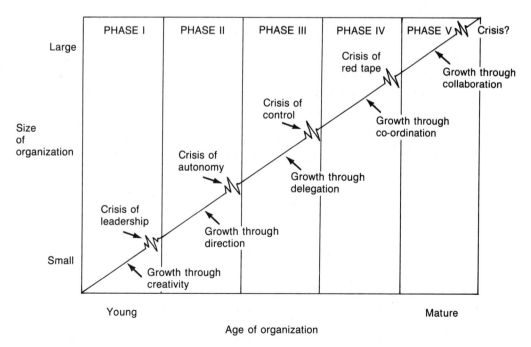

Figure 4.3 Greiner's five phases of growth.

Phase I: growth through creativity

This is the birth stage where the business is run by its founder who is an entrepreneur or inventor, but not a manager. All the founder's energy goes into creating or marketing the product or service rather than on managing or setting up systems. Communication between employees is frequent and informal in nature. Control of activities is by feedback from the marketplace.

The crisis arrives when the business has grown too large for the founder to run in an informal way. The founder is unlikely to have the talents and temperament needed to be a good manager and therefore must now employ someone to do the managing. This means relinquishing a certain amount of power: an extremely difficult thing for the founder of a business to do. If it is done successfully the business will proceed to the next growth stage; if not it will sooner or later flounder. This type of crisis has been illustrated several times by Clive Sinclair who is an inventor of extraordinary brilliance. He produced the first pocket calculators, digital watches, home computers and mini televisions. Different crises affected each of the products. For instance, one was overpriced, the next underpriced. Having learnt many business lessons he restricted himself to inventing and technical research, only to produce a product, the small electric car, which even the smallest amount of market research should have revealed as being unacceptable to potential customers.

Phase II: growth through direction

The new manager sets about formalizing activities. A functional organization structure is likely to be set up and jobs will be defined more specifically than in the past. Communication becomes more formal with the newly appointed manager making most of the decisions. Formal accounting systems for stock and purchases, incentive schemes and work standards, payroll, budgets and variance reporting will all be introduced.

The crisis arises because as the business grows the top manager still keeps all the power and does not allow lower-level managers or supervisors any chance to make decisions or shape plans. Eventually they demand this right and the manager is forced to delegate responsibility. However, this delegation may not be successful because the manager is unused to delegating and the subordinates are not practised in decision making. So the business may flounder at this stage, either through the manager not delegating successfully, or through good employees becoming disenchanted and leaving because of a lack of involvement. Once delegation takes place on a large scale, decentralization will have taken place. This is the next growth stage.

Phase III: growth through delegation

The business is now decentralized and responsibility is given to management at plant level. Head office managers restrain themselves from interfering with the running of the business at plant level and manage by exception. Head office managers will most likely occupy their minds with potential new acquisitions, takeovers or strategic alliances.

Eventually a crisis occurs since plant managers have preferred to go their own way rather than co-ordinating plans, money, technology, etc. with the rest of the organization. Head office will eventually wake up to this loss of control and in a bid to regain or reassert its authority it will grab back the reins by changing the system.

Phase IV: growth through co-ordination

Decentralized units are merged into product groups which form business units. Formal planning systems are put back and head office assumes a greater role — even to the extent of centralizing technical services such as data processing. Thus the organization is changed from a location-orientated one to a product-orientated one, and all reporting methods and standards are dictated by head office. A period of growth takes place (because of the co-ordination of the whole business) until gradually the systems instigated by head office proliferate beyond the point of utility. Line managers begin to resent the heavy direction from people at head office who are not familiar with local conditions, and head office staff may well complain of uncooperative line staff.

Phase V: growth through collaboration

With so much red tape and restriction the organization becomes rather like a dinosaur — slow to react to change. This was true of many large organizations at the beginning of the 1980s. Ross Perot, who was on General Motors' board until 1987, criticized their structure thus: 'At EDS [Electronic Data Services] if we saw a rattlesnake we shot it. At GM they put together a committee to study the situation. They then refer it to another committee, which in turn will refer it to the committee for the preservation of rattlesnakes'.[2] This shows clearly the stultifying effect of the red tape created by a phase IV organization.

In the 1970s, when Greiner produced and described his model, organizations had only just reached phase V in terms of growth and it was difficult to see how things were developing and would develop. Today we have the benefit of hindsight. Greiner, and others, envisaged correctly that the internal focus of the organization would shift to problem solving through team or task force action. This entails small teams of people coming together across functions in order to solve a particular problem or to design and follow the progress of a particular product or service. When the job is done the team is disbanded and other teams formed to work on different tasks. This requires a loose **matrix-type stucture** rather than the traditional hierarchical structure. The new structure must not be static but change constantly, as required, by means of the teams regrouping.

Contact between the different managers and teams is vital so that this flexible, fluid structure does not collapse. This may be achieved by holding regular conferences between key managers.

The structure which has emerged is not the matrix structure that had been tried and found wanting. A new organization structure was required which, as Mark Daniell, a director of Wasserstein Peella & Co. put it, 'balances the need for central co-ordination of resource allocation with the need for local initiatives in different market environments'.[2] This requires two changes to be made. Firstly the organization structure must change from the traditional hierarchical model, with its many delaying layers of management, to one which slightly ressembles a matrix — but is much improved. Secondly, the organization must be split into small sections again, as it was in phase III, but in this phase the sections must be linked together to a much greater extent than previously. Thus the problems faced at the end of phase III that were caused by decentralized units acting in their own interests and an overall lack of strategy will be overcome.

Both of these requirements appear to be met with a network structure (see Figure 4.4). The organization is broken down into many business units which are then linked, as required, to form a corporate network. The setting of strategic objectives and control of the main resources (manpower, finance and information channels) is from a central hub. If this were not so the organization would quickly degenerate into a confused and directionless state. Head office's role has been transformed from a supervisory or peripheral one into one which supports and adds to the value of all the individual business units. Thus it has become the very heart of the organization. Groups of people who were organized into departments under phase IV have been reorganized into independent companies or independent business units. Olivetti, for instance, now consists of more than two hundred different firms which are linked through a flexible network.

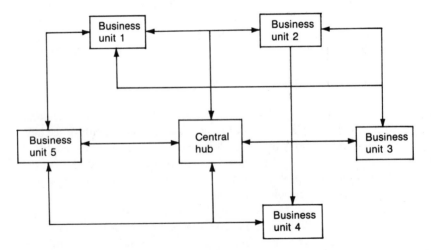

Figure 4.4 Business unit network structure.

This business unit network structure is growing beyond the confines of the organization as it is traditionally defined. Indeed, if units are legally independent can they be said to be part of the organization in the traditional meaning of the word? More than this, networks of **strategic alliances** are being created externally, that is between organizations. **Value added partnerships** and strategic alliances have, to a large extent, taken the place of the traditional, vertically integrated company.

What the next crisis will be we can only speculate. As Peter Drucker points out, reliance on task force teams assuages one problem but creates another: who will the business's managers be?[3] Will they be task force leaders, or will a two-headed monster emerge from the structure? Perhaps the seeds of the next crisis have already been sown in this particular aspect of the phase V structure.

To emphasize the point, it is not being suggested that the development of every organization may be fitted exactly into the Greiner model. However, the model serves as an indicator of the main thrusts in the development of an organization. Telecommunication and computer technology have improved considerably over the years and now offer the possibility of different and more suitable organization structures. Phase V, for instance, could not have occurred without the recent improvement in telecommunications. However, whether technology improves or not, as a business grows and strategically changes so does its structure. In the words of Alfred D. Chandler who researched into business organization in the 1950s, 'structure follows strategy'. The information system reflects closely the structure of the organization and both are dependent on the chosen strategy. This is examined in detail in section 4.7 after the illustrative case about BP.

4.6 Illustrative case: BP's phase V reorganization and restructure[4]

Early in 1990 a massive programme of change began at British Petroleum initiated by it's Chairman Robert Horton. His aim was to make BP the most successful oil company of the 1990s. Some changes, such as the creation of an updated logo, were relatively simple and painless. Others involving major changes in working methods and relationships were certainly not. The aim as far as the changes in the organization structure were concerned was to make BP as agile as a small company — not an easy task with 120,000 employees. Studies the previous year had shown that many employees felt that the organization structure was too bureaucratic. This view was not confined to office staff: employees on the oil rigs complained that a newly introduced safety programme entailed supervisors spending most of their time at a desk doing the paperwork rather than outside supervising. In addition, no decision could be made on a rig without first telephoning for permission. This often entailed a two or three hour wait for an answer.

The hierarchies which strangled decision making had to go. Thus whole layers of management were stripped out and twenty-seven committees abolished. In their place teams were created to carry out specific tasks. When the tasks were completed the teams would be disbanded. Networking was to be the 'glue' which would hold the organization together. This would mean the creation of a good information system which would allow and encourage individuals to talk both to their peers and to their bosses and subordinates. Part of this was achieved by technology and the rest by a change in attitude.

The change in structure was unusual in that it was on a massive scale and was carried out very quickly. Normally even major changes in structure take place more gradually. One of the major problems with implementing change on so large a scale is the difficulty of persuading the employees of the need to change. Therefore, before any change is made a good information system needs to be set up to inform every employee of the changes and what benefits they will bring. If this is not done then the proposed changes will not succeed. In this case BP set up many interviews and discussion groups between staff so that the proposals could be thoroughly considered. A 'card game' was even invented to assist with the implementation of the programme by reinforcing the new ideas.

4.7   The type of information system needed for each growth phase

During phase I of the model there is unlikely to be a formal communication system. Therefore an information system, as such, scarcely exists during this stage (if one excludes an informal system from the definition). The system used would be largely *ad hoc* and word of mouth with little in the way of written reports except when specifically requested. However, basic records such as payroll and accounts will of course be kept.

During phase II a formal information system is gradually set up by introducing small independent computer systems over a period of time. These independent systems or applications will be linked where necessary to save duplication in inputting data. The fewer the links the better, as passing information from one application to another is complex. This is because the applications will probably not be compatible enough to communicate directly with each other. Figure 4.5 shows the numerous links which may be required between five different applications A to E.

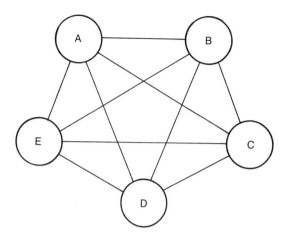

Figure 4.5 Five different systems and their links.

If two applications are linked together only one link is needed, if three applications are linked three links are needed, four applications need six links and so on. The mathematical formula for calculating the number of links is $\frac{1}{2}n(n-1)$. By the time the company has grown large and has many different systems or applications the whole is unwieldy and there is plenty of scope for programming faults and errors to creep in.

Where a large number of systems or applications are to be linked, a better and more modern method is to create a shared database, or series of linked databases. A shared database is illustrated in Figure 4.6 where each application has a single interface with the database.

A can communicate with D, for instance, by storing output on the database in standard form which can be read by D. Thus all data are available to all applications and have only to be entered into the system once, thus making the whole system flexible and simple to set up and run. This is because the programmer requires less knowledge of the detailed needs of all users of software packages in terms of data and information. This is not to say that the technology involved is simple and straightforward. In the past the formal information system would certainly have been created in stages. However, today it is possible, if the company is growing rapidly, for a complete system to be introduced. If this is the case then the central database will be, or should be, employed immediately.

Financial reporting and control systems may well not change greatly during phase III, the decentralization stage. Head office management will require reports from time to time in a standard form and in addition planning documents and budgets will be prepared. Beyond this, however, the plant manager will probably be left alone to develop an internal system for transaction processing and internal decision making. The system chosen will suit the type of business being carried out at the plant rather than the whole company. The choice of local system will only be constrained by the need for interplant communication, where appropriate.

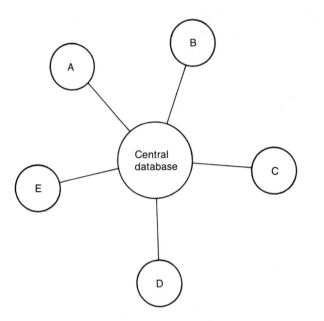

Figure 4.6 Links between five systems and a database.

The decentralization stage may entail the overall business being split vertically so that one plant manufactures the components or raw materials for the next. Alternatively, it may entail large units being split into smaller units sited near markets or resources. Interplay between the units becomes much more important than it was when the business was being run centrally by one person. This may well require a sophisticated system for monitoring production flow, stock levels, etc. An information system will be needed in order to optimize the flow of components from plant to plant or to provide a system which directs a customer order to a particular plant for manufacture. Networking which allows the transfer of computerized information from one plant to another or from one country to another, via the telephone lines, may well be necessary for this growth phase to take place successfully.

Phase IV requires an information system which links the different product group divisions to head office. Communication will be via head office and so the links between the different business units will become less important than previously. Information will flow into the centre and then be redirected by head office to whoever may require it. Typically, a large static information system which concentrates on the presentation of reports to top management is put in place at this stage. Monthly statistics are collected from the different divisions and are incorporated into the group's results. These figures are then 'locked', that is they cannot be altered, until the next month's reports are received.

Phase V requires a sophisticated system to achieve satisfactory results. The network structure of the group must be supported by a networked structure of information channels along which information can flow at any time. Information must be available as soon as the data are collected and whenever it is needed, if it is not then a flexible response is not truly possible. Therefore, employees should be able to log onto the system wherever they are in the organization, regardless of who they are, and obtain the information that they need from both the company's and a selection of external databases and systems. An example of such a system is that of IBM (see section 7.4). Information links between companies will probably be needed to provide information on customer demand and required production levels.

In order that business units may exchange information in an informal and flexible way some kind of teleconferencing system is vital (see section 8.16). Its purpose is to link a group of key managers for a conference or meeting without their needing to travel great distances. It may simply be a three-way telephone call or a more sophisticated video or computer-based system. Recent surveys show that many top managers regard teleconferencing as one of the most important recent developments in technology. Personal contact is a vital factor in any communication system: without it there may be a lack of sympathy with the other party's point of view as well as a greater chance of information being misunderstood. In today's global businesses this would not be possible without the facility for teleconferencing.

Some companies in phase V have not adopted a network structure for the internal structure of their business units. Instead they continue to use a hierarchical or pyramid structure. But this too has changed recently. In fact the traditional pyramid structure has changed considerably in nearly all large companies, whatever their phase, during the past ten years. The pyramid has changed its shape: its base has widened considerably thus reducing its peak dramatically (see Figure 4.7).

The reason for the change in shape is that the role of middle management has decreased, and continues to do so. They were the paper shufflers: the people who converted data into information to present in an intelligible and concise form to top management and who translated top management's orders into instructions for the workplace. Today this function is needed less and less. Top managers

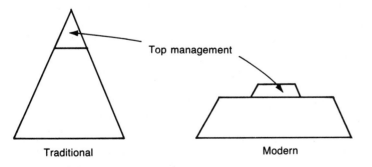

Top management

Traditional   Modern

Figure 4.7 Organization structures.

are now themselves able to obtain the information they require through executive systems. In addition improved communications technology has helped to increase the feasible span of control of a manager.

4.8 The current state of technology

The Greiner model describes a company which might have been formed in the USA at the beginning of this century and has progressed through the stages to become a powerful global business. A company which was started, say, ten years ago and is successful in terms of growth may well skip some of the stages. This is partly because a learning process has taken place from other organizations' past performance. More usually, however, it is because the potential exists for a business to grow at a quicker pace in today's global market than one formed earlier this century. In the past the majority of companies operated in the home market only because of the deficiencies of transport and communication at the time. Thus a modern organization may jump phase III, say, and go straight from phase II to IV. Alternatively, because of the nature of the business, it may adopt a matrix structure early on. (This kind of structure is not documented as existing before the Second World War when it was first used in aircraft manufacture. Presumably, therefore, it was 'not available for use' in the early part of the century.)

In addition, the technology involved in providing information and communication has improved out of all recognition in modern times. Thus today's business has quite a different set of options — and problems — from those that existed twenty, or even ten years, ago. For instance, consider a business at phase III, the decentralization stage, today and imagine that it has set up a sophisticated system connecting the different plants through one network. It is possible under these circumstances that the next crisis in the model may be avoided if the network can be used in the interests of the organization as a whole and not just in the interests of the local plant. Virtually instant monitoring and control is possible by head office managers through the medium of an organization-wide network. They may be able, or feel that they are able, to keep tighter reins on the decentralized business. Thus the crisis of control which was likely to occur previously at the end of the delegation stage can be avoided.

Similarly, because of the instant monitoring and control available through networks, the next crisis, that of red tape, may be avoided by wise management as it would seem possible to avoid the need for too much standardization and centralization. One example which helps to illustrate this is cash management. In the past, head office normally required all surplus cash to be returned to the central bank account where the chief financial officer could keep a close watch on the overall position and have cash available when needed by other business units. Today this is no longer necessary because the facility exists to transfer funds electronically from one account to another virtually immediately anywhere in the world. This means that the chief financial officer can monitor balances closely while leaving them in the accounts of the business unit. But, when required he is able to gain access to the funds quickly and direct them to a different business unit wherever it may be situated. The advantage of this is that business units are encouraged to look after and to build up their funds for their own future use. If the funds are not instantly required, it is the business unit which is credited with the interest — thus giving the business unit a much greater feeling of control.

4.9 Management style

The type of industry and the age of the company dictate to a certain extent the management style that should be adopted. As the purpose of a management information system is to provide information to help managers carry out their jobs in the best possible way it must reflect the prevailing management style, company ethos, etc. Some industries require a more formal style than others. Generally the more innovative the industry, the less formal and financially dominated both the management style and the information system should be. Otherwise there is the danger that constant monitoring will act as a brake upon innovative action. For instance, a very formal management information system, whose main purpose is to supply information to top management for the monitoring and controlling of activities, will rely heavily on techniques such as budgeting and variance analysis. This may not be suitable if the business situation is fluid and change is constantly required. The age of the business will also dictate management style. A young company will generally be less formal and more innovative than a mature one. This is due in no small part to the size of the business, but in addition the predominant management style of the era in which the business was founded will also have an influence on the style of today.

However, within these generalizations there is plenty of scope for variety and no hard and fast rules can be laid down. Traditionally, American companies such as ITT, have had very formal, paper-orientated systems. The result was that business units, wherever they were in the world and whatever the nature of their individual business, would have to plan in the same way because they were required to fill in the same forms or send the same information back to head office. Hefty procedure manuals would be produced laying down the precise way this should be done which resulted in a rigid management style and system. Other businesses within the same field profess to quite a different style of management. For example, Lord Weinstock of GEC — famed for his control methods — has said that he receives all the basic information he needs on three sheets of paper from which he can tell at a glance if something is seriously amiss.[5]

When STC took over ICL (now owned by Fujitsu) in 1984 the two companies had very different systems which reflected their different management styles.[6]. STC, which at one time was part of ITT, had an information system whose main aim was to provide reports and ratios for top managers in order that they could control the business. Therefore, its management information system was a very polished one which produced good-looking reports for the directors and top management to use. However, it was *static* in nature, in that the information was fed in monthly and then locked in the system so that it could not be altered thereafter. It was also limited in scope, the information being restricted to ten predetermined schedules.

ICL, on the other hand, had a system called the Cube (because it was three-dimensional) which was quite different. Its main aim was to help the managers who made the day-to-day business decisions by providing a database which allowed them to sort the data in different ways. Information could be provided from the database in three different dimensions: time, account and department. This allowed the user to manipulate the data in all sorts of innovative ways by making on-line enquiries. The updating of information was carried out throughout the month as required. However, it was unable to provide information in as suitable a form for the directors and top management as the STC system without considerable manipulation. Very wisely after the two companies joined, it was decided that the two information systems should remain in operation in their respective businesses. Thus there was no forcing of the one management style on the other.

4.10 Geographical spread

In the past the wider the geographical spread of the organization the more formal and standardized the information system needed to be. This was so that head office could keep control of, and co-ordinate where necessary, the different business activities. This is changing rapidly as technology improves. Teleconferencing (mentioned earlier) and other advances which are discussed in later chapters are now allowing a more informal type of information system. However, everything has its price, and it must be remembered that the equipment and its use on a worldwide basis will involve considerable financial investment. Any benefits from an improved information system must be substantial to justify the increased costs. The benefits, however, may not just be a better flow of information for internal use but may be of strategic and competitive importance to the business, such as increasing sales volume or even creating entirely new business opportunities. Such benefits are exeedingly difficult to quantify, as was discussed in section 1.8.

4.11 Political and economic influences

No organization is an island: it exists within a particular political and economic framework. A rigid and authoritarian political system tends to be reflected in the country's business organizations. These organizations tend to be multi-layered, hierarchical and rigid in structure. As a result, they have rather formal and vertically-orientated information systems. On the other hand, in a liberal democracy the opposite tends to be true. Thus organizations in such countries have fewer management levels and tend to be much more flexible. If the organization has reached phase V of the Greiner model, as is possible in a liberal democracy, the formation of task forces will further reduce layers of management and increase flexibility. The information system will need to be much broader to cope with the broader management base, and have less emphasis on control and more on the provision of information to enable all personnel to operate efficiently.

In favourable economic times the internal information system of a business is normally more informal and power is decentralized. In bad times a business tends to gather power back to the centre and a more formal and vertically-orientated information system is imposed. An interesting illustration of this, because it was one of the first and because it happened so soon after decentralization, is that of a leading Japanese sythetic textile manufacturer.[7] In 1970 this company decentralized when it became apparent that such a structure was required to achieve further growth. Almost immediately a series of unfortunate economic events hit Japan: the oil crisis, the revaluation of the yen, inflation and recession. This caused labour and material prices to rise and demand to decrease leading to intense price competition. One of the company's answers to this was to change back to a centralized functional structure which could give a more unified perspective. This helped the company through the bad period by concentrating on aspects such as minimizing short run costs.

NOTES

1. From Larry E. Greiner, 'Evolution and revolution as organizations grow', *Harvard Business Review*, July/Aug. 1972. Reproduced by kind permission.
2. Mark Daniell, 'Webs we weave', *Management Today*, Feb. 1990.
3. Peter Drucker, 'The coming of the new organization', *Harvard Business Review*, Jan./Feb. 1988.
4. From *The Money Programme*, broadcast by the BBC, 1990.
5. Walter Goldsmith and David Clutterbuck, *The Winning Streak* (Penguin, 1984).
6. From a paper by Patricia Rickard, 'Internal reporting systems' (City of London Polytechnic, 1988).
7. Lex Donaldson, 'Regaining control at Nipont', *Journal of General Management*, 1979.
8. Martin Large, *Social Ecology* (Hawthorn Press, Stroud, 1981).

FURTHER READING

Lessem, R. *Global Management Principles* (Prentice Hall International, 1989). A wide-ranging book which contains a good section on organization structures and how to organize individuals for work as businesses change and develop.

EXERCISES

1. The following three-phase model is an alternative to the Greiner model which was put forward originally by Lievegoed. The summary of the three development stages reproduced here is from Social Ecology by Martin Large.[8]

	Phase I Pioneering	Phase II Differentiated	Phase III Integrated
Approach	Personal	Impersonal	Individual
Leadership	Primal	Rational	Developmental
Goals	Directive	Purposeful	Inspirational
Structure	Simple/flat	Complex/pyramid	Open/hexagon
Response	Improvised	Planned	Evolved
Style	Active	Authoritative	Adaptive
Orientation	Outer-orientated	Inward-looking	Outer/inner balance
Emphasis	Economic	Technical	Social

Consider the relationship between the Greiner and Lievegoed models. How would the information systems change and develop during the three phases of Lievegoed's model?

2. Outline the differences you would expect between the information systems used by a corner shop, a regional supermarket chain and an international supermarket group.

Part Two

Techniques and technologies for providing information

Part One dealt with the specific information which an organization may need and the nature of the system that is likely to be required to meet its specific information needs. Part Two looks at a range of different techniques and technologies which can be incorporated into, or themselves comprise, the organization's overall information system. These techniques and technologies are, or should be, selected *only* because they help to supply the information which the organization requires. There can be no other criterion for selection.

Most large organizations will use the majority of the techniques and technologies discussed in the following chapters. Smaller organizations will have fewer information needs and may have use for only a small number of them. Each chapter covers a different topic, and in each instance examples and cases illustrate how the technique or technology may be used in practice. It is up to the individual organization to find a mix suited to its own particular needs.

It should be borne in mind, however, that a good, or even adequate, information system is not created simply by tacking several techniques and technologies together. Careful planning of today's and future needs must be undertaken and a compatible mix of systems sought.

The most important aspect that requires planning is the information or communication infrastructure of the organization. This is the base upon which everything else rests. A distributed database, for example (as discussed in Chapter 9) will operate successfully only if the communication infrastructure is in place to distribute the information conveniently and quickly from the database to the person requiring it. Expert systems (Chapter 10) can be major weapons in the fight to create a specific type of competitive advantage, but they again usually need good communication systems if they are to achieve their aims. Chapter 5 which deals with fast cycle organizations also illustrates the importance of a good information or communication infrastructure. This is because being fast cycle usually requires rapid communication of the customers' needs, stock requirements, etc.

As you read through the different techniques and technologies discussed in Part Two try to imagine how they might be used to link up to form an overall information system strategy for a specific organization with which you are familiar. How an information strategy can be formulated is discussed in Part Three once the reader is familiar with the different types of system currently available.

Fast cycle systems

5

SCOPE AND CONTENTS

A: Fast cycle companies. This section explains what fast cycle companies are and how entire industries can change their nature and become fast cycle: information systems, together with a simple logical production flow, are the keys. The case of Federal Express illustrates a variety of information systems as used in a fast cycle business. We explain how the concept of the value chain has become important in analyzing a business to find activities where time may be squeezed. Porter's value chain is explained. Lastly, the concept of just-in-time is considered to illustrate how organizations can simplify their manufacturing process or the provision of a service to become fast cycle.

B: Fast cycle manufacturing systems. A range of different systems relying on technology that may be used by manufacturing companies to become fast cycle are examined. Some of these are information systems and others control the manufacturing process. The ones considered are: MRP I, MRP II, CAD, CAE, CAM and CIM. The relationship between them is discussed and the benefits and problems of moving towards an integrated system (CIM) are considered.

C: Fast cycle distribution systems. This section deals with fast cycle systems for distribution. It covers retail organizations, specifically supermarkets and fashion retail outlets. It also considers links into value chains outside the organization, in particular forward linking in the car industry. Lastly, the McKesson case is considered as it illustrates several types of external linkage.

A: FAST CYCLE COMPANIES

5.1 What is fast cycle?

Anyone familiar with the old cowboy films will recall that the hero was inevitably 'the fastest draw in the West'. He could pull the trigger of a gun quicker than any opponent and that necessitated having the fastest reaction. The cowboy who was the fastest draw could react quicker than his opponent and thus had power both real and assumed. It is just the same today for a business. The business which can react quickest to a situation has power; power which can be turned into competitive advantage and profit. The organization within a business sector which is the first to react to a change in circumstances or to spot a customer need, pre-empts its competitors and gains increased sales and, therefore, profit, thus strengthening its position. It is not enough, of course, just to spot the change and react to it quickly. The cowboy who was the fastest on the draw had to be accurate. Almost anyone could fire a gun in a random direction very quickly but part of being the fastest draw was to be on target. Similarly an organization must be on target. It must interpret the changed needs correctly and produce a quality product or service to meet those changed needs.

The moral is, therefore, to become a **fast cycle** company and gain competitive advantage. To do this time must be squeezed out of all processes — design, production, marketing and information processes. Whole strategies have been based upon being a fast cycle company, with fast cycle systems, and it is in no way a modern phenomenon nor one which demands the latest technology, although the latest technology can help. However, it must be remembered that if the technology is available to one company it will probably also be available to its competitors — if not at present then in the near future. Therefore, as always, competitive advantage may be fleeting.

An example of a simple industry whose whole strategy is built upon being fast cycle is the tailoring industry in Hong Kong. In order to supply the foreign travellers who are spending only a brief time in Hong Kong the tailoring businesses must be fast cycle. It must endeavour to meet the customer's needs in the shortest possible time by producing, for instance, a made to measure shirt within twenty-four hours. A fast cycle system is needed, but in this case nothing complicated is required in the way of technology: one merely needs a superbly organized and adaptable workforce. This idea can be followed by virtually any organization which is willing to spend time and money to remove bottlenecks, delays and errors from their processes and to improve material and information flows. This requires organizations to rethink their procedures and to develop information systems and techniques which will improve the flow of information and goods. It may well mean throwing out many of the existing internal reporting systems and radically changing the information systems for manufacturing, procurement and customer service.

In order to become a fast cycle company attitudes have to be changed as well as systems. People in fast cycle companies must think of themselves as part of an integrated whole: a linked chain of activities and decision making points that are continually delivering value to customers. Both management and workforce must understand how their activities relate to the whole and how time can best be used. This is normally second nature in small companies where most employees work directly on the product or deal directly with the customer. But as companies grow, the aim of the business and the flow of activities and systems often become hidden from the individual employee or manager and need to be rediscovered. The managers in large organizations may, therefore, need to go back to basics and redefine the chain of activities and decision points before they can select systems which will squeeze time from those activities that are likely to generate competitive advantage. When the chain of activities is considered and analyzed it is usually the case that it can be simplified. The first task in any study of this kind, therefore, is to simplify the activities themselves and the information systems that accompany them. Simplicity allows a company to become fast cycle, and a simple chain of activities reduces the need for much management information.

5.2 Making an industry fast cycle

Sometimes being fast cycle is critical to surviving in a particular industry — as it might be in the tailoring industry in Hong Kong. Alternatively, the industry can be totally transformed by one participant in the industry becoming fast cycle and providing the customer with a better service. This, in turn, forces rival businesses to follow their lead if they wish to remain players in that industry. One such area where this has occurred is that of parcel delivery. The case below outlines Federal Express's use of a series of different technologies to provide the information necessary to become a fast cycle company. This forced the other parcel companies to become fast cycle also and completely changed the nature of the industry.

5.3 Illustrative case: Federal Express

Federal Express could not have become fast cycle without modern technology. It is, therefore, a product of the age and could not have existed in its present form in an earlier one. The founder of Federal Express had a vision of a fast cycle distribution business, and this he proceeded to create during the 1970s and early 1980s in the USA. It is a parcel delivery business that guarantees that any package sent within the USA will arrive by 10.30 a.m. the next day. In order to achieve this a good communication and information system is necessary in addition to a good transport system. The company has its own planes and vehicles and has spent a considerable amount of money on information technology. By 1988 it had two computers for every one of its 55,000 employees, and a whole range of information systems were provided for their use.

Firstly, to give good initial customer contact, centrally located telephonists answer calls from potential customers. If the customer query is 'where is the nearest collection point?', the telephonist can give precise details and directions from a local landmark that the customer knows. This information is gleaned from a computer to which the telephonist has access. Without the computer the telephonist could not give a satisfactory reply as it is extremely unlikely that the telephonist has ever visited the town in which the customer lives and certainly would not have enough information to give directions to the collection point.

As soon as Federal Express receives the parcel, a bar code is put on it giving details of its destination. This is used to control the parcel throughout its journey. The bar code can be read by a hand-held scanning pen called a super tracker. A parcel tracking system called Cosmos scans the bar code on the parcel at each stage on the journey and reroutes it. Prior to the use of the bar code a code consisting of ten digits had to be written on the parcel and had to be read at the relevant redirection points along the parcel's journey. This was a major source of error and thus of delay in the delivery, but the new system is virtually wholly reliable. Cosmos is much more than a tracking system; it generates information to control and monitor activity levels and provides the information for planning flight operations.

In addition the company has its own weather analysis centre which sends forecasts to flight centre control. Local radio masts are used to communicate with every delivery van so that vehicles may be rerouted for pick-ups. The vehicles have an in-cab computer and this, together with super tracker, means that any parcel the company is delivering can be traced within thirty minutes — wherever it may be in the world at the time.

The company also has its own satellite television for communicating with employees. New ideas and parcel regulations can be communicated to all employees almost immediately. This is particularly useful for relaying day-to-day information such as a change in the weight regulations. Alternatively, it can be used by top management to communicate the company's aims and culture to employees.

All of the different systems blend together to provide a comprehensive network of information systems that ensure the company is as fast cycle as possible. Without the systems the company could not follow the strategy of being fast cycle nor sell itself to the public on that basis. Federal Express also developed a revolutionary system for the physical distribution of the parcels. This is known as a hub and spoke system, and is now widely copied by others. The system has a central hub, that is a location where most of the sorting is carried out and through which all parcels flow. Spokes radiate from the hub to various regional airports and from the airports the parcels are taken to their specific destinations. Thus the parcels move in along one spoke to the hub where they are re-routed and sent to their destination along another spoke. (This type of model can also be copied for the flow of information. For example, data may be collected locally and sent to the centre where it is stored: then when particular information is required it is sent to the location requesting it.)

Other parcel companies were forced to become fast cycle to compete with Federal Express. The single European market has added impetus to the development of a fully integrated fast cycle parcel delivery service in Europe. For example, in the ten years to 1989 TNT UK has grown from £5m turnover to £300m and its staff has increased from 500 to 8,000. That growth is set to continue throughout Europe if the strong competition allows. TNT's hub computer has the power for 60 million instructions per second and data lines to 10,000 terminals. Together with the requisite planes and staff this allows TNT to say that they can pick up a parcel anywhere in Europe and deliver it anywhere else in Europe overnight.[1]

5.4 The value chain

Each organization is individual and has its own set of activities, quite distinct from others in its industry. These reflect the organization's history, strategies, etc. The management of Northern Telecom, Inc., a Canadian company, carried out an analysis of this when they wished to become a fast cycle company. They identified six activities to concentrate on when implementing a fast cycle strategy. These were: new product introduction and change, procurement practices, manufacturing process improvement, operations planning and scheduling, product delivery and installation-field service.[2] The activities of a business are linked in a chain. While each activity is in a sense separate, they are all interdependent. This chain was first called the 'value chain' by Michael Porter.[3] He identified 'value activities' which linked to form a value chain for a particular business and this linkage could be used to derive competitive advantage.

The value a business creates is measured by the amount that buyers are willing to pay for a product or service. A business is profitable only if the value it creates is greater than the cost of performing these activities. To gain competitive advantage a business must either perform these activities at a lower cost or perform them better than its competitors thus achieving product or service differentiation. Porter's generic value chain comprises value activities which are classified as either **primary** or **support activities**. The support activities include the setting up of an information infrastructure and the provision of information to assist and improve the performance of the primary activities. A value chain for a typical manufacturing company, showing all the primary activities but only the one support activity of information provision, is shown in Figure 5.1.

The value chain for a particular company in a particular industry is part of a larger stream of activities which Porter calls the **value system**. This includes the value chains of suppliers and customers. All value chains overlap and are linked into the overall value system. Figure 5.2 portrays such a system. The

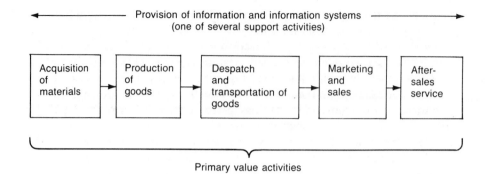

Figure 5.1 The value chain of a manufacturing company.

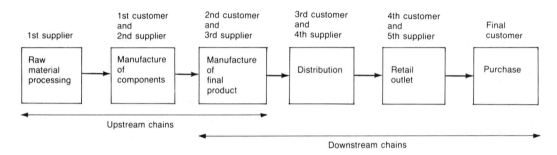

Figure 5.2 A business sector's value system.

upstream chain refers to manufacturing activities and the downstream one to distribution and retailing activities. As will be seen from the many examples quoted later in the chapter, a business does not have to stop at its own value chain when attempting to gain competitive advantage. It can link in with suppliers or customers to create a large 'vertically linked business unit'. This may have many of the benefits of a vertically diversified business without many of the drawbacks. These linkages create dependencies between the supplier and the company and between the company and the customer which, once formed, cannot easily be broken. Neither does the linkage necessarily have to be vertical. Horizontal linkages into different value chains are possible, although they are not so common. The case of McKesson outlined later in the chapter illustrates one of these horizontal links.

Having defined a particular business's value activities, the next step is to consider where time should be squeezed from the chain and how this should be done. The primary activities of the chain are those from which time must be squeezed as they normally form the **critical path** in supplying the customer with the product. In an organization which is attempting to be a fast cycle company, the support activities should never be allowed to intrude into the chain and delay supplying the customer. This might occur, for instance, if the processing of sales orders were delayed in order to batch them up before entering them into a computer. Batching up may save money but it wastes time. A company which has no pretence to be fast cycle may be quite happy to save money at the expense of time but a fast cycle company would not be.

There are many techniques and approaches which can be used to save or squeeze time in the primary activities. Many rely on technology and some of these are considered in the next chapter. However, technology is not always necessary. For example, the simpler the physical manufacturing system is the simpler the information system needs to be. This is because less information will be needed to plan, monitor and control the manufacturing process. A simple system does not require much modern technology to assist it, therefore, it makes sense to simplify the physical systems first and this will in turn simplify the needs of the information system. This is illustrated clearly by the JIT technique.

5.5 Just-in-time

Just-in-time (JIT) is a technique which requires little technology in order to operate efficiently. However, as with most techniques, technology well employed can be of considerable benefit in this context. JIT is an information system for short-term production scheduling according to the requirements of customers, and is based on a philosophy of flexibility and responsiveness. It attempts to produce components and products as they are required by customers rather than in advance of customers' needs: hence its name. The customers, therefore, dictate production by placing orders for the goods. The result of JIT production methods is to minimize or abolish finished goods stock and production work in progress. In addition, the JIT concept is applied to raw materials. The object is to minimize the stock held and only to receive materials immediately prior to their use in the manufacturing process.

JIT originated at Toyota in Japan in the 1950s after, so the story goes, a group of managers went to the USA to study factory processes.[4] While they were there they went into a supermarket and noticed that people bought small quantities of goods and that the shelves, which also contained relatively small quantities of goods, were frequently restocked. They introduced the system into Toyota's production process so that a manufacturing section or cell makes a quantity of a particular component which is then stored in a container. The containers are small and at Toyota contain no more than one-tenth of a day's production of the component. The process starts when the final assembly section gets a signal that a customer has placed an order. The assembly section goes to its 'supermarket' for material (components) and takes a container of each component needed. In each container is a kanban (which means card in Japanese). This is the authorization to produce another container full of parts. When the container of components is collected by an assembly section employee the kanban will be removed from the container by the employee and passed back to the manufacturing section thus signalling that another container load may be produced. This pattern is repeated right back through the total manufacturing process.

Thus the most beautifully simple information system is created with the kanban as its base. (The kanban does not have to be a card, at least one factory uses coloured golf balls which are put into a chute.) The only piece of paper that is needed is a master assembly schedule which will group small orders and ensure an even mix and flow of products which the technique relies on. Thus JIT requires very little technology to work smoothly. It can of course be used with a computerized information system rather than pieces of paper but this is not always an advantage because technology may be used partially to hide or 'paper over the cracks' of a poor communication or information system. The great advantage of JIT is its superb simplicity where visual signals replace computerized work in progress tracking and detailed capacity planning systems as normally found in the West. Traditionally, western businesses used a fairly complicated planning system which preplanned production using estimated production times. An electronics company which used this traditional method had eighty people working on the production scheduling and control process at a cost of £1m a year.[5] The large number of people made communication difficult and, as a result, the final production output rarely satisfied sales' requirements. When the company adopted JIT not only was stock reduced but customer service levels improved and the production control cost was cut by half.

In a JIT organization the workforce control and monitor themselves. Usually statistical control charts showing improvement patterns and performance indicators against a plan are pinned up for all to see at the point of production. If the managers want to know what is happening in relation to productivity and performance levels they go to the shop floor and look at the charts. In most other types of organization a manager would switch on his or her terminal and bring the relevant data onto the screen — or alternatively open the office door and shout for the relevant figures to be brought in.

A typical information system for a company which uses the JIT system would comprise the following three subsystems:[6]

- *Technology database.* A record store containing details and specifications of all materials, products and equipment for use by the other two subsystems.
- *Planning subsystem.* Provides information of production arrangements for the following month so that managers can prepare and organize the workforce.
- *Performance measurement subsystem.* Compares actual performance with the plan.

It is only since 1980 or so that western businesses have tried to adopt the JIT philosophy and implement JIT systems. Some have been successful, others have not. Basically it runs contrary to traditional western thought and thus its implementation has not been easy. Western organizations traditionally believed that long production runs of a standard product reduced the cost per unit and were the secret of success. This had the effect of building up large stocks. As holding stock costs money, there comes a point where the increased costs of holding large amounts of stock outweigh the benefits of long production runs. If it is possible to reduce the cost of shorter production runs then the change over point at which it begins to be worse to hold large stocks comes much sooner. Thus the costs involved in storage are reduced or forgone, but above all else the benefit of JIT is that if a company can produce to a customer's order it is able to meet his or her specific needs: this should give the business an edge over its competitors.

The JIT philosophy, therefore, concentrates on reducing **lead times** and machine set-up times. As a result, finished goods stock, raw materials stock and work in progress may be reduced to a minimum. In addition, working capital and floor space requirements are reduced. In order to cut raw material stock to a minimum, suppliers must be found who can deliver regularly, reliably and to a high standard of quality. Ford, for instance, have some of their components delivered as frequently as every two hours. Hewlett-Packard's manufacturing unit in Scotland can receive components within an hour of placing an order with its suppliers. This requires a high degree of cooperation between the supplier and the company, and usually means having a single supplier, for a particular material, who is willing to work closely with the company to meet its requirements. The reward for the supplier is a high price, as, if quality is always as specified and no storage costs are involved, the purchasing company can afford to pay considerably over the going rate. Once this arrangement has been made neither party can easily switch business and thus stability is ensured for both supplier and producer. The potential for stability has increased further in recent years with the introduction of networks which link the supplier and manufacturer together (see section 7.12).

B: FAST CYCLE MANUFACTURING SYSTEMS

5.6 Material requirements planning (MRP I)

A JIT system is referred to as a *pull system* because the product is pulled through the production process by the customer. The instruction comes from the customer purchasing or placing an order and the information flows backwards in stages through the manufacturing process. Not all organizations can operate on this basis. A hamburger fast-food outlet operates in this way but a top quality restaurant cannot. At a hamburger outlet when a customer places an order for a particular burger a pre-made one is taken from the shelf where several of each type are waiting for customers. An employee in the kitchen watches the shelf and replenishes it as necessary, while the manager watches the quantity of burgers used and will reorder when necessary. Thus the fast-food outlet operates on a JIT system. A top quality restaurant with a cordon bleu chef cannot operate such a system because of the time taken to prepare the food and dishes cannot be left standing waiting for a buyer. Instead a *push system* is needed which will produce food for a predetermined number of people. A plan will be made which determines the likely number of meals that will be served on a particular evening. This will depend on such factors as the day of the week, the seating capacity and current trends. It is the plan which determines the quantity of meat and vegetables purchased.

Similarly, some manufacturing companies cannot use a JIT system to instantly provide a customer with a product. Instead they use a system called **materials requirements planning** (MRP I) which, in jargon, 'explodes' a finished product backwards in terms of its material content. MRP I can work either from a customer order or from a predetermined production schedule which anticipates customer orders. When a customer orders a product, or a plan to manufacture a product is set, the product has to be broken down into its components and raw materials for planning and ordering purposes. Some materials have to be ordered immediately, others can be ordered later so as to arrive just in time for the production process for which they are needed. This is portrayed in Figure 5.3 in an example where, for simplicity's sake, production consists of just five processes and three materials — steel, fixings and a speedometer. It is assumed that no stock is held and that production takes place after the customer has ordered. This may be slightly unrealistic as, in practice, most companies would build some components of the final product on the assumption that they will

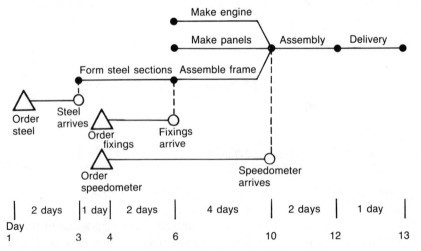

Figure 5.3 Part of an MRP I schedule for material acquisition.

be required to meet some order or another in the next day or so, thus the completion time of a particular customer's order will be cut. For instance, a car manufacturer meeting a customer order could carry out the early stages of manufacture before the order had been placed and before it became customer-specific. This could be done on the basis that a certain number of orders are received on average per day. Any shortfall or overproduction can be adjusted in the next day's production or on a JIT basis.

The improved computer and telecommunication technologies of the 1980s played a major part in boosting the adoption of this type of technique as without them it would be impossible to operate such a system successfully in a complex manufacturing organization. Some companies require as many as a thousand or more different raw materials in order to manufacture their products. With such a large number of items it can easily be seen that the arithmetic would be beyond the ability of the most able humans and that a computerized system is necessary for MRP I to operate. This is one reason why economic order quantity, a statistical method, was used in the past to determine when to order and how much stock should be held. Modern systems have the capability of making the economic order quantity calculation obsolete and replacing it with a simple arithmetic calculation.

It must be mentioned that modern systems are not perfect and may create a whole series of problems that did not exist previously. MRP I is a modern system which has its difficulties. For example, the US Department of Defense found that MRP I systems were moving materials internally among various accounts. This led to duplicate billings for materials. According to the audit agency such deficient MRP I systems have cost the US government hundreds of millions of dollars. A survey carried out in 1988 of 159 contracts using MRP I found deficiencies in the MRP I adopted by 112 of them. In 23 cases there were serious deficiencies.[7]

5.7 Manufacturing resource planning (MRP II)

MRP I is sometimes combined with another information system, namely **manufacturing resource planning** (MRP II). MRP II provides an integrated decision support system for planning, scheduling and control that covers three activities:

1. Demand management (customer orders).
2. Supply management (materials and components).
3. Capacity management (efficient use of resources).

Based upon a forecast of customer orders from the marketing department and product specifications from the design and manufacturing departments, a computer system uses details of lead times and capacity constraints to create production schedules. These schedules feed into schedules for procurement, production, manpower, dispatch and cash flow, thus influencing and adjusting the amount of each resource needed. So MRP II ties together the activities of many departments such as design, manufacturing, marketing, distribution, finance and personnel. In addition, MRP II can measure the performance of manufacturing and related departments by monitoring costs, quality, volumes, stock, etc. It can even be used to amend and improve product design in the light of problems faced on the factory floor.

The American Production and Inventory Control Society, when reporting on the installation and success of MRP and JIT systems, said that the average company finds that stock turnover increases by 50 per cent, lead times for delivery are 17 per cent shorter and that there was a 55 per cent improvement in meeting promised delivery dates. It should be stressed, however, that if a problem exists in internal manufacturing and information systems it is unlikely to be solved by technology and money. Instead, the organization should first look to improve and simplify the existing systems and only then consider the use of technology.

Every primary activity (see section 5.4) has both a physical and an information processing component. The physical component encompasses all the physical tasks required to carry out the activity. The information processing component encompasses the steps required to capture, manipulate and channel the data necessary to perform the activity. JIT and MRP II are information systems for the planning and organization of production and its associated areas. In order to achieve a properly integrated and successful business strategy the production information systems must be integrated firstly into the physical manufacturing system and secondly into the information systems for other business areas. JIT is a technique which integrates the information system into the production system in a superbly simple way. MRP II needs to be coupled with a system to control the physical manufacturing aspects of the business. We now take a brief look at the systems which control the physical manufacturing aspects of a business and consider how they relate to the information system MRP II. The survey is then gradually broadened so as to see how the JIT and MRP II information systems link into the information systems of other business activities.

5.8 Computer aided design and manufacturing

The computer and its associated technology have had an important impact on manufacturing. **Computer aided design** or **engineering** (CAD or CAE) are two such techniques now used by many companies. The former automates the design process so as to permit the manipulation of drawings, three-dimensional modelling, computer generated perspective views, etc. CAE turns the designs into manufacturable products by verifying the feasibility of the plans: this may include assessing and testing material specifications and tolerances. These two techniques should mean better designs which do not have to be modified at the production trial stage. In turn, this means that more product launches are possible, if desired, as planning and design times are greatly reduced. Other benefits can be incorporated into CAD and CAE, such as a common database of knowledge for all manufacturing and expert design systems (discussed in Chapter 10) to design to individual requirements. The Rover Group is one company to use this technology successfully: it has led to a threefold improvement in drawing office productivity. Rover regard the creation of a common engineering database, used by everyone in design, development and manufacturing, as the single most important innovation in the motor vehicle industry in the past twenty years. Rover now expects to be able to introduce a new car within four years rather than the normal seven or eight.[8]

Computer aided manufacturing (CAM) is the next step along the manufacturing chain. CAM defines operating sequences and creates instructions for computer numerically controlled (CNC) machines. It should be used with CAD and CAE to realize its full potential. For instance, tools and moulds can be produced directly from CAD and CAE data. Instructions on how to manufacture components on CNC machines can also be generated this way. In addition CAM provides a monitoring and automatic feedback facility. Thus CAM has considerable potential in speeding up production — for instance, Rolls-Royce introduced a sophisticated CAM system with the aim of cutting the production time for a car from twenty-six weeks to six weeks.[9] This not only made the company more responsive to customers' needs but also cut work in progress by two-thirds thus reducing costs.

5.9 Computer integrated manufacturing

The whole physical and information processing technology is collectively known as **computer integrated manufacturing** (CIM). As yet, total CIM for a whole factory does not exist but some companies are making strenuous attempts to achieve it and have gone a considerable way towards doing so. The aim is to link all systems such as CAD, CAE, MRP I and MRP II into a total computer system which will make many humans redundant. This linkage is depicted in Figure 5.4. CIM extends beyond mere production, however, to link all facets of a manufacturing business through a common network and database. It encompasses, or will do, design, purchasing, production, planning and control, assembly, inspection, marketing and accounting. Through CIM, therefore, it is possible to pursue new strategies. For instance, it becomes feasible to produce specialized designs for a finely tuned, small market segment, or even to produce a specific product for an individual customer. Thus products can be positioned in the market very precisely as the organization can compete with products tailored to the needs of small groups of customers in more closely defined market segments than was possible before.

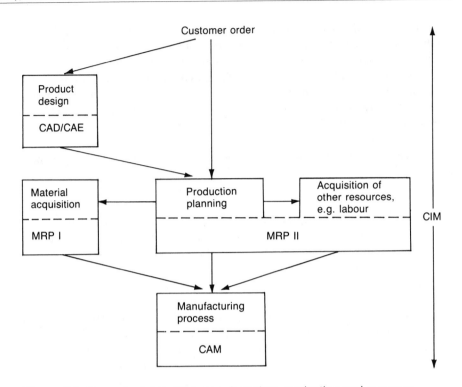

Figure 5.4 Computer integrated manufacturing: production and resource acquisition systems.

One of the major problems encountered with the installation of CIM is how to integrate the information system (which tells the machines what to build) with the physical control aspect (which tells the machines how to build and which monitors quality). One of the first companies to get close to using total CIM was Allen–Bradley, a subsidiary of Rockwell International Corporation, which manufactures industrial automation controls and systems. Allen–Bradley had an integrated CIM system running in 1986 to control a manufacturing process which produced 600 units an hour in any of 777 variations with lot sizes which could be as small as one or two items. The chief executive commented on the problems of integration thus:

> When you try to put in the information system simultaneously with the control system, the former has lots of problems. Let's say a contactor base comes to station one. The computer reads the bar code that we stick on the bottom of the base and then goes back to the information system — which governs orders and schedule — to find out exactly what kind of thing to build, how many, and so on. If the control software — 'build like this', 'inspect for that' - was not properly separated from and integrated with information software, God knows how long that base would sit there. It could sit for five minutes. You can waste a whole bunch of the computer memory — and time — looking for where the hell the data is.

So we had to find a way to partition the software. Today it takes only six seconds for station one to know what to do. We still have got all those diagnostic things running, quality inspections — practically every kind of sensor you can think of operating in real time — 3,500 automated test inspection stations.[10]

However, despite the problems, large savings of time and money are possible with CIM. IBM achieved such savings after it installed CIM technology at its thirty-five plants situated around the world. In its German plants at Mainz and Berlin the production cycle time on one product line was reduced from twenty days to six days over a three year period. Over the same period the **material turnover rate** improved from 8.7 times to 25 times a year.[8]

The speed and cost advantages of CIM can be built into specific strategies. Sometimes this is done as a positive strategy in order to strengthen an already good market position. However, it is often done when the business is in a very weak position and threatened by competition which is too strong to be fought by traditional means. This was the reason that Allen–Bradley installed their system and Xerox reacted similarly when threatened. In 1982 Xerox found itself in a rapidly worsening position.[11] It had only 41 per cent of the worldwide photocopier revenue whereas six years previously it had had twice that percentage. In addition, its costs were between 30 and 50 per cent higher than its Japanese rivals and it took twice as long to develop new products. Xerox used CAD technology to shorten development time and to cut development costs. This resulted in a cut in development time of 50 per cent. Prior to this, Xerox engineers had designed nearly all the components required for their production even though they were virtually all bought in and not manufactured by Xerox itself. Xerox reduced its number of suppliers from over five thousand to four hundred, and trained the remaining suppliers in techniques such as JIT. It also involved them in the design of new components — in some cases to the extent of simply giving the supplier a performance specification and letting the supplier design the part rather than Xerox. This resulted in rejects of incoming components and materials being reduced by 93 per cent over a four year period which helped to reduce product cost by approximately 10 per cent each year for those four years. Production lead time was also reduced from fifty-two to eighteen weeks. Thus the installation of a package of techniques and systems cut costs substantially and, perhaps more importantly, squeezed time from the manufacturing process, thus making it more responsive to customer needs.

C: FAST CYCLE DISTRIBUTION SYSTEMS

5.10 Distribution resource planning (DRP)

It is not only manufacturing businesses which can benefit from taking advantage of improved computer and telecommunications technology so as to become fast

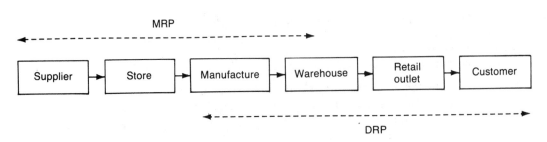

Figure 5.5 The scope of distribution resource planning.

cycle companies. Any type of business, in which distribution plays a key part, such as wholesaling and retailing can gain tremendously by installing fast cycle systems. **Distribution resource planning** systems or techniques are also based on the idea of reducing stock and abolishing the economic order quantity concept thus pulling goods through as they are ordered by customers or purchased from shops, etc. The implementation of fast cycle systems leads to major savings in storage costs for a wholesale or retail business. Thus the concepts and techniques are exactly the same but simply applied to a different section of the value system, the 'downstream section' (see Figure 5.5).

5.11   Supermarket information system

To illustrate the downstream section of the value system we consider a large supermarket chain which has a central warehouse. This feeds local warehouses, which in turn feed the supermarkets with the goods required as portrayed in Figure 5.6. Traditionally, the quantity of stock of each good to be held at each location would have been determined by statistical methods and orders would be placed every week, say, to restock each location. Today, using an electronic point of sale (EPOS) system, which will probably be a scanning wand reading a bar code, not only are the goods identified and the customer's bill added up, but a record is made of all the purchases. If linked to the warehouses this can be used as an instant information system which may be used to simplify and improve a whole range of activities:

- A visual display unit can be used within the store to inform shelf stockers which items are low.
- Stock movement from local warehouse to store becomes automatic, i.e. there is no need to check stock levels and write out orders by hand.
- Optimal vehicle loading plans and journey routes can be built into the system.
- Stock movement from the central warehouse to the local warehouses also becomes automatic.

- Information requesting more stock can be fed to the manufacturer immediately a sale is made. This may be done either automatically by linked business systems or by manual means.
- The sales of a high-demand product which is in short supply can be optimized by correctly allocating the product to the sites where it is most likely to be needed.
- Changes in the rate of consumption of a product can be easily picked up thus improving the accuracy of forward ordering. This information can also be used to assess rapidly the impact of advertising and promotional activity.
- Managers should be able to manage the business better as they have an immediate picture of customer purchases.

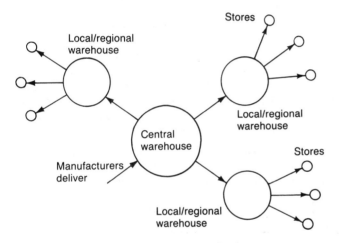

Figure 5.6 A supermarket chain distribution system.

From the customer's point of view the use of this type of system means that the shop, if properly run, should never be out of stock and the food on the shelves should always be fresh. From the business's point of view, it is meeting the needs of the customer more satisfactorily. This should generate an increase in sales volume. In addition, at least part, if not all, of the cost of the system is met by a saving of clerical jobs and storage space and their associated costs. But, of course, nothing in the world is perfect. Unfortunately, no computer system can yet take account of pilfering. If goods are taken from the supermarket's shelves without being paid for they escape the system, and similarly if they are removed from the storage area by dishonest employees their disappearance from stock is not recorded. As pilfering of stock is a major problem in all retail businesses, any computerized system must be constantly amended by a comparison between its records and the physical reality. Part of the answer is to make pilfering as difficult as possible — by attaching electronic tags to the products, for instance.

The impression should not be given with either the distribution or the manufacturing resource systems that all information is based on actual orders or purchases. This would lead to the impossible situation in which all parties would have to always respond instantly. Instead, regular forecasts are made of expected usage, and prior stages in the value chain — such as suppliers — are informed of these on a regular basis. The forecasts are updated frequently so that the actual requirements do not come as a bolt out of the blue but are very much in line with the forecasts.

While the system outlined above is designed for a supermarket chain, not all supermarket chains in the UK have such a system fully implemented at present. However, most of them are rapidly installing such systems.

5.12 Other retailing DRP systems

A DRP system also has potential in retail areas other than supermarkets. This was demonstrated when Gerald Ratner acquired Salisburys, the luggage and handbag shops, from Next. Ratner felt that the tills could generate 30 per cent more profit once an efficient DRP system was installed. This system would generate information at the checkout. This would allow for reordering several times a day rather than the once a fortnight as was the position prior to acquisition. Thus fast selling lines could be restocked much more quickly than in the past. This is particularly important in the fashion industry where seasons are brief and taste fickle, and a sale not made today is a sale lost for this particular season or maybe for ever.

Another example of a company using a DRP information system in the fashion industry (as well as CAD and CAM on the manufacturing side) is Benetton, the Italian manufacturer and retailer of sports and fashion garments. By introducing CAD and CAM the company removed bottlenecks in production and design and cut the traditional three or six monthly industry cycle dramatically. The CAD system automatically explodes a new design into a full range of sizes and transmits these through a CAM system to CNC fabric cutting machines. Benetton also developed a method by which clothes can be dyed after they had been sewn — a reversal of the traditional method. This has reduced the fabric held in stock as only a neutral colour fabric is now needed. In addition, a good DRP information system, linked to the integrated manufacturing information system, tells the company which lines are selling well, thus should be restocked and, therefore, should be manufactured. This system is a just-in-time system with the customer who buys the goods in effect placing an order for a similar item for its next buyer. This total system — design, manufacturing and distribution — has cut delivery time to fifteen days. Such speed allows for a change of emphasis in stock within the season dictated totally by customers' purchases. For instance, if sales are not going well in certain areas, no more of these items are produced after the initial run. But if, on the other hand, certain lines are selling well they should always be in stock as they can be speedily manufactured and delivered. This was impossible before recent improvements in technology. Most of the stock had to be made before the season started and very little restocking was possible if goods sold well because of the time taken in production and distribution.

5.13 Being fast cycle does not require advanced technology

It should not be imagined that the only way to become fast cycle in every industry is to install a computer system. This is far from the truth as was illustrated at the beginning of the chapter by the tailoring industry in Hong Kong. In fact, computer systems, especially bad ones, can sometimes be a hindrance. For example, a textile manufacturer who wished to reduce lead time found that the main delay was the transfer of material from the factory to the warehouse. While it took a few hours to transport the textiles, the inflexible computer information system took up to one week to provide the necessary information. When the computer system was replaced by a simple manual system the lead time was reduced to just one day.

Little has been done to date to speed up the flow and productivity in offices. It seems likely that attention will be given to this area in the near future. Bottlenecks or queues far too often build up for facilities such as the photocopier or fax machine: inadequate facilities or poor maintenance are the cause. Fast cycle telephone systems are particularly important in the office: business is lost if customers are kept waiting at the end of the telephone line or are put on hold and left to listen to irritating music. It may be financially advantageous to double the number of switchboard operators to ensure that calls are answered promptly. This is probably cheap in comparison with the cost of business lost due to telephone delays. Answering calls quickly also has the advantage of promoting an image of efficiency for the organization. Stickers on telephones telling employees how to answer a phone which is ringing at a nearby unoccupied desk also help to provide a better and more efficient image to the customer. Photocopier, fax and telephone usage are only the tip of the iceberg when it comes to potential fast cycle operations for the office. However, being fast cycle is more a question of attitude rather than of equipment. See, for example, how quickly a bookmaker at a racecourse can process information about bets placed with him using only paper and pencil.

5.14 Electronic data interchange

There is no reason why the information system running through the value chain should be confined to an internal system. Benetton is a vertically integrated company which designs, manufactures, distributes and sells through its own retail outlets but many retail organizations do not themselves manufacture. Those retailers which have close relations with their suppliers, as Marks & Spencer has, have a structure which will allow information to flow between the businesses. The potential is not, however, limited to retailing. A manufacturing company can build a similar system with its component suppliers — and an increasing number are. This linking is known as **electronic data interchange** (EDI) and involves at least two computer systems communicating directly with each other. The benefits are great. A company will already hold details of stock levels and reordering levels in its computer system and purchase orders will be generated by the computer. It makes considerable sense to connect the organization's computer to suppliers' computers so as to save postal charges and paper costs — but those savings are minor in comparison with other possible benefits. These may be categorized under the following headings:

- Cost savings.
- Elimination or reduction of errors.
- Saving of time.

Cost savings

The size of possible cost savings are indicated by McKesson's savings (illustrative case at the end of the chapter). Here the number of purchasing staff was reduced by 88 per cent as a result of introducing an EDI link with their suppliers. As soon as stock levels fall to the reorder level the organization's computer automatically contacts the relevant supplier's computer and places an order. If the organization does not hold stock, i.e. an organization using JIT, the system will be activated by customer orders.

Elimination or reduction in errors

Any system that relies on human beings is, unfortunately, prone to error. Keying into a computer system the details of a customer order is one area where errors are likely to occur. Goods and components are identified by a code of numbers and letters and one error may mean that the wrong goods are sent. Surveys have revealed that between 20 per cent and 30 per cent of all human input is incorrect; to reduce these errors and possibly eliminate them totally is a major benefit saving many hours of correction and problem solving.

Saving of time

The most important benefit of all to the majority of businesses is that EDI saves time. Although most companies initially enter into EDI to cut costs, they soon realize the benefit that time saved can give them. This may be in terms either of competitive advantage or simply of costs saved by reducing time. STC was one of those companies that initially saw EDI merely as an improved postal system.[12] STC linked up via EDI with two of its suppliers, Texas Instruments and Phillips Components. This meant that if a delivery schedule was sent to either supplier at 8 p.m. the goods would be received by 9.30 a.m. the next morning. STC soon became aware of the potential of EDI to assist in their drive towards JIT. By coupling the two techniques, lead time was reduced by four weeks. This resulted in a considerable saving in terms of stock held — quite apart from any benefit of quicker delivery to the customer.

The impression must not be given that all the managing director of an organization has to say is 'we must get into EDI' and the system will magically appear in six months' time. There are many problems in setting up such a system, not the least of which is the fact that there are no standards for EDI and different organizations have quite different information systems which are incompatible. At present the organization needs to be large enough to develop its own system or willing to use one of the existing systems offered by a network supplier. The latter entails paying a fee and then plugging in much as one would with an ordinary telephone system. The details and problems of networking are considered further in Chapter 8.

5.15   EDI in the motor industry

One of the first industries to use EDI was the motor industry. The following examples deal with linking forward in the value chain to the dealers. This was the first area for linkage to be explored, probably for two reasons. Firstly, the dealers have a close relationship with the manufacturer. Secondly, there was a considerable financial benefit to be achieved if the motor manufacturers became more responsive to their customers' needs. Links with suppliers are now quite common in the industry with General Motors leading the way. Linking is discussed further in section 8.4.

Renault introduced a new data interchange system in 1987 called direct vehicle ordering system.[13] It links the three hundred UK Renault dealers with the company's factories in France. The dealers paid only a subsidized price of about £2,000 each for the system. This is often the case as companies are so keen to get their new networks installed for their own benefit that the equipment is given free or at a reduced price to those willing to accept it. In Renault's case the equipment consists of a PC with a modem link to British Telecom's packet switching data transmission service. From British Telecom the dealers are connected via British Telecom's French counterpart to Renault's mainframe computer situated in Paris where production schedules are drawn up. Apart from speeding up the ordering process and thus supplying the customer more quickly, there are other benefits. The main benefit to the dealers is probably the ability to use the network to contact other dealers to trace the availability of a specific car for an immediate purchase. The main benefit to Renault itself, made possible by the improved communications, was an initial planned reduction in stock of around 20 per cent. This amounted to £70m in 1987.

At Toyota, one of the champions of squeezing time out of the value chain, Japanese dealers are connected on-line to the factory scheduling system so an order can be combined immediately into the production schedule.[14] Proper production scheduling is still needed despite the fact that production is executed in small lots. This is done by flexible manufacturing units and production teams thus making the change from one individual car to another very easy. The Toyota production schedules for the different plants aim to minimize volume fluctuations from day to day and to produce a full mix of models each day. On placing an order the customer receives a delivery date which will be within a week, and possibly just two days' time as the production cycle has been reduced to that extent. Suppliers are automatically notified immediately of the order and given their production schedule for delivery of components on time for the assembly of the vehicle. Thus the value chain is extended upstream to the supplier.

5.16   Illustrative case: McKesson

McKesson was one of the first companies to use technology to link its value chain with others to gain mutual benefit. Its case is still one of the best examples of linkage. In the mid 1970s McKesson (who distribute drugs to small local drug stores in the USA) was worried about its future. Its small customers faced strong competition from the big chain stores, and if its customers went out of business so eventually would McKesson. It needed to develop a strategy to help strengthen its customers and thus itself; it chose to make the ordering and delivery of drugs easier and faster. To this end a hand-held terminal was given to each of the company's 16,000 drug store customers. There was no charge to the customer, McKesson paid — they could afford to because they would soon reap some of the benefits. The benefit to the drug store proprietor was that ordering became quite easy. It was done just by walking round the store checking the shelves and ordering straight into the hand-set. The hand-set was then coupled to the telephone and the order transmitted to McKesson. Additionally, delivery times were improved to the extent that most goods arrived within twenty-four hours. Later, as technology improved, a bar code scanner which could read bar codes fixed to shelves replaced the hand-set thus making ordering even easier for the customer.

After a while McKesson realized that with its computerized systems it could pack the goods for delivery in a specific order. If the company knew the layout of a particular drug store it could provide the store with its goods packed in shelf order. This saved the proprietor considerable time when restocking the shelves. McKesson went even further in the provision of assistance. It produced price labels for the goods incorporating the proprietor's individual mark up. The result of all these improvements was that life had been made easy for the drug store proprietors and they now had a strong incentive to remain with McKesson rather than changing to another supplier. Also, freed from the chores of the running of their business, the proprietors could give more time to the consideration of the future strategy and profitability of the business. Thus by linking the value chain of McKesson with the value chain of the drug store proprietors, both had gained, and so ultimately had the customer.

The next step for McKesson was to move into the area of pharmaceutical cards. Most US customers who have prescriptions are covered by health insurance, and they reclaim the cost of the drug from the insurance company. McKesson formed a link with the insurance companies and offered to reclaim the cost of the prescription for the customer. It issued cards to those wishing to take part in the scheme which meant that the customer paid only a nominal charge for the prescription, about $1. McKesson, rather than the customer, then claimed the full cost from the insurance company. This made the purchase of drugs on prescription much simpler for the customer and encouraged them to return to a McKesson-supplied store. McKesson again went even further by holding detailed records of individual customers who wished them to do so. This meant that when a customer purchased a drug for a specific problem they could check to make sure that it did not clash with any other that they were already taking.

The final linkage that McKesson made was backwards — to the suppliers of the drugs. This tied McKesson's purchasing system into the order system of most of the large drug suppliers. The result was a saving in purchasing staff of 88 per cent. So McKesson, then, had fully exploited the value system within their business sector by forging the links shown in Figure 5.7.

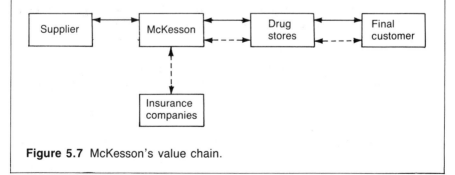

Figure 5.7 McKesson's value chain.

5.17 Illustrative case: Amalgamated Foods

Many wholesalers have followed McKesson's lead and provide ordering and information systems for their customers, retail shops. Amalgamated Foods is an example of a UK wholesaler providing such a system for the Spar and VG stores in the south east of England. The standard package consists of a computer, a modem to link the computer to the telephone, a printer, two checkouts, scanners and software.

The scanners read the bar codes on the products so that the checkout can provide a bill. The information is then transferred to the store's computer which calculates the stock position and any necessary reorders from the wholesaler are made automatically via the telephone system. Every week new prices are sent to the individual store's computer; from this, shelf price labels are printed and the checkouts are updated.

However, the system provides more than just ordering and pricing facilities. It generates a computer model of an individual retail store from which regular information on volume and profit is given. These include details such as gross profit per shelf, net profit per shelf and net profit per item. All goods sold are ranked according to profitability and fast and slow moving items are highlighted. The system also provides average information on five similar stores. This system is not free, though: stores have to pay around £100 per week, so the smaller ones may not be able to reap enough benefit to cover the cost.

NOTES

1. John Osborne, 'Freight of the art', *Management Today*, Oct. 1989.
2. Roy Merrills, 'How Northern Telecom competes on time', *Harvard Business Review*, July/Aug. 1989.
3. Michael E. Porter, *Competitive Advantage* (Free Press, 1985).
4. Edward Hay, *The Just-In-Time Breakthrough* (Wiley, 1988).
5. Stephen Young, 'Manufacturing under Pressure', *Management Today*, July 1988.
6. Sangjin Yoo, 'An information system for just-in-time', *Long Range Planning*, Dec. 1989.
7. Alan Shoulders, 'IT assisted resource planning' *Accountancy*, May 1989.
8. Nigel Coulthurst, 'The new factory', *Management Accounting*, Mar. 1989.
9. Eduardo Punset and Gerry Sweeney (eds), *Information Resources and Corporate Growth* (Pinter Publishers, 1989).
10. 'A CEO's commonsense of CIM: An interview with J.Tracy O'Rourke', *Harvard Business Review*, Jan./Feb. 1989.
11. David N. Burt, 'Managing suppliers up to speed', *Harvard Business Review*, Jul./Aug. 1989.
12. Malcolm Wheatley and Alan Patrick, 'Leave it to the machine', *Management Today*, Aug. 1989.

13. *Management Today*, June 1987.
14. Joseph L. Bower and Thomas M. Hout, 'Fast cycle capability for competitive power', *Harvard Business Review*, Nov./Dec. 1988.

FURTHER READING

Harmon, Roy L. and Leroy D. Peterson, *Re-inventing the Factory* (The Free Press, 1990). Two practitioners explain, using examples, how production can be simplified, speeded up and made fast cycle.

Hay, Edward, J., *The Just-in-Time Breakthrough* (Wiley, 1988). A good, easy to read book explaining the principles and benefits of JIT.

Platts Richard, *Computing Needs for Automated Material Handling* (NCC, 1989). Detailed treatment of systems and techniques in this area.

EXERCISES

1. Consider a transport system with which you are familiar and suggest ways in which it could become fast cycle.

2. Outline the different business approaches to car maintenance. What can a traditional repair garage do to become fast cycle?

3. Detail the information systems that a shoe manufacturer and retailer should install so that it may become fast cycle.

6 Fast cycle data entry

SCOPE AND CONTENTS

Firstly, possible uses for fast cycle systems are outlined and illustrated by an example and a case. Then various data collection and entry methods are described before taking a detailed look at some of the different technologies available. The technologies are categorized according to the data collection source. The categories are: data from documents — optical mark recognition, MICR and image processing; data from goods — bar codes and optical character recognition; data from people — magnetic stripe cards, optical memory cards, passive and active smart cards. The chapter ends with a brief discussion of the dangers of new technology.

6.1 Spotting uses for fast cycle systems

In the previous chapter the analogy of a cowboy who is both accurate and fast on the draw was used to describe an effective fast cycle organization, namely one which is both quick to react and consistently on target. To pursue the analogy further, the equipment and technologies employed by an organization may be likened to the weapon, the gun. Similarly the data collected and entered into the system may be likened to the bullets — the means of achieving the fast cycle end. This chapter is concerned with the type of 'gun' to use and the nature of the 'bullets'.

The creation of a fast cycle system requires a clear understanding of the activities which make up the value chain of a particular organization. It also requires the ability to recognize and exploit new technology, or to use an established technology in a novel way. By introducing a new data entry method an organization may be able to shorten a particular cycle or activity time. This should enable an organization to gain competitive advantage.

There are three basic ways in which fast cycle systems can be used to achieve competitive advantage:

- To use a physical system to process a customer or an order quickly. This could mean moving customers swiftly through the checkout at a supermarket or through an exit at a station. Alternatively, it could mean using a fast cycle system to provide a service or product swiftly.
- To get data quickly so as to be able to react swiftly, for instance, by obtaining data on customer needs and then swiftly producing and distributing the goods.
- To turn cash around quickly, thereby reducing working capital.

The first involves directly squeezing time out of a primary activity in the value chain. The second, by providing a better support activity, allows those involved with primary activities to squeeze time from them. The third does not have such a direct impact on primary activities unless the company is a finance organization. However, saving time in the money chain can generate real advantage. Speeding up the cash flow improves the productivity of money and the organization which can use funds to the best advantage also achieves competitive advantage. This is because it makes it possible to produce more with the same amount of money and thus cut the price per unit, offer discounts to some customers or invest in more productive processes. Examples of the different ways in which fast cycle systems might be used will be given before discussing in detail the fast cycle techniques available today.

6.2 Illustrative example: supermarkets

Most readers will have suffered the frustration of waiting in a long, slow-moving queue at the supermarket checkout after obtaining their goods from the shelves comparatively quickly. The queue is caused by two factors: the recording of purchases by the checkout assistant and the method of payment tendered by some customers. When the customer reaches the head of the queue the trolley must be unloaded so that the assistant can record the purchases and prepare the bill. Having done so and paid the bill, the customer must then repack the goods into bags. This process can be time consuming. A similar delay may occur with payment. Cash still remains the quickest method of payment at the till, but plastic cards are beginning to catch up as currently available technology is gradually implemented. Cards are an advantage to the store (even though they usually have to pay a percentage to the bank or issuer) because they eliminate the necessity to count coins and notes at the end of the day and to carry them to the bank. Some customers also regard them as an advantage because they eliminate the need to carry cash.

The challenge for a store is to devise a means whereby the existing time taken by checkout procedures can be drastically reduced or even dispensed with entirely. There is little advantage in doing this unless payment procedures are also improved at the same time. The first store to eliminate queues would have two advantages. Firstly, making shopping a truly fast cycle activity would create competitive advantage. Secondly, considerable staff savings could probably be made. However, if competitors could install similar equipment fairly quickly, competitive advantage would be fleeting. Therefore, any money spent on research and equipment would probably be considered wasted as far as the company was concerned even though all shoppers eventually benefit. This would not be true if the overall market increased as a result of being fast cycle because shoppers were won over from other types of retail outlet.

In recent years many new techniques for recording goods and prices have been introduced into supermarkets and other stores. The customer may have wondered about all this investment in new technology as it rarely speeds up the checkout procedure — in many cases it appears to slow it down. The new optical techniques often require several 'swipes' of the purchase past the reader and sometimes the assistant has to enter the details by hand. However, these systems are not designed to benefit the customer directly nor even the checkout assistant. Instead they are designed to benefit the organization by allowing data about purchases to flow back instantly to the warehouse and central office. This allows for better and swifter provision of future goods which will certainly benefit future customers. (See section 5.11.)

The organization must not fail to consider the effect of the new systems on customers and checkout assistants. If the systems do not operate efficiently staff will become dissatisfied and customers will go elsewhere. In some shops, for instance, though rarely in supermarkets, when a purchase is 'swiped' or read by a wand the terminal does not accept it because the details of that particular good have not been entered into the system by the central office. This is terrible organization and results in great delay as the checkout assistant has then to find the list of products and look through for the price and code before entering the details by hand. Technology cannot improve poor organization in administrative departments, instead it highlights it.

The technology and techniques to solve checkout problems probably exist now or will soon be available. What is lacking is someone who can devise a workable system which will use these techniques for collecting the required data and getting the customer out of the shop quickly. So, if by the end of this chapter you have solved the problem, get yourself signed on as a consultant to a large supermarket chain — a fortune awaits you. One novel solution which has been introduced in a chain of stores in the USA is to provide the facilities for customers to 'swipe' their own goods through a checkout and obtain a bill which they then take to a cash desk for payment. Whether this system is beneficial depends on whether customers feel that service is being lost by checking out their own purchases. It also depends on whether there are adequate cash desks and checkout points. If there are not the result will be two queues and a wait which may be twice as long as previously. Lastly, its success will depend on the honesty of the customers.

6.3 Illustrative case: Singapore's Mass Rapid Transport system

Few countries have used fast cycle *information* systems effectively in transport. Most systems have concentrated on physically speeding up the flow of passengers. This means devising ways of speeding up trains and moving passengers through the ticket office and barriers as quickly as possible. This has involved attempts to design trains to run faster on existing, rather inadequate track. It has also included machines to dispense tickets and automatic barriers to check tickets.

On considering the activities described in the previous paragraph, one might wonder whether most transport organizations are not more concerned with cutting staffing costs rather than improving the journey for the customer. Few transport organizations have attempted to go beyond improving the flow of passengers to improve the flow of data and information. One of the few that has is Singapore whose underground railway, the MRT (Mass Rapid Transport) system, is probably the most advanced in the world as far as data collection and information provision is concerned. Virtually everything is known about the travelling pattern of passengers. This includes:

- Where the ticket was bought.
- When the ticket was bought.
- Where the passenger entered the system.
- What time the passenger entered the system.
- What type of ticket was purchased.
- Where the passenger alighted.
- What time the passenger left the system.

These data are collected from the ticket machines and gateways. Every one of these is connected to a station computer which in turn is connected to a mainframe at MRT headquarters. Every morning a computer printout of all data is ready for the traffic managers who run the system. This shows the flow at fifteen minute intervals highlighting the peaks and troughs. If a peak occurs one day an extra train can be put on the next day to alleviate the problem. The aim is to keep the number of passengers per train to less than 1,200.

The data and information flow allows managers to match the trains to demand and provide a better service to the customer, both in terms of journey quality and speed. Few transport companies can react this quickly and change their schedules.

It is interesting to compare the approach of Singapore's underground with that of London Underground, the largest in the world. Mike Strzelecki said that when he took over as General Manager of the Central Line early in 1988 the £100m turnover business had just one computer — a PC.[1] Not only was the information generating process not computerized but it appears to have been totally lacking as the detailed budget for the Central Line was written on a single sheet of paper. It is true that too much information can sometimes be provided for managers: it is to be hoped that London Underground, which is now correcting the situation, will not over-react.

6.4 Data collection and entry methods

This chapter concentrates on fast cycle methods for the collection and entry of data into the system. Processing, transmission and storage equipment (such as an on-line database for retrieving information) may also be required to be fast cycle. These are dealt with in Chapters 7–9.

The traditional information system relies on humans to enter data. Data normally arrive at the system entry point in written or printed form, such as paper invoices or orders and labels on goods at a checkout. Gradually this is changing and, for example, many companies today use EDI (electronic data interchange — discussed further in Chapters 7 and 8). EDI allows a customer's computer to communicate directly with the supplier's when placing an order. This is obviously much faster and more accurate than a manual system. A manual system for orders received involves collecting them into a batch before a keyboard operator types them into the system. Not only is this unreliable, it is also slow because the orders are not entered into the system immediately. Thus it is difficult to be a fast cycle organization with such a system. There are two paths available to an organization wishing to have fast cycle data collection and entry systems. The first is to speed up the entry of data from paper, and the second is to replace paper with a better data collection method. The technology involved in fast cycle data collection and entry is basically of four types:

- Magnetic methods, for example the stripe on a debit card. These are fast and accurate unless the medium gets damaged.

- Optical methods, for example the use of bar codes. These are fast accurate and reliable.
- Instrument readings, for example petrol station flow meters which are attached to electronic tills.
- Voice recognition methods. This may well be the method of the future, but as yet the technology has not been perfected for use in the commercial market.

Magnetic and optical data entry methods are used in the majority of fast cycle systems and these are the two methods which will be considered in this chapter. Many of the methods are so familiar that they are taken for granted, but there is still plenty of scope to develop them further. New methods are frequently introduced and as a result some of the ones which are described here could be replaced by better ones almost before the book is published. Of course, once fast cycle book publishing methods are in place, this problem will be largely overcome.

The different methods and technology involved have been grouped, for discussion purposes, into the following three categories which are based on the how the data are collected:

- **Data from documents**. Data are collected from documents, such as orders or invoices, these are then entered into the information system on the organization's premises.
- **Data from goods**. Data are attached to goods in order to identify them.
- **Data from people**. Data are carried by people: this will normally identify individuals so that a particular service can be provided for them.

One technology may be used in two different categories. For instance, bar codes which are normally used to identify goods may also occasionally be used to identify people. Thus the following classification of technologies within the categories should not be taken as rigid.

6.5 Data from documents

Three different technologies are in use and are described below. The amount of data to be entered will dictate which is most suitable to use. It is normal to use the simplest feasible method as this will be cheaper and possibly more reliable. The first method, optical mark recogition, is suitable only where there is little variation in the data to be entered. The second, magnetic ink character recogition, is suitable for a limited amount of data of standard form, and the third, image processing, which is very new technology, can cope with the most demanding data entry requirements possible.

Optical mark recognition (OMR)

Readers who have ever taken multiple-choice examination papers will be familiar with this technology. Answer sheets are issued to examinees which contain areas to be blocked in by pencil for the recording of answers. Special equipment is used to translate these sheets and enter the data into a computer. As a result, fast cycle examination marking is possible with completely consistent grading.

Automatic data entry from optical mark recognition dates back at least thirty years and new uses are still being developed. In the early 1960s, for instance, Dunlop Rubber Company was using mark-sensed (optical mark recognition) cards for some of its stock control data collection, which was then processed on a Leo computer. Gas and electricity meter readings are often recorded using OMR. Its use in these industries in the UK reduced the time taken to invoice the customer by several days because the process of entering data into the system could be automated as a result. This in turn reduced the time taken to receive payments and thus the working capital required by the business was reduced.

Another popular application of OMR is in questionnaires. It was used in the US population census for the first time in 1990. The census had to be filled in in pencil. However, the returns for the 1990 census were much lower than in the past — it was suggested that the reason for this was the average American family no longer possessed a pencil. Alternatively, some people may have completed the form in ink before reading the instructions and not bothered applying for another when they realized their mistake. Whatever the reason, the benefits gained from automatic data transfer were totally vitiated by the increased costs of attempting to collect outstanding census forms.

Although OMR has limits, it is very simple and easy to use. There is little scope for errors in either data collection or entry.

Magnetic ink character recognition (MICR)

This technique has been used for many years on cheques where the static data (cheque number, account number, bank and branch code) is preprinted in magnetic ink on each cheque in a special typeface. When a cheque is presented for clearing the amount or value of the cheque is typed on it in magnetic ink. This makes automatic processing possible.

Another similar application is on 'turnaround' documents which are single documents combining an invoice with a payment advice note. When a cheque is sent the payment advice is detached and returned with it. Again, the payment advice contains data printed in magnetic ink for fast automatic processing.

Two standard fonts or typefaces are currently in use. One is a UK/US standard called E13B which is used by UK and US banks. The other is a European standard called CMC7 which is used by European banks and on UK postal orders. As can be seen in Figure 6.1 the two standard fonts are very different in appearance although they are both easy to read.

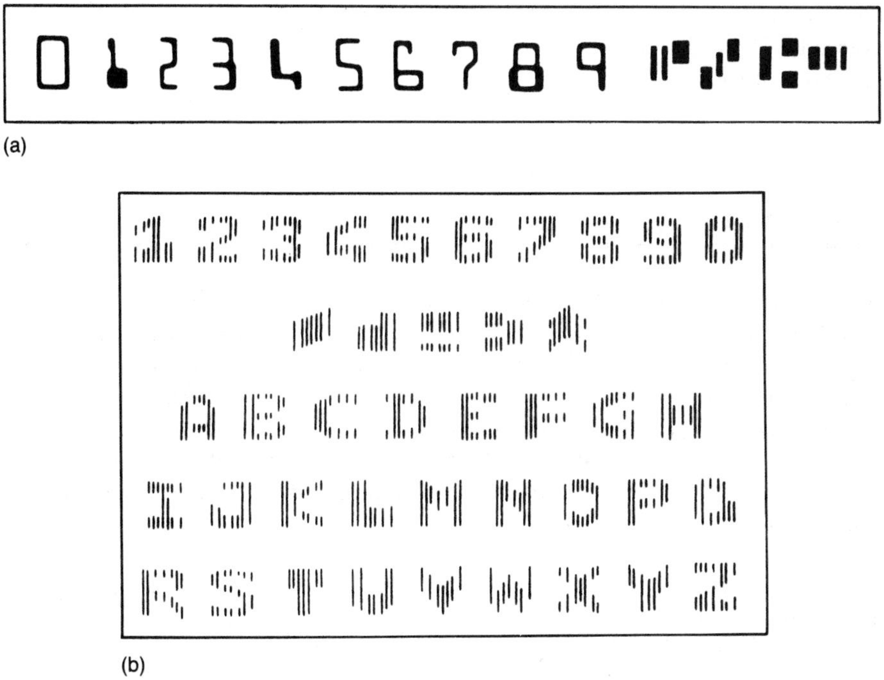

(a)

(b)

Figure 6.1 Magnetic ink character recognition fonts. (a) E13B. (b) CMC7.

There are two minor disadvantages which limit the use of this technology. The first is that the printing of the magnetic characters must be precise and of high quality if they are to be read correctly. The second is that data must be presented in a single horizontal line of characters placed in a standard position on the document. As a result, optical characters have been used on more recently developed applications. Both magnetic and optical characters have the advantage of being capable of being read by humans as well as machines, unlike, for example, bar codes.

Image processing

Complete documents, such as invoices, can be recorded on a disk. The technical name for this is CD ROM and the technology is similar to that of hi-fi compact disks. The disk has tiny pits burnt into it which can be read by a laser. Image processing is very new and is used by only a few organizations at present, therefore, it is as yet rather difficult to assess its potential and how it may be used in the future. The main advantage of the system appears to be its ability to store a considerable quantity of data in a tiny space, that is on one small disk. (It is discussed in more detail in section 9.9 as a storage medium.) However, it could also have potential as a method of entering a large quantity of data quickly and correctly. Once the data are on the disk they can be sorted and relevant parts retrieved quickly.

6.6 Data from goods

Shops have always attached labels of some sort to the goods they have for sale. These normally contain details of the product and its price. This information is needed for accounting and restocking purposes as well as to assist at the point of sale. There are other reasons for attaching labels: Federal Express attaches bar code labels to parcels which identified their destination for routing purposes; shelves or storage bins in shops or warehouses may also bear a similar label to the good so that the identity of their contents may be recorded quickly when reordering or checking stock.

Bar codes

Bar codes are the most widely used type of 'label' on goods at present and the majority of shops have point of sale systems which can read them. They are normally incorporated into the product, as they are in magazines, or into the label as on a can of beans. Therefore, they cannot normally be used to show a price which may change with time, although, or course, the bar code reader's terminal can be programmed to hold this type of current data. It is a precondition of supplying retailers that the manufacturer prints the bar code on the product or packaging.

There are two bar code standards, one for the USA and another for Europe. They are the uniform product code (UPC) and the European article number (EAN). The back cover of this book has a bar code which may be either European or US depending on the market the book was published for. The two standards are similar, the only difference being that the US version has twelve digits while the European one has thirteen. The US standard uses only one digit to represent the country whereas the European uses two; both systems use five digits for the manufacturer and five digits to identify the product; the last digit is a check digit — see section 13.6.

Bar codes are very distinct and so the relevant data can easily be read by a fixed position reader or a hand-held wand. They do, however, have to be specially printed, whereas optical character recognition equipment (see below) can read words and figures which have been typed onto a label. Bar codes also have the disadvantage of not being capable of being read directly by humans. To overcome this a translation is usually printed below or above the code in characters which can be read by optical equipment as well as humans. This allows organizations to change to an optical character recognition system if they wish.

Apart from being used to identify goods, bar codes may be used as a portable identity system. For instance, they are used in some libraries where members are issued with a card which has a bar code representing their membership number. Bar codes also have potential for identifying and tracking documents. The civil service is considering introducing bar coding to do just that. This seems like a case of applying technology to a badly thought out process. Analysis of the system in order to simplify it would probably be much more effective than introducing bar codes.

Optical character recognition (OCR)

Some retail stores, particularly clothes and department stores, use this method in preference to bar codes. Swing labels or tags can be printed with a fairly normal looking typeface which can then be read by a hand-held reader at the checkout. The data are translated into binary form which is used in the organization's information systems and also to print a bill for the customer. Many retail outlets including C&A, a British clothing chain, use this system: it is fast and reliable, especially when the till also incorporates a credit card reader.

Again two standard fonts are normally used. The US font is known as OCR-A and the European one OCR-B. As can be seen in Figure 6.2 the US standard is limited to the upper-case alphabet, the ten numeric digits and a variety of common symbols. It has a stylized appearance and the typeface closely resembles the UK/US magnetic ink font. Most UK applications use the European standard font, OCR-B, which has a more natural appearance and also contains lower-case letters. The quality of the print does not need to be as high as that for bar codes; however, the position of the print on the page or article must be reasonably precise if it is to be read by a fixed position optical reader. This problem does not arise with hand-held readers.

Optical character recognition is very flexible and has a wide number of possible applications. Although at present it is used mainly in connection with goods, it seems likely that in the future it will be used for a variety of purposes. It is already used on some 'turnaround' documents in place of magnetic ink characters. It is also used on credit cards. The large embossed digits which make up the card-holder's account number are in OCR-A font, although the other data on the card are often in OCR-B. These are printed out on the vouchers used for manually prepared card payments.

6.7 Data from people

There is a growing trend to make everything as small and as portable as possible. This fashion has been led by the Japanese who have used their skills to produce

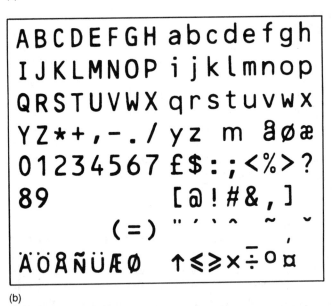

(a)

(b)

Figure 6.2 Optical character recognition fonts. (a) OCR-A. (b) OCR-B.

tiny items including radios, personal televisions and Walkmans. The Japanese have been practising the art of 'smallness' for centuries; recently this has been called the 'bonsaiation' of products. Information systems seem to be going the same way with the development of portable computers and PCNs (personal communications networks). It is also possible to get personal data stores which contain a phenomenal amount of data or information. The simplest portable forms of data are bank cards, but in the past ten years several new types of card have become available which have far greater potential. These and their relevant technology are now discussed in detail.

Magnetic stripe cards

Cards with magnetic stripes have many applications. They are currently used on charge cards, credit cards and debit or cash cards. They are also used on train, tube and car parking tickets. The use of magnetic stripe technology started with ATMs (automatic teller machines) in the late 1970s, but it had been available for a long time before it was used for this purpose. The stripe is the same type as is used for audio recording. In the late 1970s the banks were driven to the use of plastic cards because of the high costs that would otherwise have been involved in expanding the size and number of branches to meet the increasing number of bank customers. Note that the banks did not initially install ATMs to provide a faster or better service to the customer but rather to reduce costs.

One of the causes for the delay in putting magnetic stripe technology into practice was the lack of international standards. These have now been introduced by the International Standards Organization. The stripe is divided laterally into three tracks. Each of these can hold a string of magnetically encoded data which is read by a reader head or terminal. Tracks one and two can only be read. Track two is the one normally used by banks and can take an account number of up to nineteen digits. This track is written before the bank card is issued and is read each time the card is used. The account number is read and sent to the bank's computer centre for verification. Track three, which was introduced after the other two, is a read/write track. Its contents are rewritten each time that it is used. It contains an encoded version of the PIN (personal identification number) which is the number the holder enters every time the card is used. The advantage of the third track is that the ATM does not have to be on-line, as verification is done by comparing the PIN number which is keyed in with the encoded PIN number. Thus transmission costs are reduced.

Another example of the type of card which uses a read/write track is the photocopy card. When a photocopy machine is used, the number of copies made is written onto the card thereby reducing the total units available.

Magnetic stripe cards are fast and accurate but they are not as reliable or convenient as the newer optical techniques. Occasionally train, tube or car parking tickets are rejected by the machine because they have been folded and damaged. This failing is particularly unfortunate in a car-park where a lengthy queue of frustrated motorists can quickly build up behind the offender!

Optical memory cards

Although the technology is not new, the first optical memory card was introduced as recently as the early 1980s. The phonecards used in the UK are an example of this type of card. The middle layer of an optical memory card consists of a thin film of silver into which a laser writes, or burns, a pattern of minute pits. When another laser reads the card, light is not reflected back from the burnt areas. It uses the same basic technology as image processing, and like image processing it can store vast amounts of data. A card the size of a credit card can hold up to eight hundred pages of text. The information on the card cannot be erased, but new information can be written and flagged so that the old data are ignored. It can sometimes be useful to have a record of all transactions or events on the card. For instance, it has potential as a medical record card and this is one of several areas where development is currently taking place. It also has the potential to be used in manufacturing to control the different operations required of machine tools.

Passive smart cards

Most smart cards available today are passive. However, active ones (described below) are being developed. At the time of writing, therefore, a reference to a smart card usually refers to a passive one and this usage is adopted here. A smart card can take many forms but usually looks similar to a credit card. One different looking smart card is that used by US military personnel as identity tags worn around the neck.

The cards contain a microprocessor chip and have an electronically erasable memory. The standard card is divided into three sections:

- **Open section**. Data stored here can be obtained by anyone using the card. The data will probably include the account number and name.
- **Confidential section**. Data stored here are only given when the PIN is used. This section may contain details of transactions and the current balance.
- **Secret section**. Contains details of the encryption codes and is used by the microprocessor to check the encoded PIN.

Dr Kunitaka Arimura was probably the first person to conceive the idea of a smart card. He registered a patent in Japan, only, in 1970. Four years later in Europe a French journalist called Roland Moreno filed a patent for 'a card with a self-protected integrated memory'.[2] Since then France has been at the forefront of the development of smart cards and strong support has been given by the French government through their telecommunication agency.

Smart cards are used today in the French banking industry. Customers are given a card which allows them to pay for purchases. At the cash desk it is inserted into a terminal and the assistant enters the amount of the purchase via a keyboard. The customer checks the amount at another display point and, if correct, types in the PIN. The memory in the card checks for the requisite funds and tells the terminal either to accept or to reject the transaction. The card contains a monthly calendar and operates to a preset monthly spending limit. Once this is spent the card will reject further transactions. When a transaction is accepted it is recorded into the card's transaction section and a printed receipt is generated by the terminal. The terminal may be connected on-line or polled overnight for the day's smart card transactions by a central computer. Alternatively, small businesses which do not have this facility can take out the POS terminal's memory, known as a cartette, and take it to a bank for processing. A Minitel (videotex) user in France can, with a terminal that includes a smart card reader, pay for goods selected via the television using this technology.

Smart cards are used in the USA as store cards. A reader in the store can analyze the details of past transactions on a particular card. The customers' attention can then be drawn to new products or special offers in areas which are likely to be of interest. This personal approach is considered to be a more successful marketing technique than giving standard information to all customers via in-store televisions or loud-speakers.

Active smart cards

Active smart cards are very new and as yet few are in use. They are cards which contain up to date information about the holder and are designed to operate without the aid of an independent card reader. Therefore, each card has to have its own power source which is normally a lithium battery. It also has a keyboard and a liquid crystal display. One side of the card looks just like a traditional credit card but the other contains a keyboard which usually has a pad of 4×5 keys. Several letters and one number are represented by one key. A master terminal is used initially to customize the card and to download data into a PC, if required.

One card may be used for several purposes, for instance, it could contain both medical and financial details. Applications for these cards appear at this stage to be limited only by the imagination. The travel agent Thomas Cook is interested in them to provide a single portable medium for all travel details.[2] This could include details of a traveller's itinerary, reservation details, medical details and funds, the equivalent of travellers' cheques.

Roy Bright lists the selling points of smart cards, in particular active ones as:[2]

Compactness (its small size).
Conviviality (its user-friendliness).
Convenience (it can be used at all times in all places).

6.8 The dangers of new technology

The foregoing list of methods and technologies suitable to enter data into a system should not be taken as exhaustive. An organization should study the technologies available carefully as the selection of the correct one may bring considerable advantage. If the wrong technology is chosen it can be expensive to correct the mistake. Imagine the expenditure required to re-equip all the point of sale terminals in a national chain store.

In order to stay ahead, or at least abreast, of competition, managers and information systems staff should actively search for new technology and ideas for use in their organization's systems. This does not mean that all new technolgy should be automatically adopted. There is a wide array of new technology which has not yet found suitable commercial applications, and only now are uses being found for some of the technologies discovered many years ago. For instance, the discovery of 'super waves', which has led to today's fibre optic cables, was made in the middle of the last century at about the same time as the technology for telephones. The technology behind optical memory cards and image processing was first developed in the 1930s, but it is only within the past ten years that it has found commercial application.

It is important not to adopt the attitude that a use must be found for every new technology. This may be described as the 'solution in search of a problem' syndrome. Suppliers who have recently invested in developing a new technology may push it as being the answer to an organization's problems so that they may begin to recover their investment. New technologies have teething problems and, until proven to work satisfactorily, should not be adopted unless a clear competitive advantage is likely to accrue. The initial equipment may not work as well, or be as reliable, as equipment designed several years later. If an organization has invested early it may be costly to replace the initial equipment.

Sales staff are also keen to push new technologies just because they have caught their imagination. There is always a danger, therefore, in relying on suppliers' sales staff for advice. Small businesses which lack both specialist staff and the funds to correct a mistake are particularly prone to blunders of this type. As a result they may be talked into using a new technology to solve what is a quite common problem and which could have been dealt with more satisfactorily and cheaply by an old technology.

NOTES

1. Hashi Syedain, 'Underfunded overcrowded underground', *Management Today*, July 1990.
2. Roy Bright, *Smart Cards: Principles, practice, applications* (Ellis Horwood, 1988).

FURTHER READING

Clifton, H.D., *Business Data Systems*, 4th edn (Prentice Hall International, 1990). Contains a chapter on data capture techniques.
Bright, Roy, *Smart Cards: Principles, practice, applications* (Ellis Horwood, 1988). Contains details of both types of smart card and related technologies.

EXERCISES

1. Flair and Wear is a new chain of fashion shops which is currently fitting out a series of high street outlets. Give the management advice, together with reasons, on the systems that you would recommend to capture data at the point of sale.

2. What information will a manager of a supermarket, which is part of a large chain, require to run the store efficiently? How may this information be provided?

3. What problems can you envisage because of the differences between European and US standards for OCR, MICR and bar codes? What are the barriers to adopting uniform standards for these in the future?

7 Networks and electronic data interchange

SCOPE AND CONTENTS

A: Types of network and their management. This section defines what a network is and looks at both LANs and WANs. Then licensing and private networks are briefly discussed. Electronic data interchange and the development of networks to transfer funds are considered. The problems created by reliance on networks are examined. The possibility of using different types of link is examined in an illustrative case.

B: Strategic uses of networks and EDI. The possible uses of and benefits to be gained by employing networks, both internally and externally, are considered in detail. The political use of networks is briefly considered. The case of American Airlines and the growth of information systems in the air travel industry is outlined as an example of EDI and the strategic use of networks. The effect of this strategy on travel agents and the formulation of new strategies which are changing the structure of the travel industry are considered. An attempt is made to classify interorganizational information systems and to consider possible future developments.

A: TYPES OF NETWORK AND THEIR MANAGEMENT

7.1 What is a network?

A network is some kind of interconnected system. The word is often used in relation to a physical transport system: the London underground railway system is an example. It comprises many different interconnecting lines which allow a passenger to board a train at any station and take any chosen route to any other station before leaving the system. This network interconnects, to a limited extent, with other transport networks — the London bus network, the British Rail networks (such as Network South East) and air networks from Heathrow airport. Thus a passenger can board at one stop on a particular network, travel on a number of these interconnected systems (bus, tube, rail and air) and alight at a stop on a different network to that of entry.

Computer and telecommunications networks may also be considered to be interconnected transport systems. The network is the physical system which consists of, for example, computers and cables. The physical system is able to transport some sort of communication (information or data) in a range of different ways such as voice or image. Today the words 'company communications network' immediately conjure up a vision of an advanced technology network; but networks have always existed. The earliest, which still exists today, was the 'grapevine' along which a communication may be sent via a number of individuals who act as the physical transport system. These individuals pass messages via a random or deliberate series of physical meetings, thus a message could take one of a number of possible routes to its final destination.

By the end of the nineteenth century, communications systems had developed and the telephone network was created. This is another network system, one which is set up to transport the human voice. In recent years great strides have been made in developing new technology to create improved networks which can carry communication in a variety of forms. This chapter looks at the different types of communication network available for linking computers and considers their strategic uses and benefits. The next chapter considers other types of communication network and takes a brief look at the technology involved.

7.2   Internal and external networks

Communication networks linking computers and terminals may be divided initially into two categories: internal (within the organization) and external (interorganizational) networks. An external network, for example, may link one organization with its suppliers and customers — the purpose and benefits of this type of network were discussed in section 5.14. Alternatively, external networks may be wider in scope and encompass communication throughout a whole industry or business sector. The purposes and benefits of external networks are considered in more detail in the second part of this chapter.

7.3   Local area networks

Internal networks which link computers and their peripheral devices may be either **local area networks** (LANs) or **wide area networks** (WANs). A local area network provides a high speed data communications network over a limited geographical area. The range of the network is only between, say, 100 yards and several miles and therefore a LAN is normally a network on a single site which connects PCs to a variety of facilities. The original idea behind the development of LANs was to connect terminals or PCs to costly peripheral devices or to devices which were used infrequently so that these facilities might be shared between many PCs. For example, several PCs may share a printer, as illustrated in Figure 7.1.

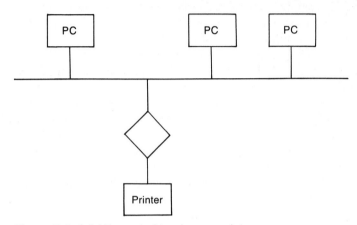

Figure 7.1 A LAN created to share a printer.

In the majority of LANs the PCs are linked to a mainframe or a minicomputer and have access to stored central data. They may also have access to the national telecommunications network in order to communicate with other systems. The PCs are connected to a particular facility via a server which provides and regulates access to the facility. An example of such a LAN is shown in Figure 7.2.

These types of LANs may be subdivided into two: those which allow PCs to draw information from a central database but do not let the PCs communicate

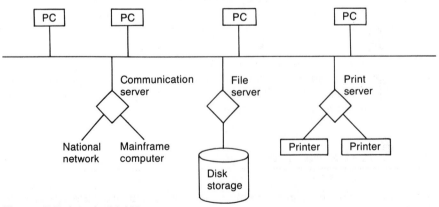

Figure 7.2 A typical LAN.

with each other, and those networks which do allow communication between individual PCs. A LAN in which the workstations do not communicate with each other has the rather predictable advantage of being cheaper. If communication between PCs is not required then this cheaper and simpler type of LAN should be used. Sometimes this form of communication can be a nuisance, as some top managers have found when using certain executive systems. These systems allow messages to be sent and received — a facility which some top managers find interrupts their concentration and wastes their time. They are used to having a secretary who filters incoming messages and interrupts only if the message seems important. Many managers prefer the telephone and teleconferencing as a means of communication rather than the computer. Whether the next generation of managers will have adapted to computer messaging systems remains to be seen. But the potential for time to be wasted by unnecessary or untimely communication is just as real as the potential saving of time by instant messaging. On the other hand, for employees who are doing sequential work on sets of data or information there is a considerable advantage in having a LAN which does allow for messages and information to be passed from one workstation to another.

Recently, however, LANs have developed more important functions than merely sharing peripherals. They are beginning to be used to facilitate the sharing of information by a group of individuals. This may simply be sequential working (mentioned above) but is more likely to go further than that. Specialized group-writing and editing software packages are available which allow people to collaborate using shared pools of information.

In addition to the change in emphasis from cost saving to information sharing, there is another recent development. More and more LANs are being set up which consist of a group of PCs only rather than a minicomputer and a number of terminals. Initially this may be more costly but the advantages in terms of the power and flexibility of the system are considerable. However, PC LANs have the major disadvantage of a loss of security in comparison with more traditional centralized computer systems.

Another way of creating a LAN is to use a PABX (private automatic branch exchange) to route data and information around the organization (see Figure 7.3).

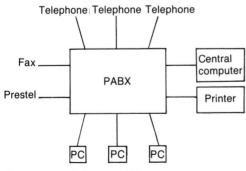

Figure 7.3 A PABX LAN.

PABXs were designed to route telephone calls but they can also handle digitized information from a PC. One of the advantages of this method is that much of the wiring is already in place. In addition, the PABXs at different sites can be linked to provide a wide area network. This gives considerable savings in costs as the national network call charges are avoided. The main disadvantage of the PABX method of creating a LAN is that a PABX cannot handle video data.

7.4 Wide area networks

LANs may be connected via gateways to public or private telecommunications networks to form wide area networks (WANs). A gateway allows two systems which communicate in different ways to communicate with each other, as it can handle any conversion of speed, coding or protocol necessary between different systems. Figure 7.4 illustrates this.

A WAN can operate, at least theoretically, on a global scale. A WAN may be either a public or a privately-operated network — usually it is a mixture of the two. It may link the different sites of one company in a large city or it may link all of the business sites of a company in one country to form a national network. It might even use satellites to link a business internationally. If an organization wishes to create a WAN it is unlikely to go to the lengths of laying its own telecommunication cables across the country to achieve this. In any case this may well be prohibited by law. Instead it will hook up to the national network so that the messages travel from a LAN on one site through the national network to a LAN on a different site. If communication is made from one country to another it will pass from one national network to another. Most national networks (with the exception of the US, UK and Japanese) are state-owned. In the UK, British Telecom is no longer publicly owned and, therefore, the main network

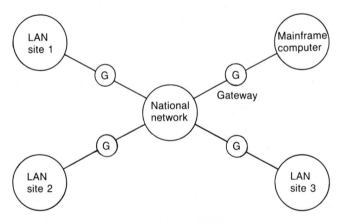

Figure 7.4 LANs linked to form a WAN.

is a private one competing with other private networks in some limited areas. In May 1981 the UK signed the Council of Europe Convention on Data Protection. This restricts the free flow of data to within the EC only. It was a protectionist measure and stopped European data being exported to cheap 'data havens' for processing. Its aim was to safeguard European jobs. The USA and Canada are the only two developed countries that have no rules on the import and export of data.

If a department's LAN is connected to a wider system it is wise to give the employees some knowledge of how the system operates and the possible routes that messages may take to reach their destination. There are quite a few apocryphal stories about situations where this has not been done. For example, messages have, supposedly, travelled half-way round the world before arriving at their destination which is a PC further along the corridor in the same building. This is extremely costly and it is even worse if the message is just to say 'I'm going to the Dog and Duck for lunch — see you there.'

Networks are, of course, costly to install and can be costly to use because of the telecommunication charges — even if used properly. Therefore careful thought should be given to the extent to which instant communication and information via networks is necessary. One company which thinks that instant communication and information is particularly important is IBM. The company installed a network in 1987 which used state of the art technology.[1] The network was set up to satisfy the five-point 'anys rule' (IBM language) which outlines the service that management wished to provide for their employees. The five 'anys' are:

That **any** employee
at **any** IBM location
should be able to go to **any** terminal
and log on to **any** IBM application
running in **any** IBM computer centre.

This system, which caters for the 20,000 IBM employees in the UK, might well be a security nightmare if it is not properly set up and monitored. This factor, together with the high cost involved, has probably prevented more companies following such an open path. It should also be asked whether such a system is really necessary now or in the future. Do all employees need to have access to such a wide range of applications and information? One view which is quite widely held by those who have studied US and UK companies is that in most of them information costs are too high. This is because an increasing amount is spent on meeting the information technology demands of staff who do not have a real need for such information. Top management should not fall into the trap of automatically meeting the priorities of users or potential users of technically advanced information systems. Neither should managers fall into the hands of technology enthusiasts who love systems for their own sake. Funds should be spent on meeting the strategic needs of the company and not on systems which may just increase the organization's overheads.

7.5 Control and licensing of networks

At present there are only two national telecommunications operators licensed by the government in the UK. These are British Telecom and Mercury, both of which can offer national and international services. All equipment that the two organizations use has to be approved by the British Approvals Board for Telecommunications. The government also controls other areas of networking by issuing licences, examples being general licences for PABXs and licences for **value added data services** (VADS) (as discussed in section 8.12). Cellular radio systems, cable television systems and satellite services are also licensed. Thus despite the fact that telecommunications and networks have been removed from the public sector the government still keeps tight control of them. This situation may change with the EC's Open Network Provision directive issued in 1990. This sets out common principles to be followed by all countries so that private service organizations can gain access to networks throughout the Community. It also intends to implement legislation to forcibly dismantle government monopolies over most telecommunication services.

7.6 Private networks

A private network may be created by an organization linking up its PABXs which are situated at different business locations. This PABX network avoids the charge per call which would normally be paid on the national system. Most of the networks being created today are known as virtual private networks. This means that they use lines leased from a national telecommunications infrastructure supplier rather than the user organization laying and using its own lines. The Alexander Howden Group (London), which is part of a US insurance group, was the first to set up a transatlantic link early in 1990. This was done by leasing lines from national operators AT&T (US) and Transglobe (Canada). The system runs on twelve lines from its London offices and can connect to fifty-six of the organization's offices. This mean six thousand users can dial just eight digits and connect with anyone else in the organization. The cost savings are expected to be in the region of 33 per cent of call costs. This system, which is called a global software defined network (GSDN), also allows for three-country teleconferences and it has its own electronic mail system. (See sections 8.13 and 8.16 for more details on these topics.) Christopher Gray, a director of the company, described the benefits of the system thus:

> What it effectively means is that I can now call a colleague in America direct and without touching the public network. I can also bring someone in Spain in on the conversation and we have also eliminated the echo problem because we do not involve satellite communications. It means that we can be much more efficient and we have the unique facility to overspill into the network during peak busy periods.[2]

7.7 Interorganizational information networks

An interorganizational information system is often referred to as electronic data interchange (EDI). Such a system comprises computers and a communication infrastructure which together permit the sharing of information pertaining to ordering supplies or reserving seats, for example. The term EDI should only be used when one computer communicates directly — without human intervention — with another. For example, a production control system in one company may communicate directly with an order receiving computer system in another company. If human intervention, such as rekeying or interpreting information, is necessary the network is not truly carrying out EDI.

Interorganizational information networks bring many benefits but they also bring many problems which must be properly considered by the participants. One major problem is that of security. An interorganizational network means that an employee in one company may be able to gain access to information, directly allocate resources or initiate business processes in another company. Before such a network is installed the management control system must be carefully revised. Another problem is that of legal liability. At what point does an electronic message passing over communication lines actually become an order? Then there may be the problem of what constitutes unfair trading. Some indication of this is given in the illustrative case of the airline reservation systems discussed in this chapter in section 7.14. Yet another problem is that of standardization of equipment and systems (discussed in detail in the next chapter). However, in comparision with some of the possible benefits these difficulties appear minor — to all but those who have to solve them.

'Section B: The strategic uses of networks and EDI' contains specific examples of EDI or interorganizational information networks and section 7.16 sums up the current position.

7.8 Finance networks

Systems for the electronic movement of funds between organizations have recently been devised. This type of system completes the paperless cycle of ordering, invoicing and paying for purchases, and makes the whole EDI process between the organization and its suppliers and customers much more satisfactory. **Electronic funds transfer** (EFT) between organizations first took place in the UK in 1968 when the **Banks' Automated Clearing Service** (BACS) was set up to provide improved interbank transfers of money. Today it offers an increasing range of funds transfer facilities between individuals and companies and can be incorporated into almost any payroll package and bought ledger system. At present it handles:[3]

> 10 million salaries per month.
> 3.5 million pensions per month.
> 1.5 million wages per week.

500 million direct debits per year.
230 million standing orders per year.

By the early 1990s BACS is expected to handle one half of all UK domestic interbank payments. One of the main reasons for its success is the cost savings it generates. The capital outlay incurred by an organization in installing a BACS system is small and the savings per transaction are considerable. It has been estimated that it costs approximately £5 for an organization to make a payment by cheque but only 40 pence with BACS.[3] The use of BACS reduces the paperwork to just an advice note and also removes reconciliation problems while at the same time giving precise control over cash-flow.

In the UK the last step in EFT development, known as 'closing the electronic loop', has recently been taken. Banks now offer a business-to-business payment system for companies using EDI on Istel and INS networks. (These networks are described in section 8.4.) Prior to this a business using EDI had to break the electronic chain to make payments, by printing out a remittance advice note, writing a cheque and then posting the two. Development was slow because of the complexities of EDI-related transactions and the banks' desire to pursue their own products rather than collaborating on one system for the whole industry. Another delay has been caused by the problem of setting communication standards. The European standards organization has only recently produced four message standards: for remittance advice, payment instructions, and credit and debit orders. The UN has backed the Edifact standard language which offers a range of messaging formats and the US has also agreed to change from its national standards towards conformity with Edifact. The banks in the USA are now pushing ahead with EDI, anxious to become involved before large EDI industry networks begin to arrange for payments between suppliers and customers quite independently of the banks and thus cut them out completely. This would deprive the banks of a section of their traditional business.

For individuals, the UK-based Homelink was the world's first home banking service. It was a joint business venture between many organizations, in particular the Bank of Scotland, the Nottingham Building Society and British Telecom. Homelink provides a range of information services for the individual apart from the transfer of funds through Prestel, a UK television viewdata system.

7.9 Electronic funds transfer at point of sale

Electronic funds transfer at point of sale (EFTPOS) may eventually replace cheques and cash as a method of payment in retail outlets. Its advantages to shops should be considerable. For instance, there is no cash to cope with and count up at the end of the day and, in addition, the customer's payment is guaranteed.

Realizing this, the banks in the UK attempted to make the retailers pay a high price for the system; this has caused a considerable amount of friction and delay in its implementation. EFTPOS should also have considerable advantages for the banks: in particular it should reduce the cost of the transfer of funds (but at present the banks dispute this). In the UK one national system is being developed which takes all cards rather than the retailer having to have a number of terminals at the checkout for a range of different cards. The system works by 'swiping' the card through a terminal, the identity of the customer is then confirmed either by a PIN or a signature on the card. The system went on trial in 1989 in Edinburgh, Leeds and Southampton and became nationwide in 1990 based on Switch debit cards, Visa and Access cards.

In Belgium the two common cash dispenser networks are Bancontact and Mister Cash. Recently they have linked up and their cash cards (with their magnetic stripe) are becoming the backbone of the EFTPOS system and are now usable as debit cards. As a result, petrol stations, for instance, are linked to one or other system thus allowing petrol to be dispensed 24 hours a day via unmanned pumps.

7.10 Network management

Information networks of one type or another will become one of the major business tools of the future. They must be simple to use and totally reliable. Companies are already finding that they rely on their networks to such an extent that even a short power cut is a major annoyance. For instance, a store might find that it could not operate its cash tills if there was a power cut, so no goods could be sold or money taken. It would be possible to issue a hand-written receipt and process the details later, but with the tills closed access to change would be impossible. No information on transactions, if there were any, would filter back through the system in order to restock the shelves or to help management make decisions. Information feeding back to suppliers may be delayed also. Toyota, for instance, has a direct link from its production control computers to Minibea, its supplier of ball-bearings.[4] This instigates deliveries from Minibea as often as five times a day. If for some reason the information did not get through, it is possible that production would come to a halt. However, the telephone could always be used to keep supplies flowing in an emergency.

A different type of industry which also relies on networks to supply instant information is that of finance. Information is the life-blood of these businesses. Thus organizations monitoring markets and dealing in shares need very reliable systems which provide up to date information twenty-four hours a day. Under these circumstances any business which did not attempt to do everything possible to safeguard its network would deserve to go out of business.

By arranging for back-up power supplies and facilities, and by good maintenance, an organization can minimize disruption to its network. Proper maintenance of the network is vital and should be planned for at the time the system is installed so that if maintenance is to be carried out in-house it is as straightforward as possible. Alternatively, maintenance agreements may be taken out with the dealer or distributor from whom the system was purchased, provided the supplier is large. There is also the possibility that the manufacturer who built the network may provide a maintenance service. If the communications network is leased from a third party whose business is communications technology the maintenance will normally be done by them under contract. Hewlett-Packard, for instance, has a system which can monitor a customer's network remotely.[5] It claims that it can pinpoint problems in minutes, and often the customer's first indication that something is wrong is when Hewlett-Packard informs them.

It is not necessary to have one uniform network. The majority of organizations do not. It is quite normal for a business operating within a single industry to have several different types of link which operate in different ways, each being suitable for its purpose. This has occurred probably because the links were set up at different times or because some customers or suppliers need slightly different treatment. The following case on Midwest Tire illustrates the different types of network that an organization may have.

7.11 Illustrative case: Midwest Tire, Inc.[6]

Midwest Tire, Inc., which manufactures tyres and has its own chain of motor stores, has a number of different network links. Some are with original equipment customers (that is supplying tyres to manufacturers of new cars) and others are with distributors and suppliers of goods for the stores. As far as customers are concerned, General Motors and Ford send information daily on production requirements via an EDI network, and Midwest sends dispatch details to General Motors every two hours and to Ford every hour. Caterpillar sends information daily on a different network. In order to obtain information on requirements from John Deere and Navistar, Midwest uses the national telephone system to call daily for a production schedule and, at the same time, give information concerning the previous day's dispatches.

Midwest also sells to tyre distributors. Information is passed on an EDI network which was developed by Midwest. This allows the distributors to make on-line orders, enquiries about the state of orders, and to check product availability. Midwest also has a number of different EDI links with its suppliers, for instance, information is passed daily to its battery supplier. Similarly, a motor freight company dials up a remote printer which is connected to Midwest's network in order to pass information to Midwest concerning deliveries.

B: THE STRATEGIC USES OF NETWORKS AND EDI

7.12 Using networks to gain strategic benefits

As networks tend to be costly to install, operate and maintain, considerable benefit must be gained from them if they are not just to increase the organization's overheads and as a consequence put up prices to the customer or reduce profits. A list of the potential benefits to an organization would be quite lengthy, but we consider a few of the major and more common ones.

Instant communication

As was discussed in Chapter 5, considerable competitive advantage may be gained by being a fast cycle organization. Obviously a network may well be a vital part of that strategy as it can provide instant communication both internally and with the supplier or customer and thus speed up the provision of the required product or service. Renault's or Toyota's dealer networks (discussed in section 5.15) are examples of this.

Removal of geographical boundaries and time limitations

In the past, the 'window' to Tokyo from London was about one hour a day — that is, both sets of employees were in the office at the same time for only one hour in the day. Thus any message between divisions or organizations had to be passed during that one hour. Now messages can be sent at any time of day either through better public communication systems, such as fax, or by using public and private computer and telecommunications networks. Not only can communications be passed but funds can also be transferred quickly. This allows two divisions or businesses on opposite sides of the world to deal closely with one another.

Improved organization and business structures

A modern communications network may allow an organization to achieve physical and operational decentralization while at the same time still maintaining strong central management control. A subsidiary on the other side of the world can be under constant surveillance by head office while the subsidiary's managers have the freedom to act and to run the business locally as they feel fit. This can result in an improved decentralized structure which is of considerable benefit to the organization. For instance, an oil company which had subsidiaries in thirty-six different countries reduced its long-term debt by $240m by setting up local bank accounts in the various countries and then making each subsidiary responsible for debt collection and payment. By monitoring the bank balances the corporate treasurer at head office knew the financial position without needing to hold the funds centrally as had been the case previously.

Better communications have given large organizations the chance to change the structure of their business activities. They can set up or acquire plants which manufacture locally and sell to their local markets products which are suited to their specific needs. This is made possible only because of a good communications network between head office and the local plants. The local plants or businesses benefit by being part of a large organization, gaining access to funds and to a high level of expertise via a comprehensive communication and information network. These benefits are unlikely to accrue to a small organization which is not part of a group as usually funds are more difficult to raise and expertise is limited.

New business possibilities created

Some businesses owe their existence to networks. Federal Express (the package delivery company discussed in Chapter 5) is one example. Another is the credit card company, American Express. Without an adequate information network American Express could not have grown to its present size or exist in its present form. Other businesses find themselves able to enter entirely new fields because they have created a good network: the case of American Airlines (discussed later in this chapter) is one example. An information network may just extend an existing business in a profitable way. Sotheby's, the international auction house, provides a good example of a communications network extending the business by introducing more potential bidders. In 1989 Sotheby's held its first intercontinental auction from its London saleroom using an international telecommunications link. Bidders in New York could watch events on closed circuit television and bid via a telephone keypad linked to the London computer via a satellite. This is discussed further in section 8.11.

Improved general efficiency

Installing a network so as to provide benefits in one area of business activity may also mean that it can be used to gain benefits in other areas. These added benefits ought to be actively sought and planned for because the high expenditure of installing a network may be difficult to justify if based only on benefits gained by a single business activity. A crucial lynchpin in Avis Europe's organization is its computerized reservation system Wizard. It is the only fully integrated rental and reservation system in the vehicle rental industry and probably played a major part in the company increasing its profits from £27.7m in 1986 to £72m in 1989. It allows customers to check out in just two minutes and check in, when returning the vehicle, in one minute. However, this is not its only benefit. It also provides a means of controlling and managing the fleet of vehicles in a way that could not be done without the information network. This gives the major benefits of improved vehicle utilization and cash flow throughout the group. Another, relatively minor benefit is that it allows the company to produce published accounts in six weeks instead of the normal three months.

Locking in suppliers or customers

In some industries it is vital to have the right network system in order to trade. General Motors was one of the first companies to initiate this by demanding that its suppliers 'got on-line with EDI or off-line with GM'.[7] In Europe, General Motors has network links with around two thousand suppliers across seven countries. This entails the suppliers having to comply with the computer hardware standards and communication protocols recommended by the Automotive Industry Action Group, of which GM is a member. Not all organizations which are encouraging their suppliers to join an EDI network need to resort to such threats as made by General Motors; in any case, the benefits can usually be perceived and realized by all participants. The same is true of links with customers. Often customers receive substantial benefits in terms of better material management, a reduction in stock holding, information on the status and location of products, and a reduction in delivery time as a result of networking.

Many of these industry networks are set up by information technology (IT) organizations keen to sell their own technology, such as British Telecom, Istel or INS (partly owned by ICL). For instance, INS operates one of several 'electronic clearing houses' for the motor industry called Motornet. How secure the future is for networks run by an IT organization, unless they offer specific benefits, is open to question as many large industrial organizations, such as GM and Ford, are setting up their own. However, benefits such as constant monitoring for faults, a guaranteed back-up network and access to networks operating different systems may well be inducement enough to attract most to networks created by IT organizations.

Because of their nature, networks have the potential to form and cement power blocks within an industry by tying suppliers and customers to manufacturers. This may lead to the formation of cartels where the status quo and market share are accepted by the participants. This could possibly have the unfortunate effect in these industries of making it more difficult for a new organization to enter the industry and of reducing competition between the participants.

Substantial cost savings

EDI comes into its own when an organization processes a large volume of orders. British Coal deals with 12,000 suppliers and receives 1.8 million invoices a year, so the advantage to them of 'paperless trading' is manifest. Although EDI at British Coal is still in its early stages, paper-handling savings have been identified and the cost of sending messages is cheaper than using the post (Istel, whose services British Coal uses, currently charges 8 pence per message against a second class postal charge of 17 pence[8]). However, there is a substantial 'mailbox' or standing charge to recoup which makes Istel's system attractive only to organizations which have a high level of transactions. IBM is another organization which is doing most of its business with its many suppliers via EDI, thus saving an estimated $60m over five years by 'paperless trading'.

7.13 Political use of networks

A quite different use of information networks was demonstrated in 1989 during the unrest in China. In 1986, Chinese students in the USA and Canada set up a computer network called Usenet. Its main aim was to keep the Chinese students studying at different universities in touch with each other. It gave students the chance simply to talk to each other or to seek advice from others. The network grew quite rapidly and became a global network which included computers in China itself. The network was used during the 1989 student protest in ways which had not been foreseen. Firstly, it was used by the students in China (until it was destroyed by the authorities) to co-ordinate protest activities in different cities throughout the country. Secondly, it was used to relay information around the world about the events occurring within China. Apart from networks linking embassies around the world, this was probably the first example of a computer network being used to convey political information.

Governments can initiate and foster networks to benefit both themselves and their countries. For instance, the government of Singapore initiated a system known as Tradenet.[7] Its aim was to improve the country's trading position by attracting more multinational business to the country. It is a system which links importers and exporters with all the organizations they might wish to deal with. These include the trade department, the customs department, the census and statistics department, banks, shipping lines and airlines, sea container terminals, and air and sea cargo agents. The potential for growth in EDI in this area over the next decade is vast and if some regions lag behind it is likely that they will face economic decline.

There is also the possibility that information systems will be misused or manipulated for political purposes. There have been quite a few examples in recent history of regimes trying to restrict the flow of information or putting out misinformation. Sometimes this is done with the intention of keeping up morale, as was the case during the Second World War when the British public was kept in ignorance of many events occurring on the other side of the Channel.

Politics, in the broad sense, reveals itself in the development of networks within particular industries. The airline reservation systems case illustrates this quite well. It also shows clearly how systems are developed over time and that initially many of the potential benefits may not be fully comprehended.

7.14 Illustrative case: American Airlines and airline passenger reservation systems[9]

One of the first examples of a fully integrated network was that developed and used in the airline business. The story starts many years ago. The original impetus behind its development was the cost saving to be gained by reducing clerical staff. When using the original manual system agents could sell seats once they had confirmed that a seat was available on a particular flight. This they did by looking at a noticeboard in the office. When a reservation was made the agent telephoned it through to the airline's central reservation office and then filled in a passenger name record (PNR). This in turn was sent to the central reservation office. The central office monitored the level of seats still available and when this dropped below a certain level a notice was sent out to all agents' offices telling them to stop selling seats. This was posted on the office noticeboard. The procedure was slow, cumbersome, and wasteful of labour. Discrepancies between the number of seats booked and the PNRs were frequent, resulting in either under- or overbooking on a flight with its consequent loss of revenue or of customer goodwill.

As long ago as 1953 the president of American Airlines consulted IBM on the possibility of an automated system. A year later a simple automated PNR system was produced but it fell well short of the fully automated reservation system that the president had dreamed of. This dream began to be fulfilled in 1964 when the first American Airlines SABRE system was launched. Three years later, terminals were placed in a limited number of travel agents on a trial basis.

Other airlines began to develop their own rival systems, and from this point until 1974 various efforts were made to establish an industry standard passenger reservation system. This was foiled by lack of agreement and financing problems. For instance, one of the bodies set up to promote this was the JICRS (Joint Industry Computer Reservation System). American Airlines was the main force behind this body which consisted of airlines, suppliers of the equipment and travel agents. American Airlines formed this body in response to an earlier initiative between the American Society of Travel Agents and a computer company called Control Data Corporation.

American Airlines felt that if this initiative had been successful the airlines would have been ousted from their position and a computer company would have controlled the access to and from travel agents. JICRS foundered when it was decided that the cost of developing the reservation system should be borne by the airlines in proportion to their size. United, the airline with the largest market share at the time, had already developed its own system (Apollo) by this stage and it was felt by United's management to be superior to the other systems. The management thought that as a result the airline would be paying a considerable amount of money for a system which would really only benefit the small airlines — as it would have the effect of reducing the advantage of size which United had gained.

When it withdrew from JICRS, United notified the other members that it would start installing Apollo in travel agents in six months' time (September 1976). American Airlines had anticipated this move and reacted immediately by putting its system, SABRE, into travel agents' offices free of charge. By the end of that year they had installed them in 130 offices and had plans to install many more in the following year. Meanwhile the rival Apollo system was put into just 4 pilot locations. Up to this stage the potential for increasing market share by using a reservation system had not really been considered by anyone except possibly American Airlines. However, that potential soon became apparent. American Airlines had estimated that its system would generate $3.1m a year in additional sales. Before the installation programme was complete the estimate was revised to $20.1m, a return on investment in excess of 500 per cent. This vast increase in bookings was due to the fact that although SABRE showed all airline flights to a particular destination, American Airlines's were shown first; and as 70 per cent of all bookings were for flights shown on the first screen the system increased revenue considerably.

The rush to get terminals into travel agents was won by American Airlines. This was most important as travel agents wanted only one terminal in the office. Therefore, once SABRE had been installed it was difficult for another airline to get its system accepted. Despite this, by 1978 things were not going too well for American Airlines in its battle for market share with United. This was thought to be because United had a better route structure. So American Airlines devised the co-host system whereby other airlines were given preferential treatment in the display of flights on the SABRE system on payment of a fee. Five airlines that had different routes which complemented those of American joined the system. Thus American's network of routes was, in effect increased and United had to fight back with a similar system. The screens of the two systems now showed the host airline's flights first, then the co-hosts' flights, then those of the airlines not thought to be a direct competitive threat and finally the remainder.

By 1980/1 American Airlines estimated that SABRE was generating $77.5m in terms of increased revenue and co-host fees were $6.9m. In 1983 the Civil Aeronautics Board carried out a study of the systems to assess the effect on competition in the industry. The Board produced a set of rules to eliminate display bias and prohibit vast fees being charged for display by those airlines that owned systems. This had a disastrous and unpredicted effect on small airlines' revenue, as without bias their flights got lost among the mass of American's and United's flights. Also the Board set fees which were considerably higher than those being charged at the time to small airlines. In fact, prior to this some airlines had not even been charged fees. Various court cases followed. Some small carriers went to court on the grounds that the reservation systems of American and United were 'a powerful anti-competitive weapon'. This failed when it was held that there was insufficient evidence of excessive profits or of overcharging. When other airlines tried to develop their own systems they had to fight to get them accepted by the travel agents because this meant replacing one terminal with that of another airline. American took Texas Air to court alleging illegal inducements were being offered to agents to convert to their system. Texas Air in turn took American to court alleging anti-competitive tactics to protect their 38 per cent of the market.

The court cases prove the importance of the flight reservation systems to the airlines. In 1985, American's profit from SABRE was thought to be $143m on revenue of $336m. This level of profit led American's chief executive officer, Robert Crandall, to say that if forced to choose between SABRE and the transport business, American Airlines, he would have to choose the information technology business, SABRE and sell the airline.

Over the years the system had grown and expanded beyond mere airline seat reservation. This was due partly to the pressure to stay ahead of competing systems by offering a better service and partly because of the potential for increased sales by giving added benefits to the customer. Today it is possible for a person in the USA who is booking a flight to the UK to book at the same time a hire car, hotel rooms, tickets for the theatre or for tennis at Wimbledon or a particular tour or cruise.

SABRE helped American Airlines to achieve the largest market share in the USA and to overtake United. This was achieved by the long-term vision of their president in 1953 which gave them a head start in the information technology business. Secondly, and most importantly, they recognized that the travel agents were their real customers because in effect they select the flight for the final customer, the passenger. Having recognized this, American concentrated its efforts on winning over travel agents by installing its system well before its competitors realized what was happening.

American did not stop there. It went on to identify that the second largest group of customers, after the travel agents, were business travellers. In order to appeal to them they introduced the 'AAdvantage' program, aimed at regular travellers, in 1981. This program could not have been introduced without their existing comprehensive network, SABRE. Every time a business passenger flew, the miles were recorded; and if enough miles were clocked up in a year the passenger was entitled to a free flight. This meant that flying regularly on business during the year could give the traveller a free holiday flight — a fact that many quickly latched onto! Thus when businesses were booking flights, employees put pressure on them to pick American Airlines. From this starting point terminals have been given to businesses who require them, and the programme is even extending to giving terminals to individuals who fly regularly.

In 1986 American Airlines appear to have realized that it could not develop its systems any further, although it is still improving some minor aspects. This being so, its competitive advantage was expected to disappear over the coming years as other airlines developed their own systems. American, therefore, began to sell its skills to other airlines, railways and anybody else who wanted them, thus putting all the knowledge they had acquired to a different use.

Meanwhile in Europe similar systems were being built. British Airways has a major stake in an international computerized distribution and reservation system called Gallileo which is backed by a consortium of airlines, including Swissair and KLM. The importance of information technology to the airline business is further highlighted by British Airways' expenditure in this area. It spends 3 per cent of gross revenue per year on this at present and expects to reach 5 per cent per year by 1990.[10]

After reading the above case about the development of an information network for flight booking and its extension along the value chain into areas which were traditionally the domain of travel agents, the reader might wonder if there is a role for travel agents in the future. Are systems like SABRE — which book hotels, hire cars and arrange theatre tickets — going to develop further and take business from travel agents? Has the structure of the air travel industry changed so greatly that they are becoming redundant? Will 'travel agents' as we know them become obsolete in a few years time? Is the travel agent business different in the USA compared with the UK and the rest of Europe? If the industry is under threat many travel agents will adapt to the changes and find a new role. Those that do not change may well go out of business. There is no doubt that the change caused by the development of new information systems based on networks and new technology has had a major impact on the structure of the air travel industry and permanently changed it.

7.15 Illustrative case: the change in structure of the air travel industry[11]

Rather surprisingly, perhaps, systems like SABRE have on the whole been good news for US travel agents. In 1976, in the USA, less than 40 per cent of airline tickets were booked through travel agents. Today this has risen to more than 80 per cent.[12] This rapid expansion has enabled the large chains to grow but has not been so good for small travel agents. Many agents were traditionally small businesses: anyone with a small amount of capital could buy a shop and start a travel agency business. In the USA today this is no longer possible because of the cost of information and technology within the industry — in particular, access to large databases is necessary for survival. In recent years, in the USA, many small agents have gone out of business or have been taken over by larger companies. This has been caused partly by the change in the nature of competition and also because of the need to develop databases. As travel agents fight back against the airlines by creating their own holiday reservation systems even the larger businesses need to grow in size to absorb the cost of the databases required.

However, simply fighting on the same ground as the airlines by creating one's own information database is not very imaginative and might not succeed as a strategy on its own. Some US travel agents have realized this and have shifted ground. For many companies, expenditure on travel is the third largest expense category, after wages and salaries and communications. In an effort to control expenditure some of the larger companies have begun to look to large travel agents, such as Thomas Cook or American Express, to handle their travel needs for them. The travel agents work on the basis of a commission paid by the airlines and are now beginning to split this commission with the purchasing company. In addition, bulk buying of hotel rooms or airline tickets can usually be done at a discount to the travel agent which can be passed on to the customer if desired. This, together with a special 'control package' for businesses, such as American Express offers, means that large travel agents have a new role and can survive. The business control package includes reports to enable management to control and audit the expenditure on travel. The reports also give the opportunity to obtain quantity discounts from hotel chains and car hire companies by recording the company's use of the resource throughout the world. Price Waterhouse has developed an 'Air Auditor' package which it is selling to travel agents and businesses. At present, travel agents are using it as a marketing tool to win the business of large companies.

Travel agents are also extending their service, to cover not only hotels but such items as the arranging of meetings, meals, taxis, and 'incentive travel' with the arrangement of trips to major events. The consulting segment is growing too, whereby travel agents take over the managing of travel in order to minimize cost and boost the productivity of expenditure on travel.

In the UK, holiday bookings are a much greater part of a travel agent's business than in the USA because there are many fewer business passengers making internal flights. There are also fewer airlines. As a result, holiday companies have followed the US airlines' lead and gone into booking technology. This may help small independent travel agents to survive. In the UK, Thompson Holidays has developed a system called Tops which is a videotex-based booking system for use by travel agents. As Thompson has by far the largest market share, its competitors have been forced to follow and make their information available in the same form. Thus a *de facto* industry standard has been created.

7.16 Different types of interorganizational information systems

Interorganizational information systems are in their infancy and the different types of system have not been properly classified. Figure 7.5 shows a classification adapted from work by Benjamin *et al.*[6]

1. **Fixed link EDI** (electronic data interchange). This is the type of system in which specific links are created between suppliers and their customers so that *data* relating to stock required or despatched can pass between them. Most current interorganizational information systems are of this type and are known simply as EDI systems.

2. **Fixed link DSS** (decision support system). This is the type of system where specific links are created so that *information* may pass between the two parties. This might include information which can be analyzed and used to make decisions or used to assist in component design (CAD). Amalgamated Foods' information system (discussed in section 5.17) which links it to the stores that it supplies and provides them with information to assist in ordering is an example of such a system.

3. **Networked market EDI**. This is a market where suppliers and customers conduct business electronically through an intermediary. *Data* on the product or service are transmitted and the customer can browse through

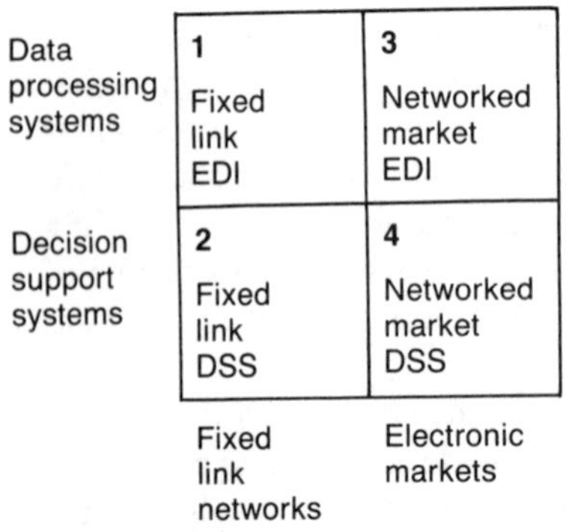

	Fixed link networks	Electronic markets
Data processing systems	**1** Fixed link EDI	**3** Networked market EDI
Decision support systems	**2** Fixed link DSS	**4** Networked market DSS

Figure 7.5 Categories of interorganizational information systems.

the offerings of various suppliers before ordering the product or service of a particular supplier. The airlines' seat reservation systems is an example of such a system.

4. **Networked market DSS**. This is a market which offers more than just data. *Information* for making decisions is provided. Few examples of this type of system exist as yet. Some financial systems are moving in this direction so that more information than merely the price of shares or commodities is given in order to assist the user in decision making. (The system must also include the facility to buy and sell as well as providing information for making decisions on whether to buy or sell.).

Most interorganizational information systems fall into category 1 at present but within a few years a rapid movement should be seen towards the other categories. If this occurs it will follow the same sort of pattern as computer systems took as they gradually developed. Originally they dealt only with routine data processing before moving into decision support systems and beyond.

NOTES

1. Richard Sharpe, 'IBM's five star plan', *Management Today*, June 1987.
2. *Daily Telegraph*, 19 April 1990.
3. 'BACS to basics', *Management Accounting*, July/Aug. 1989.
4. Clive Jackson, 'Building a competitive advantage through information technology', *Long Range Planning*, vol. 22, no. 4, 1989.
5. *Daily Telegraph*, 26 Sept. 1989.
6. Robert I. Benjamin, David W. de Long and Michael S. Scott Morton, 'Electronic data interchange: how much competitive advantage?', *Long Range Planning*, Feb. 1990.
7. Janice Burn and Eveline Caldwell, *Management of Information Systems Technology* (Waller, 1990).
8. 1990 prices.
9. Much of the information in the case is from Duncan G. Copeland and James L. McKenney, 'The airline reservation systems: lessons from history', *MIS Quarterly*, Sept. 1988.
10. Sir Colin Marshall, 'Information technology moves centre stage' paper, Hoskyns Group plc, Oct. 1990.
11 William J. Doll, 'Information technology's strategic impact on the American air travel service industry', *Information and Management*, no. 16, 1989.
12. Max Hopper, 'Rattling Sabre: new ways to compete on information', *Harvard Business Review*, May/June 1990.

FURTHER READING

Idrees, Muhammad, *Design and Management of Distributed Data Processes: A practitioner's approach* (NCC, 1990). Contains chapters explaining the technical aspects of networks.

EXERCISES

1. Examine the different information networks which are available to you in your institution or organization. Draw a chart showing how they interrelate and indicate the scope and purposes of each.

2. Prepare a brief report on the advantages of EDI for the management of a major soft toy manufacturer.

8 Communication networks

Standards, applications and techniques

SCOPE AND CONTENTS

A: Standards. This section looks at the problems involved in setting international standards and the progress made towards this. It covers the standardization of computer operating systems within an organization and briefly considers Unix. Then it deals with external linkage via national or private networks and the progress towards OSI — detailing the seven layers. The ideal of one standard network for all information purposes and the steps being made through ISDN towards achieving this are outlined.

B: Other networking applications and techniques. This section covers a range of applications which rely on communication networks. The first is the use of networkers or homeworkers. Then the rapid growth in telemarketing centres and their technology, including ACDs, is discussed. The different types of teleconferencing — audio, video and computer — are briefly mentioned, as is satellite communication. A brief section on other developments completes the chapter.

A: NETWORK STANDARDS

8.1 The need for standardization

Most organizations' computer systems have grown up over the years in a piecemeal manner. This might have been adequate in the past but it is no longer satisfactory for an organization to allow this haphazard growth to continue. Management must have a proper strategy for planning and investing in information systems which is in keeping with the overall aims of the business rather than letting the different systems grow like 'Topsy', i.e. in a random incoherent way. Furthermore, past piecemeal growth has, for many organizations, resulted in a plethora of computers which cannot communicate with each other due to different operating systems. It is likely that different computers and systems will be incompatible unless all the equipment is purchased from the same manufacturer. This is because there are no generally accepted standards for computer technology — a state of affairs that is not unusual in a new and growing industry. For example, the railways in the UK developed without standards with different companies operating on different widths of track and with different rolling stock. Today there are still problems as the width of British rolling stock is narrower than continental rolling stock although both travel on the same gauge track. This means that some bridges and tunnels in the Midlands and the North will have to be widened before French trains can travel through the Channel Tunnel to the north of England. Thus the systems of the different railways have been, and in some cases still are, incompatible and in a similar way different computer systems are incompatible today. Incompatible systems make any interconnection extremely difficult and act as a brake on the development of a fully integrated network or system.

8.2 Systems incompatibility

The incompatibility of computer systems was tolerable, though not very satisfactory, until businesses began to realize the strategic potential of their information systems. There are severe problems in linking computers externally but the problems of linking internally should not be underestimated either. Specific applications were in the past purchased from the supplier who best met the need of the particular group or activity within the business. Different suppliers were better at providing different types of application, hence the diversity of systems within a single organization. Local authorities, for instance, face considerable problems with their wide range of activities which include finance, property, libraries, highways and school administration. Surrey County Council found that it could not integrate two systems which should be compatible for the smooth running of the organization, namely the centralized word processing system and the council-wide office system.[1] It tried for three years to exchange documents from the word processing centre to the mainframe system. One consequence was that if departments used the office system to produce a report they could not paste in paragraphs which were already held on the word processing system, as would normally be possible. Instead, the paragraphs had to be retyped.

The previous example may seem a relatively minor problem — after all, twenty years ago the words would have had to be retyped anyway. However, more serious difficulties are often faced in achieving total integration of management and other information systems after a takeover or merger. The case of the merger between ICL and STC has already been mentioned in section 4.9. After the merger, the two organizations kept their own, very different systems. This was mainly for cultural reasons but undoubtedly any integration of the two would have been difficult, if not impossible, technically. Phillips Polygram International, the records subsidiary of Phillips, had problems with different computer architectures as long ago as the 1960s after the merger of the Phillips and Siemens labels.[1] More recently, when the merger with Warner's WEA was considered the management realized that they had two incompatible systems, Wang and IBM. The strength of Wang's system was in communications where Phillip's IBM system was weak. But Phillip's strength was in mainstream data processing where the Wang system could not cope with the volume of business that the merged firm would generate. The management faced a major problem in deciding which system should be kept. Before they could make the wrong decision, however, the merger was vetoed by the Federal Communications Commission.

8.3 Standards

The need for computer standards or an open system, as it is called, has been realized for at least a decade, but until recently little progress had been made towards standardization. Action is at last taking place, led mainly by frustrated customers and governments worried about the lack of standardization harming trade. Part of the problem in the past was the equipment manufacturers' initial reluctance to standardize. It could be argued that while each of the large manufacturers produced equipment and systems which were incompatible with each other's they were safeguarding their future market share by tying customers to them. In addition, any change in specification would have been costly and would have caused problems of incompatibility with their own previous models.

In reality, *de facto* standards have existed and survive today. IBM, because of its vast size in relation to the other suppliers, has often set the standard. Software suppliers have made their products IBM-compatible in an attempt to gain a larger market share; small equipment manufacturers have made their products compatible in order to obtain any share at all. IBM's management has gone along with this because it has had the effect of strengthening IBM's position relative to its larger competitors.

Another very real problem with setting standards in the past was that the industry and technology was changing rapidly so that any standard would always be out of date in a few years. While this is still true, recent pressure has been so great that standards of a sort have been set. There are two areas where agreed standards, of a fashion, exist. They are computer operating standards and standards for the transmission of data between computers. In 1984 a pressure group of computer suppliers called X/Open was formed to accelerate the standard-setting process with regard to computer operating systems. It chose Unix, a system developed by the US company AT&T. Unix is now licensed to several hundred suppliers and is the nearest thing to a standard that exists in that area. It has been endorsed by the Open Software Foundation which is a group of leading computer companies which includes IBM and DEC (Digital Equipment Corporation). At present most organizations use other operating systems, and it has been suggested that even in 1992 only 25 per cent of multi-user systems will operate on Unix. Recently, however, Unix has received a boost — IBM has foresaken its own proprietary operating system in favour of Unix for its latest range of System/6000 series workstations. Tony Cleaver, chief executive of IBM UK, is reported to have said at the product launch: 'IBM is market-driven and we have therefore dedicated ourselves to achieving systems leadership in the Unix world. We're serious about Unix.'[2]

8.4 Linking networks

There are problems linking internally with LANs. There are two main types of network: Ethernet developed by Xerox and made by DEC, and Token Ring which is used by IBM. IBM is progressing towards a partial solution, as in the future IBM computers with a revised operating system will be able to link to Ethernet. Other systems are being developed which allow the user simply to plug a PC into a wall socket to connect to the network. This is known as structured wiring and has the great advantage of doing away with the mass of cables that exist in some organizations because of the different networks. It also gives the user almost total flexibility over the siting of the PC, thus an individual wishing to move office can just plug the computer into a socket without the technical department having to install new cables. Even this may soon appear out of date as cordless LANs (and PABXs) are being developed which use radio frequencies rather than cables.

By far the most difficult problem to solve, however, and the most crucial for many businesses, is that of external linkage. As far as the physical network is concerned there are three choices in the UK at present:

- Use the national or public network — British Telecom or Mercury.
- Subscribe to a third party network — such as Istel or INS networks.
- Invest in a private network.

It is initially very costly for an organization to set up its own private network. However, it is now legal in the UK to lease any spare capacity to other organizations thus reducing the financial burden. The main advantages of a private network are the chance to optimize the design and configuration of the network and the ability to tailor security (a major problem in external networks) to the organization's needs.

Leasing from a third party, by subscribing to a specific network, means that all interface problems are handled by the lessor. All the subscribing organization has to do is to plug the equipment into the network and to provide the information in the required format. This will necessitate buying software to format the messages. The two main suppliers in the UK are Istel and INS (International Network Services) which is an ICL/GEC joint venture. British Coal, for instance, uses Edict on Istel's Infotrac network for communication between its suppliers and customers. Third party EDI networks (see section 7.7) normally link suppliers and customers within a particular industry. Istel concentrates on the engineering and manufacturing sectors, and INS on the retailing and health care sectors. For example, CEFIC is a network within the chemical industry and Odette is one of several within the motor industry.

A major difficulty arises if a business wants to link with a supplier or customer which is not within the industry and, therefore, not on the same network. Westland Helicopters have this problem as the European military aerospace companies use the AECMA network, the civil aerospace companies use ATA, and US military aerospace companies use CALS. Westland also deals with many suppliers from the motor industry who use the Odette network. This dreadful situation is gradually being improved, however, as there are now limited links between the networks of INS and Istel.

The problem is not limited to technical difficulties with networks. Each system varies and uses different types and styles of 'forms' for orders, invoices, etc. Until standard 'forms' are agreed and used, problems will still exist and business with a new customer cannot be started until computer system enhancements have been acquired. The Tradernet standard, which is a clothing industry standard and includes definitions for orders and invoices, is already being adopted by a number of organizations in the clothing industry. In the meantime large retail organizations, such as British Home Stores, have the power to require suppliers to comply with their own standards. This gives the retail organization considerable savings but the suppliers face an increased cost as they may need to buy as many as fifteen different computers/systems.

8.5 International standards

The ISO (International Standards Organization) put forward a standard in 1978 for the transmission of data between computer systems. This is known as the **OSI reference model** for open systems interconnection. However, standardization progressed slowly until 1987 when the European Commission issued a directive requiring all public agencies to specify open systems in their future IT purchasing. This meant that any supplier wishing to sell to governments or public bodies, which comprise a substantial part of the market, must use the OSI model and sell products which comply with it. This has given a certain impetus to the movement towards standardization despite the fact that the EC does not appear to enforce the directive.

The objective behind OSI (open systems interconnection) is to enable systems which meet the standard to be linked together easily. OSI takes the whole job of communications and splits it into separate tasks. These tasks are carried out by separate blocks or 'layers' of software and OSI defines the way the 'layers' communicate. A communication system may be divided into two parts — the network which carries data between systems and the software which makes sense of the data so that it may be used by programs or understood by humans. OSI consists of these two elements as two major 'layers' separated by what is known as a transport layer which standardizes the interface between the two.

The two major layers are each subdivided into three, making seven in all (including the transport layer). The first three layers are the OSI standards for networks, and three highest are the application protocols which handle data for different uses such as electronic mail or factory automation. The seven layers are shown in Figure 8.1.

NETWORK LAYERS	1	The **physical** layer — the plugging in and connecting of equipment to the network, e.g. the 25 pin connector
	2	The **data link** layer — groups binary characters together for transmission and detects and corrects errors due to noise during transmission
	3	The **network** layer — selects the route the information will take to its destination
TRANSPORT LAYER	4	The **transport** layer — responsible for the reliable and efficient transportation of data; it preserves the integrity and controls the flow of data
SOFTWARE LAYERS	5	The **session** layer — controls the dialogue for each application and makes sure that messages are sent as directed
	6	The **presentation** layer — translates data to and from the language and format used by the application
	7	The **application** layer — the specific application

Figure 8.1 The seven layer OSI reference model.

A message sent from one system to another is relayed through the seven layers of the sending system, 'over the wire' and back through the seven layers of the receiving system. Thus it passes 'down' one system and 'up' the other. Each layer communicates with its opposite number on the other system. To do this it adds its own tag to the data which are understood and removed by the equivalent layer in the receiving system.

An organization choosing an OSI system must first decide what is required from the system, that is, what the computers should be able to do and over what type of network. Then the organization can select the most suitable network standards for the three lowest layers and the application protocols for the highest layers. For instance, layer 7 options include X400 electronic mail. Corporate networks operating to X400 may be linked to public mail services, such as Telecom Gold or Mercury Link 7500, and to EDI networks such as Istel's Edict or INS Tradanet. Layer 3 options include X25 which defines the interface to wide area networks, national or third party, and Ethernet and Token Ring local area networks.

Aston University in the UK has pioneered OSI in the academic world by installing a campus-wide network of computing and other equipment. Students and staff are linked to services such as electronic mail, satellite communications, video broadcast, and national and international networks. This means that students can, among other things, search library catalogues and collect copies of articles via their own PC, submit their essays to their tutor over the network and view satellite transmissions.

There is no guarantee, however, that two products which supposedly conform to the OSI standards will in fact work together as the standards are not precise enough at present and are open to different interpretations. This is because they are a compromise. The problem with setting any standard for EDI is that networks are still developing and manufacturers have to guess future standards now and also to integrate current standards with their existing product range. The result is only a half-open world and some dissatisfied customers. Nor is there a proper method for checking equipment to see whether it does comply with the OSI open standards. Independent tests are available but suppliers are reluctant to put their products forward. The Networking Centre at Hemel Hempstead is probably Europe's leading centre for testing, having been appointed in 1987 by the European Commission to test for OSI conformance. After the first two years only one product had passed!

Meanwhile, a few businesses have become either frustrated by the whole situation or have seen a chance to gain strategic advantage by dominating the development of networks. General Motors developed its own network, and therefore its own standards, some years ago. In 1985 GM told its suppliers that they must join and conform to their network by 1989 or it would not be possible for them to continue to do business together (see section 7.12). Ford has also developed its own network. Other large organizations in different industries have followed this lead though not necessarily with the compulsion on suppliers. Will the industry networks change and conform to the standards in the future? Or will they decide that they have no reason to comply?

8.6 One all-purpose network

When an organization plans ahead in terms of installing networks, it has not only to determine existing needs and uses but also future requirements. This is by no means easy as the range of possible activities and uses is considerable and still growing. The activities and equipment may include the following:

- Communication of data or information — EPOS and PCs.
- Transfer of funds — EFTPOS.
- Text processing — word processors and telex.
- Retrieval of information — PCs, query systems, executive systems and databases.

- Voice transmission — telephone, teleconferencing and public address systems.
- Transmission of images — video, satellite television and fax.

To what extent an organization will require these different facilities is unlikely to be known with accuracy for more than, say, a year ahead. This makes planning for an adequate network that will meet all future needs for all the different types of facility very difficult. A single, all-purpose, standard network which could handle all types of communication would considerably ease these planning problems.

8.7 Digital networks

All data leaving a computer are in digital (binary) form, but traditionally telephone lines have sent information in analogue (sinusoidal wave) form. A modem is necessary to modulate the outgoing signals from the computer so that they can be transmitted via telephone cables and also to demodulate incoming signals. Gradually, digital technology is being adopted for all forms of communication, not only for digital data and text. This opens up the prospect of a single, global, all-purpose network being a practical possibility in the future. This concept is referred to as **integrated services digital network** (ISDN) and will eventually enable a combination of voice, text and images to be transmitted. This would mean that PCs could have, for instance, an integral telephone or video link and that a caller may transfer and discuss sets of figures during the course of a telephone conversation.

British Telecom launched the world's first commercial, non-standard ISDN service in 1985 called Integrated Digital Access, but companies have been slow to use the product. However, a recent prediction by a firm of London consultants was for growth across Europe from the existing 900 ISDN connections to 740,000 by 1994. France and Germany are developing their own nationwide systems, and France expects to have 150,000 users by 1992. Meanwhile, Singapore has moved ahead and become the first country to make ISDN available nationwide. Any system that is developed should be based on global standards but as yet these have not been laid down. Thus the realization of a standard network for the whole world is still some way in the future.

At present, ISDN consists of a set of guidelines which are meant to direct future development. The guidelines are being developed by the Consultative Committee for International Telephone and Telegraph (CCITT). They are similar to, and compatible with, the seven layers of protocol of the OSI. The CCITT's recommendations are based on three stages for the development of a totally standard system.[3] The first is turning the analogue telephone network into digital form. The second stage, narrow band ISDN, will integrate all communication services at speeds of up to 64K bit per second using the existing copper telephone cables. This will allow for transmission of voice and data. The final stage, broad band ISDN, will incorporate much faster speeds and, therefore, more services including pictures.

The first stage is well under way, with most trunk lines already converted. The conversion of the 'tails' (i.e. local lines, which account for 70 per cent of the UK network) is a major task and one that will take some years to complete. The main benefit at this first stage is that once it is fully implemented, information will pass more quickly and more accurately than previously. The next step will be to integrate voice and data. At stage two, according to Kennedy and Yen,[3] the CCITT is proposing two types of service using the existing lines. These are the basic service for residential and small business users, and the primary service with integrated access for larger business users (private automatic branch exchange users). The final stage, many years from now, will transmit entirely over fibre optic cables rather than the existing copper ones and use satellites to provide a global service.

There are many obstacles in the path of the full development of ISDN. One of the most important is perhaps the questions of who will control the operation of the global ISDN service? In Europe's highly regulated or government-owned telecommunication industries this is not such an important question, but in the USA this is a real issue. There are fears that ISDN could return the US telecommunications industry to a regulated, monopolistic operation. In addition, organizations which have in recent years developed their own private networks may be reluctant to give up their independence and allow a telecommunication organization to take control. There may also be issues of security which could further exacerbate the position.

Another major problem is cost. It sounds marvellous in theory to have one system which will handle all types of communication to all destinations — but at what price? It is not known yet what the tariffs might be, but some sources say that the rates will be twice the existing level.[3] Small businesses and residential users may not wish to use the enhanced service at that price. Some years ago several experts predicted that fax would not find a large market because it would soon be overtaken by ISDN technology. In reality many organizations and individuals were not prepared to wait and probably prefer the cheap, simple to use and reliable service that fax offers. There is also at least one system in use which allows people who use the telephone to transmit hand-drawn information to each other via a desk-top graphics writing pad. As it is low in cost and transmits in colour it could well be the type of system that will satisfy most individuals and small businesses. Meanwhile British Telecom have launched their ISDN 2, a service which carries voice, text and pictures over the telephone network and is aimed at small and medium businesses.

There are many questions, therefore, hanging over the full development of ISDN apart from the rather obvious one of new technology. At this stage it is too early to predict with any degree of certainty how ISDN will develop in the future and to what extent it will be used.

8.8 The structure of the telecommunications industry

The structure of any industry determines how that industry will develop in the future. The telecommunications industry is no exception. It is very important for a country to have strong, technically advanced telecommuncations and information technology industries. This is because the communication/information infrastructure is just as important as the road and rail infrastructure or the availability of labour in the fight to attract business from abroad. (See the illustrative case in section 15.13 where Singapore's information technology systems are discussed.) There are basically three hierarchical layers in the industry, see Figure 8.2. The international network is formed and controlled by the national telephone organizations but many different organizations may operate at the lowest layer in a deregulated industry.

At the time of writing there are two telecommunications organizations operating at the national level in the UK: British Telecom and Mercury. Mercury became a national telecommunications company in 1983 when deregulation started and was given seven years of protected status. At present Mercury has only 2 per cent of the business but now has a trunk network which covers 60 per cent

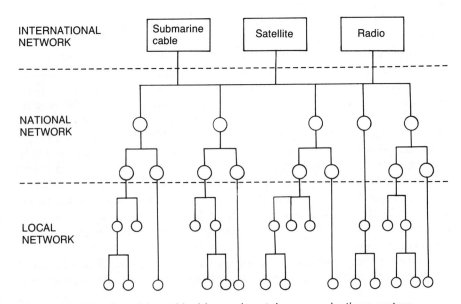

Figure 8.2 The three hierarchical layers in a telecommunications system.

of the country. The seven years end in November 1990 and then Oftel, the government watchdog, must decide the future of the industry in the UK.

Mercury is not interested in laying local lines in competition with British Telecom. However, cable television companies such as Windsor Television are. The fibre optic cable laid for television can also be used for telephones, thus in the areas which have cable television an alternative telephone service may soon be available using trunk lines leased from Mercury.

A new development in telecommunications is that of **personal communication networks** (PCNs). It is believed by many that these will take over from cellular radio (see section 8.17) as they will provide a communication system between people rather than places. In the UK three consortia have been licensed to develop this technology, one of which is Microtel (a UK consortium). Microtel also wishes to install its own national trunk lines for two reasons. The first is to be able to guarantee the quality of its service. The second is to reduce costs as it wishes to use microwave links rather than having to lease from British Telecom the high speed digital Megastream lines used in private networks. If this is permitted by the Government it could be opening the door for US and European organizations to enter the arena and become involved in the provision of the national trunk network in the UK.

Another potential player in this arena is British Rail which already has a national communications network consisting of links between every booking office and station in the country. BR wishes to put its spare capacity to use by leasing it to private companies or cable television companies. Mercury already leases some of the network.

The decisions made in the UK at the end of 1990 will, therefore, have a major impact on the development of the industry within the country and to some extent Europe. They will also influence the speed at which technical change is introduced.

B: OTHER COMMUNICATION NETWORK APPLICATIONS AND TECHNIQUES

8.9 Working from home

For some years a small number of organizations have used **networkers**, i.e. employees who work at home and communicate with the office via a computer and telecommunications network. Sometimes networkers are ex-employees as some companies have encouraged staff to become self-employed or part of a newly formed company whose major customer is the original company. Rank Xerox has some sixty-two networkers, about 5 per cent of its central office staff.[4] The networkers perform a range of jobs such as marketing, marketing research, business planning, security and tax advice. There are two main advantages to an organization in using networkers:

- Reduction in overheads.
- Increase in output per employee.

In London and other large cities the cost involved in occupying premises (e.g. rent, rates, light and heat) can be very high and the actual usage of office buildings very low. For instance, unlike a factory, an office is often used for only eight hours a day, five days a week — that is, 24 per cent of the total time available. Occupancy is further reduced by holidays and absenteeism. This means that the cost per employee of occupying space is high. In 1982, when networking started at Rank Xerox, it was calculated that for a gross salary of £10,000 the employee received £6,700 while the company paid a total of £27,000 inclusive of space costs.[4] It has been ascertained by several organizations that employee productivity increases by 20–30 per cent as a result of networking. This is due to three factors. Firstly, the networker will have slightly longer working hours — because there is no travelling to work. Secondly, the networker will be fresher for work. Thirdly, if the networker is self-employed, he or she is likely to be more motivated than the average employee.

The use of a network does not have to be expensive for the organization. This is because networkers tend to download information via the telephone lines, work on the information obtained, and then transmit amended information or a report back over the telephone lines. However, there can be problems with networking, notably in the management and development of staff, and this may have deterred other organizations from following Rank's example. There is also the problem of isolation which a person who suddenly becomes self-employed may feel. In Rank's case the Xandu Association was formed to help overcome this feeling and to act as a forum for such things as the exchange of information and services and to provide group purchasing facilities.

Networking does not necessarily involve any very modern technology. However, as technology advances, more opportunities will arise for home working. As a result of recent developments in digital telecommunication technology stockbrokers can now work entirely from their home if they so wish. This has the great advantage that they can do deals not just during their working day but twenty-four hours a day. This is very important when it is necessary to monitor a highly volatile position.

Other countries have been quicker than the UK to realize the potential of home working. In Scandinavia, for instance, about two hundred rural 'telecottages' were set up during 1985–90 to stop the decline of the rural population. Similar systems are beginning to be set up now by private enterprise in the UK in an attempt to match the skill shortages in towns with the labour available in rural areas.

8.10 The use of new communication systems in training

There is quite a range of recent developments in technology which can assist in training. Fibre optic cable is one that has been in use for several years. Its great advantage is in the provision of a two-way link of both vision and sound. For instance, an instructor can carry out a particular task while explaining what he is doing and why he is doing it. Trainees can watch at different locations and interrupt to ask questions. This technique is in use in the London teaching hospitals, where a surgeon carries out an operation watched by medical students in lecture theatres at the different hospitals. The students can hear and see the proceedings and the surgeon can hear and see them and answer their questions directly.

Satellite communication, discussed in the next section, offers great possibilities for training and may eventually replace the seminars and conferences at expensive hotels which have proliferated in recent years. The advantages of satellite communication for this type of training are the saving on travel time and hotel accommodation plus the fact that the employee remains on the company's premises and can thus cope with any crisis which might occur. This type of education and training has already been introduced for computer and telecommunications professionals by Data Vision. In 1990 this organization set up Computer Channel, a computer-related current affairs and interactive training channel which aims to take over the seminar market in that sector.

Interactive systems which incorporate text, voice and pictures are being developed at present and these may replace the current interactive video in training within a few years.

8.11 Communication via satellite

Satellites are very useful for the international transmission of information and also for communications with remote places where telephone cables do not exist. Small dishes, four feet wide, can handle voice grade transmissions. These dishes are called **very small aperture terminals** (VSATs). There are around 25,000 VSATs in use in the USA. In Europe, where the telephone systems are largely state-controlled, development has been slow — thus the cost of a VSAT has been held artificially high and development and innovation stifled.

In the UK, which is the most advanced EC country in this area, six organizations have been awarded licences by the government to provide satellite services and have been given the name **Specialised Satellite Services Operators**. These organizations include British Aerospace, Satellite Information Services (SIS) and Maxwell Satellite Communications. The licence allows only one way transmission from up to three points in the UK to anyone with a receiving dish. Two-way communication and transmission to Europe are not allowed, and this severely limits the usefulness of satellite communication for business. For instance, with two-way transmission a large food retailer could use a satellite for transmitting details such as stock requirements, delivery schedules and point of sale information across Europe. It has been estimated that it would be the cheapest form of communication between five thousand or more outlets spread over Europe. If this is so then it would be an ideal medium for a credit card company, say. Limited though one-way communication may be, some organizations are finding it helpful. SIS's main application to date — and the largest television satellite network service in the world — is its live horse and dog racing pictures which are relayed to more than eight thousand betting shops in the UK.

Sotheby's has used satellite Television to enlarge the bidding audience at an auction. A prospective bidder in New York can watch an auction taking place in London on a closed circuit television. Bids are made via a push button telephone key pad which is linked to London via a satellite. A swipe-through credit and identification card completes the deal. The system used by Sotheby's was not expensive — it was developed for just £300,000.[5]

8.12   Value added networks and data services

Value added networks (VANs) or **Value Added Data Services** (VADS), do more than just transmit information. They provide some extra or enhanced service, hence their name. In the UK, only British Telecom and Mercury are licensed to provide the basic national telephone and data transmission service. Other organizations can lease these facilities or set up their own, providing they have obtained a VADS licence from the Department of Trade and Industry. To obtain a licence, the system must conform with the OSI reference model. Licensed VADS suppliers can then sell their services as long as they provide more than the basic infrastructure service. The value added part of the service may include storage or manipulation of information such as database and information access services. Alternatively, a VADS could be any of a wide range of services which includes computer conferencing, personal answering services or automatic ticket reservation. Some of these are discussed later in this chapter.

Viewdata, or videotex, is one type of VADS which uses an ordinary television, a telephone and a key pad as its terminal. British Telecom's Prestel is an example of a such a system, but this is not as popular in the UK as it is in most other European countries. France, in particular, has developed this type of system, to the extent that all telephone subscribers have viewdata terminals instead of telephone directories.

8.13   Electronic mail

Electronic mail is a system which allows messages to be sent between computers. A message can be sent either to an individual or to any number of individuals who have access to the same network. It has great advantages over the telephone and internal mail. It is considerably quicker and cheaper than the latter, as it cuts out much of the work in company post rooms. It can also be said to increase the confidentiality of information because it does away with pieces of paper in internal envelopes. Its main advantage over the telephone is that the recipient can deal with the message whenever he chooses rather than perhaps having his chain of thought interrupted by a relatively unimportant telephone call. Studies have shown that it takes twenty-five minutes of undisturbed work to build up to a level of concentration suitable for high level knowledge work. If this is so, just receiving one telephone call an hour reduces a manager's productivity by half. It has also been suggested that the average manager spends forty-five minutes a day sorting through paperwork which accumulates on his desk. Paper messages are too easy to put on one side to deal with tomorrow; in the mean time they clutter up the in-tray or desk.

Price Waterhouse suggests, in a report published in 1988, that electronic mail has another benefit, that of reducing political infighting. Memo wars do sometimes develop within an organization, usually between two individuals in different departments who both feel unsure of their position and react by trying to hide this by writing acerbic memos to one another. This kind of behaviour does little to improve relations between the different departments and functions of the business. Anything that reduces such friction must be beneficial. It is even claimed that electronic mail actually improves co-operation between departments. For instance, general requests for information or assistance can be sent. People in different departments, who were previously unknown to the sender, may reply and thus cross-functional links are gradually built up and improved.

Any system which has benefits invariably has drawbacks. Electronic mail is no exception. Because sending messages to all and sundry is so easy, their proliferation can become a problem. This may result in many general messages being ignored. A user who has the answer to a general request may fail to reply thinking that someone else is bound to answer. Alternatively, the user will not read all the messages as he will become selective and read only those from individuals that he is familiar with. Even worse, important messages will not get through quickly enough because they are mixed in with the many general ones. What is needed is a filtering system to sift out the general messages and give priority to the important ones. Such systems are being developed; they require messages to be sent on standard templates so that an individual can request that all memos from his superior, among others, are given priority.

8.14 Fax

Given some of the startling technological innovations for the flow of information it is easy to overlook the simple fax machine. Its phenomenal rise in popularity was largely unpredicted but has undoubtedly been due to its simplicity of operation and its ability to produce hard copy. The number of faxes in Britain increased from 25,000 in 1983 to 550,000 in 1989 and the current annual growth rate is

50 per cent. Fax was first used in Japan in response to the need for transmitting Kanji characters. The Japanese language uses about ten thousand different characters and this makes it unsuitable for typewriters or telex.

Fax has great advantages when communicating with a country on the opposite side of the world as a message can be sent during office hours to await the entry of the recipient the next morning. It also has advantages when communicating with parts of the world where telecommunication infrastructures are poor such as Eastern Europe where it may take hours to be connected by telephone.

The G4 fax machines operate on digital as opposed to analogue telephone lines and, as a result, the quality of reproduction is far superior. However, these faxes can only be used at present on private networks or on certain leased lines. Everyone else will have to await the coming of ISDN. Michitoshi Koshiyama, the telecommunications marketing manager for Hitachi, suggests that demand for G4 may trigger the overall spread of ISDN services in Japan.[6] This may be an optimistic view as in the past the demand for upgrading picture or sound quality has always been perceived by technical experts as being greater than it really is.

The major drawback of fax is its lack of security. This was graphically illustrated in the UK in 1989 when the Ministry of Defence sent two fax messages about security at a naval depot to a small recruitment agency in error! There is no check or recall if the wrong number is entered.

8.15 Telemarketing centres

There has been a rapid growth in recent years of telemarketing centres as organizations become aware of their potential. Telemarketing encompasses such things as contacting potential customers, giving information to potential customers, providing a customer service and information centre, researching markets and running promotion campaigns. Not only do telemarketing centres give information to customers, or potential customers, they also provide management with valuable information about potential problems with products, the type of individual buying the product, potential sales leads and so on. The US company General Electric was one of the first to set up such a centre in 1981 in response to customers' poor opinions of the company and its products. Telephone calls are free to the enquirer and the centre's running costs are more than $10m a year; even so the rewards have been considerable. As a result of the valuable back-up service provided by the centre, sales volume has increased and the company is able to charge more for its products, thus increasing the profit margin.

Many companies prefer to use agencies to do this type of work because of the high cost of setting up such a system and the uneven use that one company is likely to make of it. For instance, a special promotion or advertising campaign will necessitate many telephone lines being made available, but the majority of these lines and the staff to operate them would not be needed by the organization under normal circumstances.

Most agencies, and some companies, use automatic call distributors (ACDs) within their telemarketing system. ACDs sort the calls coming into an organization or agency and report on their handling to ensure an efficient service is provided. Although they are expensive at present they have considerable benefit when a large number of calls are received. With a large number of incoming calls it is vital to control the cost and to make sure that productivity is high while still providing the highest possible level of service. The more sophisticated ACD systems help to do just this by generating daily management reports on the following:

- The number of calls received and made.
- The duration of the calls.
- How long the caller had to wait for attention.
- The percentage number of calls put on hold.
- How many calls were transferred to back-up staff.

In addition, ACDs give managers the facility to listen in to calls with a view to discussing and possibly changing an individual or a group's answering technique. More advanced ACDs also help the telephonist to respond more quickly by identifying which client is calling. Together these factors result in real cost savings — some organizations have reported productivity increases of 60–70 per cent.[7]

American Transtech is an organization which has grown rapidly by providing telemarketing agency services for other organizations.[8] The calls are routed to the agency which answers them and provides or receives information on behalf of the organization. Telemarketing requires a combination of telecommunication and computer technology. The hardware required will probably include an ACD to send calls to appropriate agents, processors and databases to record incoming data and to access data to answer enquiries, LANs to distribute incoming calls and input voice units to record messages to be sent. American Transtech uses ISDN to further improve the service they give as follows. A caller's area code and telephone number can be captured instantly and sent to a customer database. On the agent's screen the customer's name and the business or work involved is displayed immediately so that the agent answers the telephone knowing who the customer is and any details of work being done for the customer. An additional database can be searched to retrieve the name and address of the dealer nearest to the customer and this can be displayed as the agent answers the telephone. This procedure drastically reduces the time of the call, making the agents more productive and thus saving on telephone charges. It also helps a company to appear more aware and appreciative of the customer.

The use of ACDs is not limited to telemarketing: they can be used as part of a reservation system. Trust House Forte is one organization which uses them in this way. All reservation telephone calls are routed to sales agents in Aylesbury, Buckinghamshire, who make the bookings in the company's computer system.

A copy of the booking is then printed out in the office of the relevant hotel for the staff's information. Apart from the normal details about how many calls each agent takes and their duration, this system also notes the time of day when they are made and how quickly calls are abandoned.

8.16   Teleconferencing

The word **teleconferencing** is used to describe any interactive electronic communication system between individuals or groups in different locations. There are two quite different types of system. The first, audio and video teleconferencing, is a system which normally links two or more conference rooms for instant communication. The other type is a computer based messaging system which allows messages and comments to be sent and incoming messages to be received. The communication takes place over a period of time, probably weeks or even months. This system is known as text-based teleconferencing and was first used in the late 1970s. One way it has developed recently is into 'groupware', mentioned in connection with LANs in section 7.3.

Audio teleconferencing began as long ago as the late 1960s. At that time one or two go-ahead companies in the USA had conference rooms with audio conferencing systems which allowed managers at one location to speak with managers in conference rooms at distant offices. This saved the pressure and money involved in commuting across the USA to meetings and conferences. In the mid 1970s IBM took this further by developing its own in-house system for still-video conferencing which allowed still pictures to be transmitted together with an audio conferencing facility.[9] This was especially useful for communications of a technical nature where diagrams and charts were needed to clarify words.

The next step was the development of moving-picture video teleconferencing using a satellite hook-up. This began in the early 1980s and is particularly useful if top management wishes to talk directly to a group of its employees in order to put a particular view or give instructions. In the UK, Ford and BP both use this type of system which allows their top managements to address all employees in the UK simultaneously. Moving-picture teleconferencing may also be used to instruct a salesforce about a new product. New features can be demonstrated and the members of the salesforce can put queries to the staff who developed the product. Thus all the salesforce are instructed simultaneously and they have the chance to gain more accurate and specific information about the product. Video teleconferencing can also be useful for trouble-shooting or rectifying machine breakdown. An expert who is located elsewhere can watch the video and suggest possible causes for the problem. In the USA it is used by some organizations to hold weekly meetings of key managers in different locations.

However, despite its apparent usefulness the growth of video teleconferencing has been slow and its use is still the exception rather than the rule. Whether its use will increase or whether developments in the range of facilities provided by workstations with ISDN will overtake it remains to be seen. In the meantime, teleconferencing simply by means of the telephone is gaining considerable popularity. This allows more than two people to be linked up via their telephones. If this is coupled with faxing visual information beforehand it becomes a very useful informal communication system.

8.17 Mobile telephones

There are about 1 million cellular telephones in the UK and this figure is increasing by about 30 per cent annually. The current technology is based on a cell-like network of low power transmitters which cover a radius of a few miles each and connect to the national telephone network. The telephones automatically tune to a common radio frequency and this is used as the communications channel for receiving and transmitting. When an incoming call is about to be received the telephone will be directed by a computerized switching centre to tune to a different frequency, currently unused, in order to receive the call. This is done automatically so that the user is unaware of the process, unlike short wave radio on boats. If the telephone is in a car which travels from one cell to another during the call the frequency is likely to be changed. This means that frequencies can be used efficiently as one call does not need one frequency: the same frequency can be used in different cells provided they are not adjoining.

There are other newer, competing developments in this field such as Telepoint and PCNs (personal communications networks — see section 8.8) but being the first into the market, cellular telephones will be difficult to compete with and replace. The first European cellular system covering seventeen countries will be introduced between 1990 and 1995. Scandinavian countries (Denmark, Finland, Iceland, Norway and Sweden) have operated a standard system since 1982 called NMT (Nordic Mobile Telephone). In terms of penetration it is the most popular mobile service in the world: one in every two new telephones lines in Sweden is for pocket or car telephones.

8.18 Other developments

Data can also be broadcast by terrestial means via BBC Datacast or Aircall Teletext which uses the spare capacity on the BBC and ITN networks. The benefit of this system is its cheapness as it saves the cost of leasing telephone lines. It is, therefore, suitable for small organizations wishing to make contact with potential customers as a nationwide fast response service can be established without the expense of a telemarketing centre.

In some circumstances it is particularly important for an individual to be able to give and receive information or instructions without having to use hands to adjust dials or type messages. For instance, an airline pilot would find it useful to give instructions verbally rather than having physically to adjust the controls. The adjustment of controls may include changing and selecting radio stations. Computers which understand language are being developed either to react to a command or to monitor conversation and make sure that humans take action. The technology for voice synthesis is also just developing but already, for instance, weather information can be given to a pilot in synthesized speech. Words may be stressed or unstressed which makes the speech sound reasonably realistic by putting emphasis on particular words much as a human being would do. This is obviously one area for the giving and receiving of information which has considerable potential.

8.19 Conclusion

Networks have proliferated in recent years. Most organizations have far too many of them — one company's internal survey revealed nineteen different networks. Gradually, organizations are combining and rationalizing their networks, but there is still the problem that there are no absolute standards, no integrated systems, and many different products and manufacturers. Telecommunications planning is, therefore, extremely difficult at present and should concentrate on meeting the requirements of the company as far as they can be perceived and providing a reliable and simple to use system. Those options which are cheap and flexible, in the sense that they can be disposed of if necessary without too much financial loss, may be best during this turbulent period. The opposite, which may commit the organization to an expensive long term programme that may prove to be ill-fitting or not the best in the light of future developments, could prove very costly.

The lure of modern technology should not cause organizations to ignore the traditional telephone which still has great potential. Little monitoring of telephone systems appears to be carried out by organizations. A recent survey found that 90 per cent of modern large company telephone systems had undetected faults and that more than 50 per cent had external lines which were being paid for but were not used. In addition, one in fifteen incoming calls were lost — this could well represent a large loss of sales revenue for the organization. So perhaps the moral for an organization should be to make the systems currently available work efficiently before looking for more advanced ones.

8.20 Illustrative case: Reuters's financial information and news network[10]

Reuters has grown since 1964 from a small, highly regarded news agency into a major global player in the provision of financial information and news.

This has been done by forward-looking investment in the right information technology and networked systems.

Reuters took its first step along this road with Stockmaster which, at that time, collected information on particular commonly traded stocks. This information was held on about thirty computers around the world to which Reuters's clients had access via a terminal at a computer site.

The end of the Bretton Woods agreement in 1973, which had regulated and controlled the movements in currencies, created a demand for really up to date information to cope with floating exchange rates. Reuters stepped in to meet this need with Monitor, which soon dominated the world market for foreign exchange information. Monitor consisted of computers located at the world's major financial centres which were linked by lines leased from British Telecom to form a network. Rather surprisingly for an organization introducing this type of new technology, Reuters asked the banks, who were the customers, to pay to display their information and also to pay for the terminals they needed to view the information — which they did. This is in contrast to the normal situation where the instigator of the system gives the equipment to the customer free of charge in order to get as many users as possible. The instigator's benefit, such as increased market share or a stronger competitive position, normally more than pays for the cost of the whole system.

Monitor was an entirely separate network from Stockmaster, providing different information to different customers. It grew rapidly and was soon Reuters's biggest source of revenue. In 1981 a dealing facility was added enabling subscribers to carry out transactions. Dealer Service was again run as a separate network as it was a private network for subscribers and needed for security reasons to be inaccessible to outsiders.

Although Reuters had pioneered the use of computer and network technology in its sector, by the early 1980s it was facing problems about the future which had to be considered and solved if it was to maintain its position. The problems that Reuters saw were:

- That customers would soon be demanding real-time information on items such as currency, equity markets and commodities.
- Its existing network would be unable to cope with increased demand at some point in the future.
- The growth in the use of PCs and LANs in the early 1980s was creating a demand for information in digital form rather than in the well-established page-based format which Reuters was using at the time. A digital format gave the user the ability to manipulate information and to incorporate it into other programs.

So development began in 1982 of a new digital network called IDN which is divided into three regions: USA, Europe and the Far East. There are databases in New York and London which are linked and synchronized. (The Far East obtains its information by high speed links from London.)

Information sent from London to other European cities goes via satellites. It is picked up by Retrieval Data Centres which house MicroVAX computers networked using Ethernet. The MicroVAXs hold all current data to which Reuters's clients have access via dedicated lines. Storing the data near the client is an advantage for the client even if it created problems initially for Reuters in developing a system to move so much data speedily around the world. After five years of development it was estimated that it had taken at least three hundred man years of work to design and implement the system which began operating in May 1987. The first service provided was Equity 2000, which carries 55,000 real-time quotations from seventy-five exchanges. There is a similar service for commodities, Commodity 2000, which has details of 18,000 commodities from thirty exchanges.

The system is, of course, still developing. One aim is to provide City traders with all the information they need on one screen, as opposed to the three that most traders have at present. Reuters's Dealing 2000 is getting quite close to that by allowing four simultaneous trading conversations to be shown on one screen. Reuters are not alone in the dealers market and face strong competition. For example, Telecom's City Business System has a 40 per cent market share and Telerate has a system called The Trading Service which can link up with any of the thirty-two world trading centres within less than two seconds.

NOTES

1. Ian Meiklejohn, 'Slowly, slowly into the open', *Management Today*, Aug. 1989,
2. *Daily Telegraph*, 19 Feb. 1990.
3. Andrew J. Kennedy and David Yen, 'The coming of ISDN', *Information and Management*, no. 17, 1989.
4. Phillip Judkins, 'Working from home: the Rank Xerox experiment', *Multinational Business*, no. 3, 1988.
5. *Daily Telegraph*, 23 Nov. 1989.
6. *Daily Telegraph*, 4 Oct. 1989.
7. 'Better phone service is just the ticket', *Modern Office Technology*, Oct. 1986.
8. W.F. Cobbin, K.A. Kozar and S.J. Michaele, 'Establishing telemarketing leadership through information management', *MIS Quarterly*, Sept. 1989.
9. Robert Johansen and Christine Bullen, 'What to expect from teleconferencing', *Harvard Business Review*, Mar./Apr. 1984.
10. Andrew Lawrence, 'Reuters dealing in DDP', *Network*, Feb. 1988.

FURTHER READING

De Noia, Lynn, *Data Communication — Fundamentals and Applications* (Merrill, 1987). Provides a detailed, but clear and simple, look at computers, telecommunications and their standards.

Gunton, Tony, *Infrastructure: Building a framework for corporate information handling*

(Prentice Hall International, 1989). Provides detailed information on all aspects of an organization's communications infrastructure.

McNurlin, Barbara and Ralph Sprague, *Information Systems Management in Practice* (Prentice Hall, 1989). Contains a good, readable chapter on building the telecommunications highway, which covers OSI and ISDN.

EXERCISES

1. 'Setting any type of standard puts a brake on the development and improvement of the system to which it is applied and is therefore only to be tolerated under extreme circumstances.' Discuss this statement in relation to computer and communication standards and in relation to other standards you are aware of, for instance, statements of standard accounting practice (SSAPs).

2. What future do you envisage for teleconferencing assuming that progress in developing ISDN continues much as envisaged in this chapter?

3. Consider what deregulation changes Oftel, the UK government watch-dog, recommended at the end of 1990 and whether these were implemented by the Department of Trade and Industry. How has, and will this, affect the industry? What possible developments and changes in the industry have been postponed or stopped by this structure?

4. 'The telephone has proved to be the most important invention in the last 150 years.' Discuss this statement stating why it might be possible to hold this view.

5. 'Developing standards in any new industry has its problems but the computer and telecommunication industries are faced with more difficulties than most.' Discuss and explain the state of development in international standards in the equipment and techniques of information systems.

6. Describe how an organization can use computer and telecommunication technology to improve its marketing performance.

7. Consider the scenario that all London universities and colleges (or those of any large city) are connected via a video teleconferencing link. Suggest ways in which the link can be used by both staff and students to improve education. Would the teleconferencing link pay for itself?

9 Databases

SCOPE AND CONTENTS

A: Technical aspects of databases. This section starts with a description of what a database is and then traces the development of databases from data storage in application packages to the development of a central database system for an organization. Consideration is given to the advantages of physically splitting databases and the different ways in which this can be achieved. The terms data dictionary and database management system are explained. Hierarchical and relational databases are briefly mentioned. Finally a quite different method of storing data is considered — image processing.

B: The different uses of databases. Consideration is given to whether databases may be used to reduce staff costs. Then a detailed examination is made of possible strategic uses for databases — these are illustrated by examples from specific organizations. The uses covered are: to serve the customer better, to enter a new product area and to increase sales volume. Customer databases and database marketing are considered in detail. Finally the different types of external database are examined, in particular the growth and extent of the external database PIMS.

A: THE TECHNICAL ASPECTS OF DATABASES

9.1 What is a database?

A database is a collection of data stored in a way which allows *information* to be drawn from it in a range of different ways and formats in order to answer a range of different management questions. In a traditional batch-type transaction processing system, the data relating to transactions are collected and stored initially on operational data files (prior to being transferred to the database) whence they may be drawn for a particular purpose by a manager via a specific **application package**. This sequence of events is depicted in Figure 9.1. The operational data files hold a vast quantity of data for a short time. Selected data from the operational data files are transferred to the information database where they are stored for a much longer period in readiness for use by managers. In the more up to date, on-line transaction processing systems, data flow directly into the database without the need for the operational data file.

9.2 Database development

Originally, each applications package used by an organization, such as a payroll or stock control package, held its own data — thus each application had its own small database. The effect of this was that some data had to be entered manually several times if they were required by more than one application. This was wasteful of time and led to a large number of errors. Every time the same piece of data was entered there was the possibility of an incorrect figure or code being entered into the system. In addition, if the different sets of data were obtained from different sources, there was the possibility of further discrepancies. These errors resulted in a lack of confidence in systems, because one manager would produce one set of figures on a particular topic and another manager using a different application would have quite different figures. Much time was wasted as a result arguing about who had the correct set of figures.

These problems were partly overcome by the next step in the development of databases. This was to connect the applications together so that in effect a

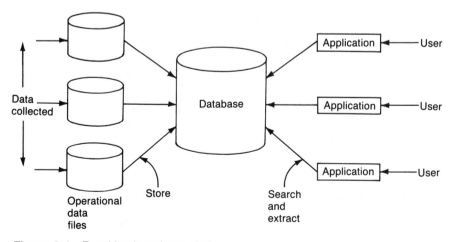

Figure 9.1 Data/database/user chain.

large database was formed, thus avoiding the problems created by entering the same data several times. Passing data between applications, however, was often awkward and complex due to the incompatibility of the software of the different applications. The required data flows have to be determined before the links between the applications are set up and, obviously, as data can pass only where links have been made, the total system is not very flexible. The number of connections increases rapidly as more applications are acquired. This is illustrated in Figure 9.2 where three applications require only three links whereas six applications require fifteen links to be fully connected. This results in a proliferation of wiring which requires maintenance. In old buildings this often poses problems, firstly of finding enough space for the wiring and secondly of gaining easy access to it for maintenance. A further disadvantage of this method is that the user has to have knowledge of the application which stores the data in order to gain access to it, as well as knowledge of the application which is currently being used.

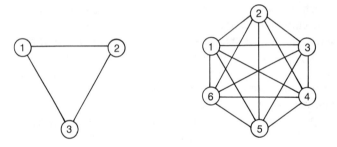

Figure 9.2 Connections between applications without a database.

A much better method, which overcomes these problems, is that which is illustrated in Figure 4.6 where each application is connected to a shared database which stores data in a standard form. The user will perceive this system as a single database and so we will refer to it as such. In practice, however, it is extremely unlikely to be a single database; instead the system will usually consist of a series of linked databases which act as one. Any application can send data or information for storage and gain access to any of the data or information stored on the database. This not only simplifies the connection and compatibility problems, but also makes the retrieval of data much simpler for the user of an applications package. This is because it is not necessary to have any knowledge of any other application nor is it necessary to know where the data are stored.

9.3 Centralized or distributed databases

At present it is normal to set up a series of databases, each organized to cover a specific area of business such as a product, function, division or business unit. This gives organizations the choice of locating the whole database centrally or spreading it geographically by locating individual databases within the divisions or business units. Where a central database is in operation in a geographically spread organization, the cost of obtaining information from it will be high. Gaining access to a local computer is cheaper than one a long distance away — just as local telephone calls are cheaper than long distance ones. This problem delayed for several years British Rail's adoption of a computerized database for train timetables. British Rail had to wait until technology had advanced enough to compress the database so that it could be stored locally on smaller computers. The British Rail database is considered in more detail in section 9.12.

A geographically spread database may be controlled either centrally or locally, but local control is usually to be preferred. This is because any central provision of a service tends to be unresponsive to the specific requirements of local or business unit managers. Furthermore, if local business units are charged with the cost of the central service, it is likely that the managers will consider the charge to be too high and not use it. This might well be because the quality of service provided is better than that required by some users. The quality will be set to meet the needs of all users and so the service provided must meet the highest needs required: thus exceeding some users' needs. If a high charge is made for the central information service, local offices are often tempted to take over part of the role of the central service and store some data themselves. The criterion applied will be whether they can store and gain access to the information on their system for a lower cost than that charged by the central information service. If this is the case and local offices duplicate part of the central service to avoid part of the cost, this in turn increases the overall cost to the organization of information provision. There is also a problem of control when data and information are held centrally. All parties tend to deny any responsibility for it and as a result there is a danger that data and information may be either out of date or inaccurate. This is because the departments which collected the data do not store them and, therefore, do not feel responsible. Likewise the computer or information department does not accept responsibility as it did not collect the data.

The answer to all of the above problems is to decentralize the responsibility for and storage of data and information by splitting the database into suitable sections. This gives local managers more control over the data obtained and reduces their reliance on what is often seen by them as an unsympathetic central information systems department. Such a system, where the overall database is split over several sites, is referred to as a **distributed database**. It has the following advantages:

- It gives local managers the freedom to handle information in their own way to meet their specific needs.
- Local managers are more accountable for the data and information generated.
- It reduces the impact of equipment failure, sabotage and industrial action.
- Security may be improved by creating several smaller databases at different locations. Against this it might be argued that it is easier to set up a security system to properly safeguard one single central database.

- The introduction of new technology is easier if done in small stages on a more frequent basis. This is only possible with a distributed system.

There is a further important reason for multinational organizations to have distributed databases and that is the problem of transferring information from one country to another. Many countries have laws which make it difficult or impossible to send data or information for processing to another country, so there is a tendency for multinationals to set up at least one database in each country.

Distributed databases, however, are not perfect. They have several drawbacks. These are mainly technical and concern the integrity of the data. With a centralized system an audit trail will always exist whereas this might not be the case with a distributed one. In any system an error may not be noticed until some time after it occurred. This delay makes tracing it or backtracking to a correct position difficult. The difficulty is exacerbated in a distributed system. To obviate this it has been suggested that all pieces of data should carry codes indicating the last operation through which they passed in order to assist in any reconstruction of the position prior to the error.

A distributed system soon becomes chaotic if it is not properly supervised centrally. There is always the need for someone to take a corporate view and to advise business units on the systems and data required. This is best done by the central information systems department, or information centre as it is more often called nowadays. This department's role has changed with its name and it now has more of an advisory and monitoring role as opposed to just supplying a data service to user departments.

There are several different types of system which are collectively referred to as being 'distributed'. Technically this is incorrect as only the last one to be considered below is a true 'distributed database'. The different systems are suited to different information needs. The three main systems are now described.

9.4 Replicated databases

A replicated system is only a partially distributed information system and, therefore, not all of the benefits of distribution are realized. It requires a full set of data to be held centrally and working copies to be held locally. Every morning, subsets of data are distributed to the locations where the data concerning transactions will be collected. The subsets are updated during the course of the day, and in the evening the up-to-date data are sent back to the central office ready to be added to the central database overnight. If it is necessary for the records to be kept absolutely up to date, the transactions can be sent to the central database in real time — at the moment they take place rather than once a day. Each subset of data must be discrete for this method to work — that is, the data of one location must not overlap with another subset. This system is particularly suited, for instance, to purchasing requirements in a supermarket chain where each location or store is independent of all of the others. An example of this method is Halfords' Halo system which is described in section 3.4.

9.5 Dispersed databases

With a dispersed database the updating of information is carried out locally at, or close to, the place where the data are collected. Summary data, normally required for the control of the organization, are sent periodically, probably monthly, to head office where the corporate system is located. This is not usually done by means of a computer-to-computer transfer; instead some human intervention is needed to manipulate and rearrange the information for the corporate system as the different systems are not usually fully compatible. This was the case with STC and ICL's information systems discussed in section 4.9.

A dispersed database is perfectly satisfactory where time is not an important factor or where the activities of the locations do not have to be co-ordinated. Thus it may suit a diversified organization which has a traditional organization structure and where head office requires no more than monthly control information.

9.6 Fully distributed databases

Fully distributed databases are similar to dispersed ones but are more sophisticated in that data and information are sent from the local database systems at the moment an individual at another location wishes to use them. This may involve some data being stored in several places within the overall corporate system in order to reduce the cost of gaining access to the data. With a distributed database anyone, anywhere in the organization can gain access to any piece of data regardless of where it is stored — subject, of course, to authorization. The user does not have to know where the piece of data is stored because the software finds it. Each site operates as a database in its own right and yet the systems work together to provide any user with data or information. Each database is locally owned and managed, and security is also normally considered to be a local concern. This is obviously a more sophisticated system than the previous two and technology has only just reached the stage where it can provide such a system. An example of this type of database is IBM's, which is described in section 7.4.

Databases should be organized so that communication costs are kept to a minimum. On-line databases may not be necessary, in which case data can be transferred at a lower cost at night. It is very cheap for a user to gain access to a database at the same site. This is not the case if the required information is in a database at a different site, access to which is via the national telecommunications network. Often it is cheaper to duplicate some data so that transmission costs may be reduced. Duplication also has the added advantage of making the system appear more reliable by creating, in effect, a back-up system, as the following example shows.

Let us assume that a credit card company has a distributed system. The company has divided the country into three areas and each has its own database. When a credit card is offered as payment in a shop, the shopkeeper will 'swipe' it through a reader which is connected to the nearest database management system. The details of the card will probably be stored on the local database, but, if not, the computer will route the enquiry automatically to the correct database. Negative files, that is details of bad-risk customers, can be kept by all the databases. These files would be updated periodically rather than instantly. If one of the databases goes down any enquiries will be passed to one of the others which will check against the negative files before accepting the card. Thus a simple back-up system can be built in when distributed databases are used.

9.7 Data dictionary

A **data dictionary** is a necessity when a distributed database is in operation as some users of the system may be unfamiliar with the way in which the data are collected and aggregated. The dictionary allows the user to call up on the screen a definition of a piece of data or information held in the system. The definition will be required to ensure that a correct interpretation may be made of the data provided in the reports drawn from the database. Furthermore, the whole distributed database must operate on consistent and approved definitions of data. If this is not so the information generated will be inconsistent and, therefore, not reliable for decision making. Thus the purpose of a dictionary is to define data and information with the aim of eliminating ambiguity and errors of understanding and interpretation. The data dictionary should include the following information:

- A list of the different names associated with the piece of data. (Slightly different names may often be used by different users and applications to refer to the same piece of data.)
- A description of the piece of data.
- Details of ownership — that is which department generates the piece of data and is therefore responsible for it.
- Details of who uses the piece of data and of the systems and programs that refer to it and update it.
- Details of the piece of data in terms of the number of characters, whether numeric, etc.
- The security level attached to the piece of data in order to restrict access to it.

The data dictionary can be expanded to include file descriptions and subprograms which are used by a number of applications. It can also be used in system development and thus has become an important tool of the analyst and programmer. It is also of considerable use to both internal and external auditors. In short, the data dictionary has grown into a very useful tool and in some cases its name has grown too — into system encyclopaedia.

9.8 Database management systems

The different application packages obtain the data from the database via a **database management system** (DBMS). This is a large piece of software which organizes the data so that they can be stored in a suitable way ready for immediate retrieval, modification or updating. Each application interacts with the DBMS rather than the data files themselves. Having the DBMS as an intermediary means that the type of data stored in a particular database file may be changed independently because the structure of the data is separated from the program. The type of DBMS used is dependent on the way in which the data are stored. The older databases tend to be based on a 'family tree' structure with parent–child relationships between each node. This **hierarchical** type of database is illustrated in Figure 9.3. It is a good system for gaining access to standard combinations of data on account of its speed. Sometimes pieces of data are duplicated so that they are stored next to other data likely to be required at the same time. This makes retrieval easier and speedier as the data are retrieved via the hierarchical pre-set paths. The system does not work so well when management calls for pieces of data which are not located anywhere near each other in the family tree. This would occur when the connection between the data was not foreseen at the planning stage when the system was originally set up. As managers tend to make more and more requests for *ad hoc* and non-standard information the hierarchical database is beginning to have severe limitations.

Network databases were developed in order to solve some of these problems. With this type of database any node can be connected to any other in order to

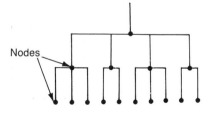

Figure 9.3 Data links — hierarchical database.

form a link. However, the links need to be predetermined and the system is slower to operate than the hierarchical type.

Much more popular today is the **relational database**. This was pioneered by E.F. Codd and his colleagues at IBM Research. It is based on the mathematical disciplines of set theory and predicate logic. A relational database does not require links to be predetermined and, therefore, this type of database is much more flexible than its predecessors. It consists of a series of tables with data stored in columns and rows within each table. Each row represents an individual record which can consist of several individual pieces of data or details. Each column is referred to as a field and contains a different detail, or piece of data, for the set of records. An extract from a relational database of student names and addresses is set out in Figure 9.4.

Ref. no.	First name	Surname	Street	Town	Postcode
90867	Jane	Hawkins	55 High Street	Chelmsford	CM4 5PQ
90764	David	Brown	2 Mead Close	Bristol	BR1 3UT
89555	Bill	Smith	7 Sussex Road	Exeter	EX2 5JT

Figure 9.4 Relational record — student.

The terminology 'record'and 'field' have been used because they are easily understood by those who have no knowledge of computers. However, they should only be used when referring to the physical representation of data whether on disk, tape or paper. When talking about the logical representation of data the terms 'entity' and 'attribute' should be used in place of 'record' and 'field'. A data entity represents a 'thing' that is to be stored for future reference. An attribute is a single piece of information that describes a data entity. So in Figure 9.4 the entity is STUDENT (this is always written in capitals) and the data attributes are the reference number, first name, surname, etc.

Some entities will have a relationship or data association with others. For instance, the entity STUDENT may have a data association with another entity called, say, ECONOMICS. This entity will be the examination grades attained in the economics course. This is shown in Figure 9.5. It will be noted that the student reference number appears in this entity as it did in the previous one. This links the information in the two tables so that data can be extracted from both of them and is known as the primary key attribute of the STUDENT entity.

Ref. no.	Date of exam.	Q1	Q2	Q3	Q4	Q5	Total	Grade
90555	3.6.90	15	—	10	12	14	51	2.2
89654	3.6.90	6	12	—	10	9	37	F
90754	3.6.90	12	12	—	15	15	54	2.2

Figure 9.5 Relational record — economics.

In the ECONOMICS entity this attribute is known as a foreign key. A database designed this way can easily be accessed by a modern query language. Despite the terminology, it is also much easier for those who are not computer specialists to understand.

The first relational database, Oracle, was introduced in 1979. IBM released one soon after which used the fourth generation language SQL (standard query language). SQL was invented in the early 1970s at IBM Research. SQL was adopted as a standard fourth generation language (4GL) by ANSI (American National Standards Institute) in 1986 and as a result most suppliers today use it in their relational databases models. However, it must be said that SQL is not particularly well thought of as a language and there are several better ones available.

The relational database has taken over from the hierarchical and network types for four main reasons:

- **Simplicity**. It is refreshingly simple both for the user of information and for the programmer. Codd and Date illustrate this by listing the number of statements needed in a machine shop scheduling application coded in CODASYL(DBTG)COBOL and a relational language.[1] CODASYL had sixty statements and the relational language just three. As a result vast simplifications in data manipulations are possible and programmer productivity increases by between five and twenty times. Normally even a relatively unskilled programmer can use the system.
- **Flexibility**. Previous databases were *ad hoc* in that they provided solutions to the specific problems faced at a particular point in time. Once the data had been organized in a specific way within the database, and the nodes had been connected as required, they were very difficult to alter. This meant that they addressed the problems of the day well enough but could not cope with the uncertain future. This was illustrated in section 3.9 by the example of the bank which could not provide a better service to its customers although its database contained the required data.
- **Theoretical base**. Because relational databases are based on mathematical theory, they behave in ways that are logical and can be predicted.
- **Necessary for distributed databases**. Distributed databases must be relational. As they grow in popularity so must relational database management systems.

9.9 Microfilm and image processing

Microfilm and image processing are techniques which are totally unconnected with computer databases except in so far as they are concerned with the storage and retrieval of data. **Microfilm** is not new: it was supposedly invented during the Franco-Prussian War when miniaturised films of troop positions were sent via carrier pigeon. Its great advantage in business lies in the fact that the original copies of most documents need not be kept. Instead microfilm copies may be made of all documents received, and computer produced microfilm copies may be made of all outgoing paperwork. Microfilm copies are beneficial because much less space is required for storage. According to some enthusiastic users it can reduce the space required by as much as 98 per cent. A microfilm document is also much quicker to retrieve from the archives — it can be located in a matter of minutes rather than hours as is normal with paper systems. However, microfilm has two failings. Firstly, a search for specific details which are contained within documents cannot be made and, secondly, another process has to be carried out if a replacement hard copy of a document is required.

Image processing is only just being developed but appears to have great potential and overcomes the two failings of microfilm. Indeed, it will probably replace microfilm given time. Image processing allows a vast quantity of archive material such as invoices, to be sorted very quickly and relevant parts extracted within minutes. This is a process which might well take several days by hand, assuming the organization had the space to store all the documents. Furthermore, a hard copy of the document is obtained which is a very close copy of the original. Image processing's technical name is CD ROM and it is similar to the hi-fi technology of compact disks: the disk has tiny pits burnt into it which can be read by a laser. The whole system is relatively cheap and consists of a high resolution image scanner, a computer optical disk storage system which holds images of the numerous documents, and a laser printer. A search can be instigated for a single word or group of words; when these are found the image is produced on a screen and re-emerges as a paper document. A network of workstations can be created which together have the capacity to hold millions of documents.

It is thought that the role of image processing may develop beyond space-saving and make inroads into areas of data storage and retrieval that are currently met by on-line databases. Already there are image processing publishing companies which sell disks containing databases of information such as company performance. Some companies are beginning to use their in-house image processing system to do jobs that a database is more often used for. For example, Ansaldo Spa (a large electro-mechanical engineering company) initially installed image processing because it calculated that it lost 7,500 man-hours a year in manual searches for documents.[2] The image processing system proved so beneficial that it was soon expanded. Now 30,000 documents are regularly accessed, and every day an additional 200 documents are added. Ten departments at different locations can obtain access to the information: thus the system may truly be considered a database. The Italians have led the way in the development and use of image processing: other Italian companies which use it include Fiat and RAI, the broadcasting corporation.

B: THE DIFFERENT USES OF DATABASES

9.10   Potential uses of databases

When managers first consider the benefits to be gained from, and possible uses for, a database, they may well think in terms of creating one which will contain employee or product details. This is, however, a very limited concept of the use of a database. Organizations have long held details of employees on payroll packages and this can easily be extended to give details of such particulars as training, qualifications, and managerial experience. This should assist in the management of employees but will not normally have a major impact on the profitability of the business. Databases have far greater potential than as mere record stores, and may be used, for example, to increase profit or enter new product or market areas.

9.11   Use of databases to reduce staff costs

It is often the case that databases are first set up by organizations in an attempt to reduce staff and thus cut costs. Many organizations that set up databases for this purpose find that this was not the prime benefit of the database and that any savings in staff costs are at best marginal. Governments, however, tend to hold vast amounts of data on a wide range of matters and thus stand to gain considerable financial advantage by computerizing the storage and retrieval of data. Therefore, some of the largest databases are ones set up by governments to hold details about individuals for one purpose or another. Whether they succeed in their aim of saving money is dubious, as the following example shows.

The DSS[3]

In the UK the Department of Social Security (DSS) has been working for ten years to replace paper files with computer records. This process is due to be completed in 1992 and will give staff instant access to clients' records and deliver benefit cheques within twenty-four hours. The system has to be able to handle 60 million records — one for every person over the age of sixteen plus details of the recently dead in order to pay widows' pensions.

Although it was a very costly project, it was thought that it would pay for itself by requiring twenty thousand fewer staff to run the offices. Whether this will be the case remains to be seen but it looks dubious at this stage. The project, which was orginally expected to cost £700m, is now expected to cost £2,000m. Large cost overruns are not uncommon with this type of project, but in this case it is particularly high. Furthermore, the program has not been written on a self-explanatory, user-friendly basis. The result is that fifty thousand staff will have to be trained in its use — at a cost of £2,000 each. Presumably this is because it was not written in a modern self explanatory language having been initiated ten years ago before computer languages had developed to their present level. This highlights one of the problems when installing very large systems: they tend to be technically out of date by the time they are completed. However, adequate amounts for staff training should always be included in any costing of a new information system.

Pressures to implement the program on time have probably been the cause of faulty software being introduced. (All new software should be thoroughly tested before it is put into use to ensure that it is not faulty.) One DSS office claims that it lost £140,000 from a fund over night and others say that some claimants can only be processed manually. Despite all the problems the system may eventually pay for itself. It was also planned to link it with the system run at the Department of Employment. If this could be done satisfactorily some saving should be forthcoming. However, it now seems likely that this will not be possible because of the regulations of the Data Protection Act (see section 13.20).

Four areas where databases may be used to give an organization positive benefits are:

- To enable the organization to serve the customer better.
- To enter a new product area.
- To increase sales volume.
- To improve the quality of decision making (see section 9.20).

These are not the only ways in which databases can be used but appear to be the areas which are most popular for development at present. Each one is considered in detail in the remainder of this chapter.

9.12 Use of databases to serve the customer better

The example of the DSS database could also have been classified under this heading as it was intended to give a better service to the user by speeding up the receipt of a benefit cheque. Serving the customer better and more efficiently is a popular strategy today (as it should be) and many organizations have set up databases to achieve this. One example of this is Federal Express's database of directions and locations which is used by telephone operators to direct potential customers to their nearest parcel drop-off point (see section 5.3). In the UK, the emergency telephone service uses a database to determine the nearest police station to the telephone caller.

British Rail's enquiry database[3]

British Rail developed its Computerized Assisted Timetable Enquiry system (CATE) to improve the quality of service to the customer. Traditionally it took about five minutes to answer a customer's timetable or route enquiry. It involved leafing through a 1,500 page timetable and the booking clerk or telephonist had to have knowledge of the best route connections to make. CATE has cut the time to one and a half minutes for the average call and the best train connections are always built in. The timetable was computerized in 1983 but it was not feasible at that stage, on the grounds of cost, to link BR's 70 telephone enquiry bureaux and 1,500 ticket offices directly to it. Now, however, the large mainframe database has been compressed so that it can be incorporated into local systems and nearly all the bureaux use CATE. When a travel enquiry is made, the operator asks for the destination and starting stations, the date of the journey and the desired time of arrival or departure. Once this information is keyed in the most suitable train or trains is displayed within two seconds. It has proved such a success that versions are currently being developed for travel centres and for self-service operation by customers.

9.13   Use of databases to enter a new product area

Many companies have adopted the strategy of entering new product areas which would not have been possible without the prior existence of a suitable database to assist in reaching potential customers. Whether, when the companies first started to set up their databases, they realized their potential in this regard is a matter for conjecture. For instance Marks & Spencer built a customer database when it started issuing its own credit cards to customers. It later used the database to help expand its product range into financial services such as unit trusts and PEPs (personal equity plans). This was done by searching the database of existing credit card customers and selecting people who might be interested in the new services. **Telemarketing** was then used to contact these potential customers.

Saga, which provides holidays for older people, used its database in a similar way to expand into sheltered accommodation and insurance for older people. In the past, organizations with databases or lists of customers, such as mail order companies, have been able to sell this information to other organizations. So, in effect, they have entered into another product area — that of selling information. Professional organizations also, in effect, sell their database of members' names by agreeing to distribute a mail-shot for other organizations. In the future this market may no longer exist as more and more organizations begin to build up their own specific databases.

9.14   Use of databases to increase sales volume

Many organizations are finding that databases can be used to increase sales volume because of their great assistance in building up customer records and in recording a wide range of details about customers. (As this is currently such an important area for the development of database systems, a discussion of what information a marketing database should contain and how it may be stored is given in sections 9.15–9.19.) Information on customers has always been available to an organization willing to spend the time collecting it, but for some reason most businesses have failed to collect and use it properly until recently. It has been suggested that this is because sales staff are more keen to move on to the next sale rather than to keep detailed records of sales already made. With a database, however, sales staff get benefits themselves from the data they have logged into the system and so are willing to process the data. This is illustrated below.

Hewlett-Packard's customer database[4]

In the early 1980s Hewlett Packard had a direct salesforce of about two thousand who, on average, spent only 26 per cent of their time with customers. The rest was spent on administration, travelling and at internal meetings. By 1987 each member of the salesforce had been given a portable computer and printer. The computer could act as an address book, a time and expenses recording system, a word-processor and, most importantly, could be used to gain access to information stored in the corporate databases. The corporate databases held information on product availability and pricing, customer order status, leads and prospects as well as including a customer profile database. A member of the salesforce could key in information about orders and quotations and retrieve information, such as references and equipment specifications, that would assist in making sales. The installation of the system immediately had the effect of increasing orders, increasing the time the salesforce spent with customers and reducing the time spent at internal meetings. However, improvement in the performance of the salesforce was not the main benefit: the database was a stepping-stone to further developments.

Two years later a direct marketing centre was set up to obtain, and then qualify, leads for the salesforce as well as responding to enquiries for literature and information. The customer database was enlarged when the centre was set up and divided into three sections: customers, prospects and suspects. Selected names are mailed and enquiries returned to the marketing centre. The results of the enquiry, following qualification and possibly a visit by a member of the salesforce are then fed back into the database, continually updating and improving it.

Four telemarketing centres have also been set up to handle sales to different segments of the existing customer base. The telephone operators work with the direct salesforce by calling customers at regular intervals to arrange interviews. They also gather information about customer requirements, whether installed equipment is working well, contact names, budgets and competitor activities. This unified marketing approach which relies on databases of customer information has had a major impact. Sales volume has increased by 15 per cent while cost per order has dropped 10 per cent and only 10 per cent of sales leads are now discarded. Furthermore, the information has allowed a full analysis of specific promotions and has improved the quality of mailing lists.

9.15 Customer databases and database marketing

The use of customer databases is often part of a broader approach known as database marketing. The computer has made it possible to keep details of thousands of customers or prospective customers on a database. This allows the information to be reclassified in a suitable way for a particular use — such as by life style, socio-economic group, age or geographical location. This information can be used for targeting promotion campaigns to particular customer groups or better relating the products to the needs of particular customer groups. It may even result in a brand new product launch.

Traditionally, there are three major areas for obtaining information about customers and potential customers: internally from the sales invoice and from information gathered by the salesforce, and externally from published documents or statistics and external databases.

9.16 Sales invoice

The sales invoice has always been available as a source of data and has been used to a greater or lesser extent over the years. It usually contains the following information which may be stored and analyzed as required at a future date:

Customer name
Contact name (name of an individual within the buying organization who is the business contact)
Customer address

Delivery address
Date of sale
Items ordered
Quantity
Prices
Discounts
Terms and conditions
The identity of the individual making the sale.

These data allow an analysis of sales to be made, for example, by:

- Sales territory: to measure the individual performance of members of the salesforce.
- Customer type: judged by size or frequency of purchases or product type.

9.17 Information collected by the salesforce

Information gained from the direct salesforce or telephone operators dealing with enquiries has not been collected and recorded properly in the past. Individuals have kept information to themselves and have not co-ordinated their activities and efforts on a company-wide scale. Often, sales people have recorded the information weeks after the event — far too late to chase a lead for example. The direct salesforce, suitably equipped with a means of recording information, can build up a useful bank of knowledge (as was illustrated in Hewlett-Packard's case). The direct sales force have to be able to use the information they record for their own benefit, otherwise it seems they will not see the need to record it properly. A portable computer for their personal use seems vital to ensure that information is recorded properly, and it is best that it is linked to an electronic diary so that calls and follow-ups may be scheduled by the individual. It is helpful to supply word-processing facilities so that standard documents can be processed on the spot. In addition, it is advantageous to have a means of communicating orders directly to the office when they are made and, finally, to have a system by means of which the sales people can monitor their own performance in terms of ratios and targets met.

9.18 Central database

The customer database can be organized in a variety of slightly different ways so that the specific needs of the business are suited. The model considered here is a direct mail database. This must be a relational database (see section 9.8) and is subdivided into three sections for convenience, as illustrated in Figure 9.6.

The information in the three sections can be related to each other through, for instance, a customer account number.

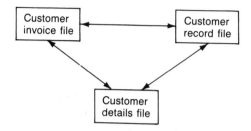

Figure 9.6 Customer database.

The customer invoice file contains all the information from the invoices. The customer record file contains the details for mailing, i.e. name and address. It may also contain information which can be used to segment the market, such as the post code for a retail customer, or an industry sector code for an industrial customer. The customer details file contains all of the extra pieces of information that are collected, such as age, life style, occupation and creditworthiness.

There is an external database called ACORN (A Classification of Residential Neighbourhoods) which can be used for analyzing existing customers or for reaching potential customers. It is obtained by analyzing census data and categorizes a neigbourhood by house type, size of household, employment sector, etc. It contains thirty-eight categories such as:

Areas of farms and smallholdings.
New detached houses, young families.
Interwar council estates, older people.
Villages with older wealthy commuters.

An organization can use ACORN together with the electoral roll and the post code to assess existing customers and from that gain knowledge to target a likely group of potential customers.

To illustrate the use of an internal database in finding potential customers, let us take as an example a company's need to increase the volume of sales of a particular product. Firstly, the database will be used to obtain a list of all customers who have bought the product in the recent past. They will then be analyzed by age, sex, income, ACORN code or whatever is considered appropriate. From this a picture of the characteristics of past customers can be built up, leading to the identification of the characteristics of potential customers. The organization's database can then be searched for existing customers who have bought other products but because of their characteristics may also be interested in this particular product. The potential customers' attention can be drawn to the product by either telemarketing or mail shot. If it is thought desirable to widen the customer base, external mailing lists may be bought which list people with the required characteristics or ACORN codes. These may then be used to target potential customers.

9.19 External databases

There is a great variety and an ever increasing number of external databases for an organization or individual to use. Some are simply reference databases such as Lexis (Law [*lex*] Information System) which holds details of every UK law case since the Second World War. Lexis also holds information on Australian, New Zealand and American legal cases. Then there are those which contain up to the minute information, such as Datastream which holds details on equities, bonds, futures, options, market news and economic indicators. Information on share price movements gleaned from this database is reported on British radio stations. These databases are funded by the user who pays a registration fee which normally also includes the hire of special terminals. In addition, the user may have to pay a fee for using the service.

Several specialist 'host' companies have grown up which market a range of databases. These companies offer an international, on-line connection to their database products. The databases may be information only, such as abstracts of publications — an example of which is Reuters's Textline. Alternatively, the databases may contain information which can be downloaded onto a customer's computer. Examples of this type are databases which contain chemical, financial, medical or engineering details. In the near future every significant body of knowledge should be accessible via external databases.

9.20 PIMS database

The fourth profitable use of a database identified at the start of this section was to improve the quality of decision making. This objective may be achieved by using an external database such as PIMS. PIMS (profit impact of market strategy) is the most extensive strategic information database in the world. Its roots lie in the 1950s when the United States corporation GE (General Electric) changed its organization structure to a divisional one based on the different types of business within the organization.[5] It was soon noted that different types of businesses had different return on investment percentages. This knowledge was considered further when in 1960 the marketing services vice-president set up a research project to consider the relationship between market share and operating economics and the effect on return on investment. A profit optimization model called PROM was created which aimed to help GE predict the future performance of its different business units.

Gradually, the model grew in size and Harvard University developed it further. In 1975 the database was extended to cover other organizations and moved to Cambridge, Massachusetts, where it was set up under the wing of Harvard University at the Strategic Planning Institute — and the PIMS database was born. Its objectives were:

- To develop an up to date database which truly reflects the business experience of the participants.
- To discover through research the 'laws' of the market place.
- To make its findings available to the participants.

Today the database contains details of over three thousand business units. These are mainly American but European representation is growing. Every organization pays a fee and supplies information on its different businesses; in turn it receives a variety of reports and information. PIMS helps decision making within an organization by providing information on a wide range of matters by using the database to find similar businesses which have faced similar situations. Some of the services offered by PIMS are:

- **Benchmarking**: developing performance norms and targets, including a par ROI, i.e. a 'normal' return on investment for the particular business based on market forces, competitive position and value-adding structure. Benchmarks for target-setting and improvement tracking are also available.
- **Margin control**: calculates a high contribution level and a low fixed cost level for a particular business unit.
- **Quality strategy**: an assessment of perceived quality which includes a 'value map' of relative quality plotted against relative price for the business unit under consideration and for its competitors.
- **Market share strategy**: the effect of changes in the product offering or in pricing can be tested on market share. Changes in profit or cash-flow as a result of a change in policy can be assessed.
- **Productivity strategy**: identifying untapped profit improvement and setting targets for future performance.
- **Start-up strategy**: a review of target market, competitors, end users, distributors and quality of the product.
- **Innovation strategy**: covers how much money to spend on R&D and how it should be targeted, based on the process of measuring the technology's value for money and assessing its take-off potential.
- **Acquisition strategy**: screening a target company and comparing the actual ROI with the par ROI. This helps in assessing the development potential of the target company.

PIMS uses a regression model which consists of thirty-seven independent variables which are thought to explain more than 80 per cent of profit variability. When a participant asks a question on a particular proposed strategy the database is searched for similar business units which have carried out similar strategies.

The effects of the strategies on those business units are then averaged and an answer is given. Obviously, the more participants there are in a particular business sector the more reliable the findings are likely to be.

Such a database takes some of the 'hunch' out of planning. Indeed, this may be said to be the main benefit of many databases. Past information can now be made available on a scale that was not possible until recently to enable better decision making — whether planning business strategies or targeting customers. Therefore the use of databases may be said to result in less 'hunch' and more informed decisions. This assumes, of course, that past information will be a good guide for future decisions.

NOTES

1. E.F. Codd and C.J. Date, 'Interactive support for non-programmers: the relational and network approaches', *Relational Database Selected Readings* (Addison-Wesley, 1986).
2. 'Paper in and paper out but no storage problem', *Management Accounting*, Jan. 1990.
3. *Daily Telegraph*, 27 Oct. 1989.
4. Ian Meiklejohn, 'Window on the sales world', *Management Today*, July 1989.
5. P. McNamee, *Tools and Techniques of Strategic Management* (Pergamon Press, 1985).

FURTHER READING

Atre, Shaku, *Database — Structured Techniques for Design, Performance and Management*, 1988. Covers virtually everything one could want to know about databases.

Date, C.J., *Relational Database Writings 1985–1989* (Addison-Wesley, 1990). Writings in support of relational databases.

EXERCISES

1. A manufacturer of board games wishes to set up a marketing database so that it may:
   (i) Be in a better position to meet sales at periods of high demand.
   (ii) Better understand its market.
   (iii) Be of help in developing new products.

   (a) Suggest what data need to be collected and from whom.
   (b) How the database may be partitioned and the data stored.
   (c) How the information would be used to meet the three objectives.

2. Find out what databases you have access to from your institute or company. Enter them and assess the information and the way in which it is presented. Could they be improved? Consider how you might use each to assist you in your studies.

3. Which databases, maintained by the following bodies, do you think your particulars appear in?
   (a) Your college or university.

(b) Local and national government.

(c) Other organizations.

What problems, advantages and disadvantages are there in linking the different databases which you have listed?

4. What dangers and problems are there in attempting to forge links between databases kept by different business organizations?

10 Expert systems

SCOPE AND CONTENTS

Expert systems are defined and the difference between rule and frame based systems is explained. How an expert system may be created is briefly discussed, as is the difference between an expert system and a traditional computer system. The advantages of expert systems are considered in detail with examples. The advantages are: better decisions, reducing the time taken to make decisions, cost savings and assistance with training. Diagnostic and selection systems are discussed and DEC's planning systems are considered. The integration of expert systems into other information systems is examined as are 'off-the-shelf' systems. Finally the ownership of knowledge and knowledge based systems of the future are considered.

10.1 What is an expert system?

Expert systems are sometimes referred to as being a form of artificial intelligence. This is misleading as they are not systems which are capable of thinking for themselves; instead they use and sift through human knowledge in the specific order in which they have been programmed. Therefore expert systems can hardly be called artificial intelligence within the true meaning of the term. Their other name, knowledge based systems, is much more appropriate as will become clear from the description below. However, we prefer to use the name expert system as it is the one in common usage.

Expert systems are programmed with knowledge supplied by a person or a group of people with expertise on a particular topic. These people are referred to as 'experts' because they have some specific body of knowledge which is not shared by the majority of other people. Once their knowledge has been incorporated into it the system becomes an expert system. However, the computer does not use the knowledge to reason for itself, instead it follows the reasoning pattern supplied by the expert. It is, however, capable of explaining the logic it followed and why it arrived at a particular conclusion. An expert system reasons in a similar way as a person might when playing 'twenty questions' or 'animal, vegetable, mineral'. A series of questions are asked whose answers narrow down the problem or choice until a diagnosis or answer can be provided.

An expert system consists of two parts:

- A knowledge base.
- An inference engine.

The knowledge base contains the factual or judgemental knowledge of the expert. The inference engine controls the process of reasoning, that is sifting through the knowledge in a predetermined sequence so as to arrive at a conclusion. The word 'knowledge' does not normally refer only to the acquisition of facts: it also includes good judgement based on experience. This is the case with expert systems: they contain both factual and **heuristic** knowledge. Knowledge is also often incomplete and uncertain, that is it lacks a full set of facts and incorporates the words 'probably' or 'more likely' into any judgement. This can be coped with in an expert system by building confidence factors into the system.

An expert system, as such, is not usually purchased by a business: instead it builds its own, incorporating the expertise of its staff. An expert system can be built from scratch but it is more common, when only a small system is required, to purchase a 'shell'. This is an empty program into which knowledge can be placed in a logical order. Most expert systems in use in the UK are small ones that operate on PCs. In fact, the UK has been criticized for sticking to small applications rather than developing expert systems on a grand scale.

10.2 Rule based systems

Expert systems may be constructed in two different ways. The systems may be either:

- rule based, or
- frame based.

Frame based systems present a more passive view of knowledge and consist of a series of frames, each containing a list of properties and associated values about the object under consideration. The frames are linked in a network, thus a knowledge base is built up.

This book considers only rule based systems because they are the more popular and appear to offer more scope for future development. Rule based systems operate on the 'if then' form of reasoning. A series of 'if thens' are linked up to form a type of decision tree. Rule based systems may have backward or forward chaining. Backward systems are goal driven systems: that is, the goal or conclusion is known but the path leading to it is not. Mycin, the expert system for diagnosis of infectious blood diseases, is one such. It diagnoses and recommends a course of treatment based on about 450 rules. Any diagnostic system will be a backward one because it has to start with the result and look backwards to the cause. Another example might be a car breakdown diagnosis system. The conclusion or result is that the car does not start. Why? Has it petrol? Is the carburettor flooded? Is the battery flat?

A forward system, on the other hand, starts with a set of conditions and moves towards a conclusion. This type of system is used in business to design products to the customer's specification. Two well known early systems of this type are DEC's Xcon and Xsel systems which are described in section 10.11.

10.3　Setting up a system

Rule based expert systems are very easy to operate and quite easy to program using a purchased shell. For example, an individual would probably need to spend two or three days becoming familiar with the basic concepts and the particular system, and then another two days' work would produce a simple expert system consisting of, say, 150–200 rules. However, an organization will probably wish to build a much more complex system consisting of, say, five thousand rules: in which case it is usual for two or more people to work together. One person will be the 'expert' who has the knowledge to be put on the system. The other will be the 'engineer' who understands the system and who will sort the knowledge into a logical order and put it into the system. This approach is usually necessary because the expert will probably not be capable of expressing facts and feelings with the clarity necessary to commit them to a large system. Neither will the expert think logically enough to put the knowledge onto the system. So an engineer is needed to shape the knowledge into a precise and logical form.

Sometimes it is difficult to extract knowledge from experts. Cooper Lybrand used a novel way when it created its system ExperTAX.[1] They arranged their tax experts on one side of a table and put a 'client' with a set of data on the other side. The table was divided by a screen so that the experts could not see the data available. This meant that the experts had to ask for every piece of data they needed for tax planning and they had to explain why they wanted it. This was the beginning of the expert system and was captured on video tape so that it could be worked on and improved at a later date.

10.4 Difference between expert and other computer systems

The reader will be aware from the above description that expert systems, or knowledge based systems, differ from more traditional computer systems in two ways. Firstly, they do more for the user, and secondly, they function in a different way. Expert systems have extended the traditional information system beyond the provision of information to the point where a decision is made by the system rather than the user. This extension is portrayed in Figure 10.1 which is an extended version of Figure 1.2.

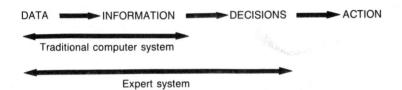

DATA ➡ INFORMATION ➡ DECISIONS ➡ ACTION

◄──────────────────► Traditional computer system

◄──────────────────────────────► Expert system

Figure 10.1 A knowledge based information system compared with a traditional one.

Expert systems use different programming languages from traditional computer systems. These are normally either Lisp (which was invented in the late 1950s and is a language based on symbols) or Prolog. Prolog is a logic based system and became popular when the Japanese said that they would use it for the **Fifth Generation Project**.

10.5 Why use an expert system?

An organization may require an expert system for any of the following reasons:

- **To improve the quality of decisions made**. The expert system can be programmed with the best knowledge available which will be based on the best expert working at the top of his or her form. Therefore consistently better decisions can be made regardless of the level of skill of the individual in charge of making them.
- **To reduce the time taken in making a diagnosis**. An expert system can be used to save a considerable amount of time in the analysis of a problem and in making the diagnosis. In a range of quite widely differing systems the amount of time taken for diagnosis is reduced to about one-tenth

of that taken by humans. It seems reasonable, therefore, to assume that this level of reduction is possible in most instances. Specific examples will be considered later in the chapter. But note that the system does not 'think' ten times faster — it is the overall process which is reduced in time.

- **To achieve cost savings**. Considerable cost savings are possible. Often, systems pay for themselves within the first year and most have recovered the initial outlay by the end of their second year of operation. This saving in cost is generally achieved by speeding up the decision making process or by improving the quality of the decision.
- **To train staff**. There is plenty of potential to use expert systems to train staff both on and off the job.

Specific examples of expert systems will now be considered, categorized under the different headings.

10.6 Improving the quality of decisions

A small but useful expert system is that operated by the Department of Social Security to determine pension entitlement. The regulations governing pension entitlement often appear very confusing to applicants and on some occasions, prior to the use of an expert system, appeared to be open to different interpretation by staff at different DSS offices. This has proved particularly true as regards the pension rights of females who only worked for a few years around the period of the Second World War. An individual who has paid only part of the contribution, or who has paid no contribution at all for a short period, may be unclear about the effect on his or her pension rights. This is just the type of situation where an expert system can work well — where only a small body of knowledge is needed but where humans have difficulty in comprehending and assessing the situation.

When a query is raised by an individual visiting or writing to a DSS office, the assistant retrieves the individual's electronic file from the mainframe computer and prints a hard copy. The assistant then feeds the expert system, which is on a microcomputer, with the relevant information and thus obtains an answer to pension entitlement. This two-step route may seem strange and is certainly time consuming. (Apparently it was set up this way to overcome the problem of persuading the information systems people that an expert system should be attached to 'their' mainframe computer.) The two-step route probably has the advantage of producing a more human and reliable face to the individual with the query. In fact the public has been so impressed by the improved service that quite a few have actually written in to thank the DSS.

The purpose of the pension expert system was to improve the quality and consistency of the decision making on pension rights but it had the added advantage of saving nearly £1m in 1988, its first year of operation. The main saving in cost was one of time, as under the manual system people who were told they were not entitled to pensions tended to go to another DSS office and put their claim again in the hope of a different answer.

American Express has an expert system called AMEX which assists in credit authorization.[1] American Express has no general credit limits for competitive reasons, instead a credit level is determined for each customer. Each time a large purchase is made, the shopkeeper telephones the office and asks an employee using an AMEX terminal about the credit rating of the purchaser. A quick decision has to be made — and with the expert system it is made within seconds. It scans up to thirteen databases before making the decision. This kind of thoroughness was not possible prior to the installation of the expert system because of lack of time — it would have taken staff about thirty minutes to reach a similar decision. As a result of the use of AMEX, the quality of the decisions on credit rating has improved and this is shown by a reduction in losses due to overextending credit. In addition, the productivity of staff has increased by 20 per cent. As was the case with the DSS, better quality decisions save money as well as providing the customer with a better and more consistent image of the organization.

10.7   Reducing the time taken to make decisions

The AMEX system was so successful in making better credit rating decisions because it was faster than a human being and, therefore, could be more thorough in analysis. A quite different area where time is important is in the analysis of finger prints. Studying and identifying finger prints is a skilled job and not one that can be rushed. If a finger print is obtained from the scene of a crime, the time consuming job of comparing it with all similar finger prints on record will begin to take place in the hope of identifying its owner. The finger print expert identifies prints by noting special points of difference or individuality on the print in question. These points may be, say, fifteen small areas, and the time taken for comparision is long. A computer using an expert system can make the comparision much more quickly: it can compare the print with eighteen thousand others in less than two minutes. If the search does not provide a perfect fit, the computer will provide several similar ones for consideration. When a new finger print of a criminal is put on file the expert system reads it and compares it with the existing ones on file on all outstanding cases in the hope of solving earlier crimes.

This expert system clearly saves a considerable amount of time and requires fewer staff to be trained in the exacting task of identifying prints. Time is often of the essence in solving crimes and tracking down criminals. Speeding up finger print analysis and, therefore, widening the scope of comparability, should lead to better crime detection rates at a lower cost.

10.8 Cost savings

Toyota uses an expert system which reduces both time and cost and which also provides the customer with a better service.[2] Cars have nowadays become very complicated with the development of in-car computers. In addition, car mechanics are always in short supply and sometimes lack the skills necessary for fault diagnosis. Toyota, therefore, developed a system called Atrex which comes into operation if the mechanic requires it. The mechanic will carry out the diagnosis and repair in the traditional manner if possible. However, if he cannot solve the problem he can make a telephone call to a Toyota office where an assistant is located with Atrex. The mechanic gives details, rather similar to a medical check-up, of the car's history, the symptoms and other relevant factors such as the ambient temperature. This is fed into the system by the assistant. The expert system then asks questions and finally suggests a remedy. If the problem is not solved as a result of the first diagnosis, the mechanic can call back for further advice. In addition, the mechanic receives a printout with the expert system's reasoning for future reference and so the mechanic is in fact receiving on-the-job training as well.

Atrex has cut costs considerably by saving time. A problem that would take two to three days to solve previously can now be solved in two to three hours; and one which took two to three hours in five minutes or so. Costs have also been reduced because the number of expert mechanics required at central sites has been reduced by fifteen. The customer has also benefited as the car is out of action for considerably less time and the fault is less likely to recur on account of an incorrect diagnosis. Other companies are working towards this system. General Motors hopes to have an expert system in every workshop. Toyota reply to that by saying that cars should not be faulty and that they are working towards that aim.

10.9 Training

With an expert system there is no need to train all the staff that do a particular job to such a high level as was the case previously. This helps organizations when there is a shortage of skilled labour because it becomes acceptable to employ people with less knowledge who, with an expert system, can operate to the same efficiency level as an individual with more training and experience. There is a slight danger in the future, therefore, that the majority of staff could receive less detailed or technical training than at present.

Expert systems can also be used to train staff in particular skills, especially diagnostic ones. Programs can be used to put trainees through their paces by setting a problem and inviting the trainee to suggest a solution. If the answer is wrong the trainee can be taken through the decision stages step by step and given a printout of the correct decision process. Working alongside an expert system can also improve the knowledge of a relatively inexperienced employee. Toyota's system is an example of a working system which also incorporates training.

ICI has created a system at a polypropylene film coating plant which has both raised the level of knowledge within the company and has assisted in training. The system contains the technical expertise of one particular individual. When this person tried to pass on his knowledge to others at the company he found it impossible and efficiency dropped. By putting the knowledge onto an expert system the company has saved £140,000 a year in the expert's time and improved efficiency. Furthermore, the system is used for training and as a source of information at the plant.

10.10 Classification of expert systems

The expert systems discussed so far have been classified according to the benefit which the organization hopes to gain by installing them. They could, however, have been classified according to the nature of the expert system employed, namely:

- *Diagnostic* systems, such as Mycin and Toyota's Atrex.
- Systems for *selection*, such as the finger print system.
- *Planning* systems, such as those of BP and Clarks (mentioned below).

A system for selecting between different options is often useful when detailed knowledge is needed to make the decision. DuPont has a system for selecting the correct plastic wrapping for use in the packing of particular goods. This might not seem a difficult choice to make, but in fact there are more than twenty different grades of plastic available and the choice depends on such things as whether it is to be heat sealed or whether the goods have sharp edges. Another example of a selection system is one which could be used by the fire brigade to assess what to do about a particular chemical spill. There are two hundred or so different chemicals which might be spilt as a result of an accident, and so selecting the correct method of treatment in an emergency is not easy. If the wrong method to deal with the spillage is chosen matters could be made worse rather than better.

10.11 Expert systems for planning

Expert systems can be used to plan a design or configure a product and DEC was one of the first companies to use it this way.[2] DEC produces computer systems from a wide range of components which can be configured in many different ways to suit the customer. Traditionally, the sales representative's order, which specified the system, was checked by technical editors (experts). They made sure that the computer system had all the necessary components and drew the diagrams showing how to assemble the system. The result was that more than 50 per cent of the initial configurations had errors or omissions, some of which were so serious that the sales representative had to go back to the customer and renegotiate terms. Neither were the technical editors perfect at configuring; this meant that virtually all the systems had to be checked again by assembling and testing them before taking them to pieces again for transportation to the customer. This process was obviously wasteful and could no longer be tolerated if DEC was to achieve the desired sales growth. Xcon, an expert system, was part of the answer. It checks the order and designs the layout of each computer, and is much more reliable than the human experts. As it is equivalent to the best human expert on a good day there is no longer any need to assemble and test the configuration before sending the components to the customer's premises for assembly.

There were many problems in developing Xcon. The major one was the difference in performance between the academic prototype and the real system when it was first installed. Nor did it solve the problem totally as orders were still returned to the sales representatives on occasions for renegotiation. Another system called Xsel, developed some years later, proved to be the answer to that problem, but again there were severe problems to be overcome before it became totally satisfactory. Being one of the first in the field is always difficult but no large expert system is likely to be developed without some pain. Xsel was originally planned to have two thousand rules, but by the time it was up and operating the number had doubled. Then, once it had been made to work properly, the salesforce were loath to use it, probably because not only did they not want to change procedures but also they remembered that in the early days it had had a habit of breaking down. The introduction of a series of new product ranges saved Xsel: as with so many new components and updates to remember the sales representatives were almost forced to use it. Then, once they had used Xsel, they found they could not do without it.

There are several important lessons to be learned from the development of DEC's expert systems. Firstly, new technology may promise great benefits but the result may be difficult to achieve because of unforeseen problems with the technology. Secondly, the system may prove to be too costly to develop — costs often double, or treble, before the project is completed. Thirdly, and most importantly, not all staff embrace new technology with open arms. They may be afraid of it, feel threatened by it or, alternatively, they may not trust it, as was the case with Xsel. This was caused by the premature launching of the system. Any system must be tested, retested and tested again before it is put into common use, as once it gets a name for unreliability, just like any product, it is exeedingly difficult to remove the stigma.

Expert systems are used by some organizations to plan production routes and levels. One of the largest British production planning systems is BP's Escort system at Grangemouth where synthetic rubber is manufactured. The system contains details of all the engineering knowledge about the basic operations and also the idiosyncracies of particular pieces of plant — such as how the wind direction affects performance. This latter knowledge can only be obtained by an individual working with the equipment for some years and represents one of the benefits of using an expert system: the knowledge does not leave the organization when the employee leaves.

Clarks Shoes uses an expert system for planning the different sizes, styles and colours to be made in batch production.[3] The benefit to Clarks is flexibility of production. This degree of flexibility could not be achieved if humans did the planning. The system allocates the workload and anticipates bottlenecks. It consists of four parts: a simulator, a statistics package to analyze the results of simulation, an intelligent database for spotting problems and suggesting remedies, and a database editor.

10.12 Integrated expert systems

Clarks Shoes is working to integrate its expert system with other production information systems, in particular the work in progress and data capture systems. There is great potential with integration for reaping even more benefits. One area in which progress has already been made is by integrating CAD (computer aided design) and expert systems to provide a 'thinking' system which, for instance, is aware of weight and stress bearing requirements in a particular design. Progress towards fully linking CIM (computer integrated manufacturing) and expert systems is beginning. Expert systems are available which operate in real time and which can monitor several thousands of variables at the same time. These can be used for process control. Thus not only is the manufacturing process automated but all the decisions behind it are as well. These expert systems are not at all the same as the simple 'shell' systems that the chapter commenced with and to which we return below.

There are, in theory, three choices when integrating an expert system with a conventional one. The first, and most popular to date is to make the expert system the main controlling program. This is relatively easy because most expert systems have facilities for getting data from databases, spreadsheets or other programs. The second choice is to do the opposite and use a conventional computer language to write an expert system application. However, it is hard to do this with a conventional language. The third choice is to connect an expert system with an application written in a traditional language. Here neither would dominate but the operating system must be one which allows programmers to write in the different languages. Therefore it must contain Lisp or Prolog for the expert system and, say, Pascal or Fortran for the traditional application.

10.13   Off-the-shelf expert systems

All of the systems considered up to now have been developed by an organization for internal use to solve a particular problem. It is possible, though, to buy off-the-shelf expert systems to give specific advice. One example is Butterworth's (the legal publishers) system on 'latent damage law' which is considered to be an obscure area of law of which few have much knowledge. The system, which comes together with a booklet, consists of about a thousand rules and was launched at a price of £64 in 1989. In comparision with the price of legal books this is relatively quite cheap, but it is aimed more at law firms rather than the general public or law students. An example of an expert system aimed at the general public is the one produced and sold immediately after the Chancellor's Budget every year which deals with the changes in the tax system. This system sells for around £10.

10.14   Ownership of knowledge

Ownership of knowledge appears to be one area which has not yet been properly considered. Who owns the information and knowledge on the expert system? Is it the individual whose knowledge is on the system, the organization (employer of the human expert) who uses the system, or the 'publisher' of the system? Clearly it would be illegal to make copies of the system much as it is illegal to make copies of videos or books. One could take the matter further and suggest that the individual whose knowledge is on the system should receive a royalty for its use: that is, every time the program is run some small payment in recompense should be made.

There may well be certain disadvantages for an expert who is an employee if he puts his knowledge onto an expert system for use within the organization without receiving proper recompense or acknowledgement. An unscrupulous employer could, for instance, make the employee redundant once his skill had been captured on a system. More likely, however, other slightly less skilled employees might be made redundant. For instance, some companies use an expert system for maintenance of plant and equipment in a factory which operates twenty-four hours a day. Previously, three maintenance experts would have had to be employed to cover the three shifts a day. However, once an expert system has been made there is no need to employ an expert on the night shift as the expert system can be interogated for a diagnosis of the fault.

10.15 Knowledge based systems of the future

There seems little doubt that expert systems, or knowledge based systems, will become a greater feature of most people's lives whether in the factory, office or home. One of the aims of the Japanese when they set up the Fifth Generation Project was to produce systems which had knowledge based processing directed towards solving problems for users rather than the mere execution of programs. Matsushita and Hitachi have recently launched a new type of washing machine which makes the decision on the correct washing program to employ for the user. The most appropriate washing cycle is selected based on data collected from sensors about the type of fabric, the degree of dirt, the washing powder used and the volume of laundry. The machine incorporates a fuzzy logic microprocessor which makes the decisions. Fuzzy logic does not require simple yes or no answers but can cope with imprecise concepts such as 'could be' or 'almost'. It has been described as thinking in 'shades of grey'. Other products using this technique are coming onto the market and it has also been used by the Japanese in controlling the movement of trains.

NOTES

1. D. Leonard-Barton and J. Sviokla, 'Putting expert systems to work', *Harvard Business Review*, Mar./Apr. 1988.
2. E. Feigenbaum, P. McCorduck and N.P. Nii, *The Rise of the Expert Company* (Macmillan, 1988).
3. C. Gabriel, 'Clearing the hurdles', *Infomatics*, Feb. 1989.

FURTHER READING

Feigenbaum, E., P. McCorduck and H.P. Nii, *The Rise of the Expert System* (Macmillan, 1988). Contains many examples of expert systems in practice.

EXERCISES

1. Briefly explain what is meant by an expert system and how it operates. Outline three instances in which expert systems could be of benefit to a manufacturing or service organization. Explain in detail the benefits that would be derived.

2. Expert systems are also called 'knowledge' systems. Select an area of knowledge which you possess and describe how a computer system using this knowledge could be constructed.

3. A rather old-fashioned local railway/underground transport organization wishes to improve its image and to provide the customer with a better service. It feels that good information systems may go much of the way towards achieving its aims. Consider what information the commuters may need and what types of system could be used to give the information. Draw up a list, in order of priority, for installation and show how the systems will interconnect.

Part Three

Formulating and implementing an information strategy

Part Two examined the major techniques and technologies which are currently available for an organization to use when creating its overall information strategy. Part Three continues by considering the way in which such a strategy may be formulated. Once an overall strategic plan has been devised it has, of course, to be put into practice; and Part Three also considers how this should be done. In order to make a chosen strategy 'happen' the infrastructure must be set up, equipment bought and software either written in-house or purchased.

There is, however, considerably more to successfully implementing an information strategy than simply purchasing the correct equipment and software. Staff must be trained, data transferred correctly and the whole process must be planned and monitored closely. But *good* implementation involves even more than this. Chapter 13 considers the need for good controls to be built into the system in order to make sure that the data and information supplied are correct and free from error. Good security is needed to protect the systems, and the data and information that they contain, from accidental or deliberate damage caused by employees or outsiders.

Another important area to be considered when installing new systems is the behaviour and attitudes of employees. Often, new technologies and systems are perceived as an aggravation or even a threat instigated by top management. These matters, together with the influence of governments on information technology, are discussed in Chapter 15.

In many ways this part is the most important of the book. In recent years many organizations have invested heavily in information technology and yet have reaped few benefits. The problem has largely been either a poor strategy or poor implementation which lacked management commitment and failed to get over to the employees the importance and purpose of the systems. Furthermore, if an organization ignores security, it does so at its own peril; and not a few organizations that have done so have paid the ultimate penalty of going out of business as a result of losses incurred.

11 Formulating an information strategy

SCOPE AND CONTENTS

This chapter starts by differentiating between strategy and tactics. It considers the role of an information director before examining the planning sequence in detail. The formation of a business strategy and some of the planning techniques involved are considered briefly. The formulation of an information strategy, its links with the business strategy and the use of an information strategy matrix are discussed. Finally the thorny problem of cost–benefit anaylsis is examined.

11.1 Strategy and tactics

> All men can see the tactics whereby I conquer but what none can see is the strategy out of which victory is evolved.
>
> > General Sun Tse, 5th century BC[1]

Strategy — the art of directing military movements so as to secure the most advantageous positions and combinations of forces.
Tactics — the art of manoeuvring military forces especially in actual contact with the enemy.[2]

The quotation above from the writings of the Chinese general Sun Tse was written about military warfare rather than business warfare but the principle is the same and the statement is as true today as when it was written. Most organizations tend to concentrate on tactics at the expense of strategy, and to the detriment of the long-term welfare of the organization. The usual reason for this is that tactics are so visible and therefore relatively easy to quantify, whereas strategy is not. This concentration on tactics has been particularly true of planning for the provision of management information within an organization. A recent survey of sixty UK companies found that only 34 per cent had a strategy for the provision of management information. Some companies consider that planning is adequate if the plan goes as far as specifying the type of PC to be purchased and the particular spreadsheet package that all employees should use. This is tactical planning only. The tactical plan may be well thought out but it will always be inadequate unless it is conceived within a proper longer term strategic framework which ties disparate short-term tactics together and links them to a properly planned information strategy.

It is not adequate simply to have an information strategy. The information strategy must also be linked to a well thought out business strategy if the organization is to prosper in the longer term. If the two are not linked, the information provision is very unlikely to meet the future needs of the organization. By 'business strategy' we mean the overall strategic plan for the whole organization. Recent surveys in the UK have established that the information strategy is frequently not linked in any way to the business strategy. Long-term information strategies are often not taken seriously by management and, in one survey, 25 per cent of companies claimed that decisions on the provision of information were less important than other management issues.[3] These organizations may well realize the fallacy of this within a very few years.

11.2 Information director

Top management often tend to accept unquestioningly recommendations concerning decisions on the provision of information if they are made by information technology specialists. This is often because the managers have no idea about systems and equipment themselves. Information managers, on the other hand, frequently feel left out of the main decisions about future business strategy as they do not participate in boardroom discussions. Thus neither party is happy and decisions about information provision are made with incomplete knowledge of future business strategies. This situation is changing gradually as some organizations, particularly large ones, are now appointing information directors. If there is no director responsible for the provision of information then it is unlikely that adequate emphasis will be given to information when setting the overall business strategy. Nowadays, good provision of information is just as important to an organization as, for example, a good marketing function, since without either the business would not continue to survive for long. What is required, therefore, is a manager at the highest level in the organization who takes part in the formation of the business strategy and who can ensure that the information strategy fits into, complements and influences the overall business strategy.

11.3 The strategic planning sequence

It is difficult to lay down rules and sequential steps for the procedure of strategic planning. It is, in fact, rather like attempting a jigsaw: different individuals will wish to complete the jigsaw in different ways, by starting it in different places and working in different patterns. Some like to start the jigsaw with the frame whereas others prefer to select a colour. Whichever way it is started and worked through, the completed jigsaw fits together perfectly. Similarly, different types and styles of organization will wish to start the planning process in different places and to plan in different ways. Within the completed overall business plan there must be individual plans for all aspects of the business and these must fit together perfectly and complement one another. The jigsaw analogy ceases to be valid at this point, however, because the business plan is not rigid and static. Instead it ought to be flexible, open to amendment and modification at any time, in order to cope with changing circumstances. This aspect of building a strategic business plan is expressed clearly by James Quinn:

> The total strategic process is anything but linear. Integrating all the subsystem strategies is a groping, cyclical process that often circles back on itself, encountering interruptions and delays, and rarely arrives at clear-cut decisions at any one time. ... The strategy's ultimate development involves a series of nested, partial decisions [in each subsystem] interacting with other partial decisions, like fermentation in biochemistry, rather than an industrial assembly line[4]

The information system is one of many subsystems, or business activities, within an organization. Its relative strategic importance in relation to the other activities varies over time. In recent years the information system has gained a greater importance than hitherto — hence the need for the information director. Business strategy is influenced by decisions taken within the subsystems just as the subsystems are influenced by the decisions taken about business strategy and the future direction of the organization. In other words, it is impossible to formulate an information strategy in isolation and, therefore, we briefly consider how a business strategy is formulated before considering the information strategy.

11.4 Business strategy

The process of determining and implementing a business strategy is known as strategic management. Johnson and Scholes's model showing the elements of and influences on strategic management is illustrated in Figure 11.1. They wrote that they prevented it with some trepidation 'as a means by which students of strategy can think through complex strategic problems. It is not, however, an attempt to describe how the processes of strategic management necessarily take place in the political and cultural arenas of organizations'.[5] Thus in no way does the model consist of a series of processes or sequential steps which all organizations must take in a predetermined order.

The model shows three interlinked elements of strategic management. One is strategic analysis. This is an analysis of the strategic position of the organization. Three factors influence this: the environment, the resources available to the organization and the organization's culture. An analysis of all three should be

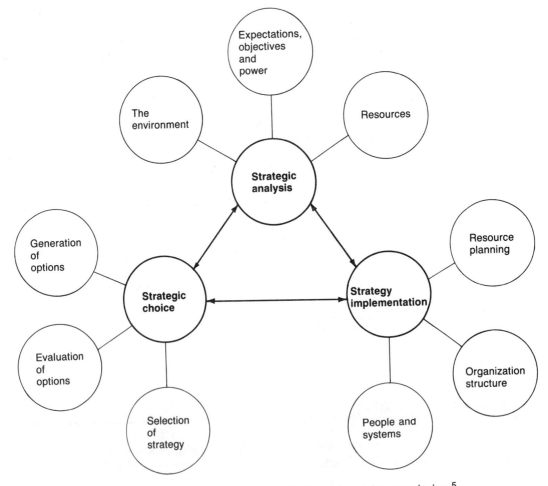

Figure 11.1 The elements of strategic management. Reproduced by permission.[5]

made continuously and automatically by good managers, although it is usual to revise the analysis formally once a year. The analysis should cover:

- What is occurring or what will occur in the business environment and its effect on the organization. These include changes of an economic, social, technological and competitive nature.
- The resources of the organization (physical, financial, skills available, etc.) in order to determine the shortcomings and strengths of the organization.
- The organizational culture, that is the management style and power of individuals or groups of individuals connected with the organization.

Another element in the model is the formation of the strategy itself. This involves generating a number of possible strategies, evaluating those that seem plausible and selecting the most suitable one. The final element, which is more usually referred to as tactics or operational strategy, is the implementation of the strategy. This is considered in detail in the next chapter. It involves the acquisition and deployment of resources, the analysis and implementation of any changes needed in the organization structure and the adaptation of systems and people to the changes in policy.

Whatever strategy is decided upon after the analysis has been made, it must take into account the attitudes and expectations of the people within the organization and all those who have contact with it, for example suppliers. The strategy must be a product of what the people involved want the organization to be, to do and to achieve. If it does not it will surely fail. For instance, a high-risk strategy would be entirely unsuitable for a mature and heavily financially orientated type of organization.

11.5 Frameworks to assist in strategy formulation

A range of methods or frameworks are available to carry out the strategic analysis of the business environment and of the organization's resources; some of these have already been mentioned in Chapter 2. One is to determine the critical success factors of the business and to build the strategy around them. The critical success factors of an organization are those crucial to its future success. Once these factors have been identified a strategy can be formulated which emphasizes them. It is essential that only a small number of critical success factors, say four, are identified. If there are more, management effort will be dissipated and few will be achieved. If, for example, a good distribution system is identified as one critical success factor, a strategy for achieving or improving it must be devised. That strategy might involve a better communication system between the customer and the organization in order to speed up reaction to a customer's request and thus shorten the response time.

Another method for formulating a strategy is known as SWOT — strengths, weaknesses, opportunites and threats. This covers both the analysis of the business environment and the internal resources. An analysis is made of all external factors to determine present and future opportunities and threats; these include such factors as new technology and new entrants into the industry. Then the organization's own resources are put under scrutiny to determine its own strengths and weaknesses in relation to the changes in the environment and competition. Any sound business strategy must build on the organization's resource strengths, remove resource weaknesses, mitigate external threats and take advantage of any opportunities which may present themselves.

A slightly different way to begin to formulate a strategy would be to use the strategic triangle — discussed in section 2.8 and illustrated in Figure 2.1. A detailed list of the information needed to make strategic decisions for each factor or player was given in that section. The interaction and possible future changes between the different factors (namely, the company, its customers and competitors and the economic and political environment surrounding it) should be considered and analyzed. This will lead to the identification of areas where the organization is not performing adequately, or may not in the future, and where potential for development is likely to lie. For instance, one important area for consideration might be the comparision between the organization and its competitors in order to determine the areas of special or distinctive competence which the organization has, or may have, which will make it stand out from its competitors. There will also be areas where competitors have distinctive competences and thus competitive advantage. The organization must form a strategy to mitigate these either by gaining these competences itself or by concentrating on and stressing other competences to its customers. This takes us back to the concept of value as perceived by the customer and to the value chain concept discussed in section 5.4. Distinctive competences can only be built along the value chain itself or along the value system within the industry. An example of the former might be a new production control and information system which permits the organization to meet customer requirements much faster than any competitor. McKesson's external links described in section 5.16. were an example of the latter.

There are many other methods that can be used and considerably more to determining and implementing a business strategy than can be mentioned in a page or so in a non-specialist book such as this one. Our aim has been to simply provide a guide which will assist in considering information systems management and in determining and implementing an information strategy. These are considered in detail in the next paragraph. Firstly, however, a word of warning. It is generally thought that most innovative and creative strategies emerge opportunistically rather than as an outcome of formal planning. Indeed, too much rigid planning can strangle imaginative thought. On the other hand, without a rigid framework too little attention may be given to the future. Achieving the correct balance is rather like walking a tight-rope.

11.6   The art of strategy formulation

Formulating a business strategy is not a science but rather, as the initial dictionary definition at the beginning of this chapter stated, an art. Rigid rules cannot be applied and the best strategy does not emerge from a mathematical or logical formula. A successful strategy instead depends on the correct reading of the signs on what the future holds, combining them in the correct way and thus producing a plan or direction for the future development of the organization. Portents of the future cannot be predicted with mathematical precision but nor are they obtuse indicators which are difficult to see. They should be visible to any competent manager who stops to look properly. John Argenti described looking for changes in the environment as being like looking for strategic elephants. This description is apt — future changes are often obvious, sometimes extremely obvious.

   The Japanese have a far better concept of strategy than do most westerners. Western organizations tend to go into too much detail or produce too rigid a strategic framework. Japanese organizations, on the other hand, usually produce what are called statements of 'strategic intent' which give the broad directional thrust for the future development of the organization. Middle and lower management then formulate substrategies within this framework.

11.7   From business strategy to information strategy

The model shown in Figure 11.1 of the elements in determining and implementing business strategy was two-dimensional. Imagine a model extended into the third dimension by the different subsystems or business activities of the organization. Some of these elements will almost totally overlap. All will be connected to a number of other elements but the linkage will be constantly changing in emphasis, thus creating a loosely connected globe whose form is ever changing. It might be likened to a chemical molecular structure. Taking a slice which represents the information part of this 'globe' would produce the model shown in Figure 11.2.

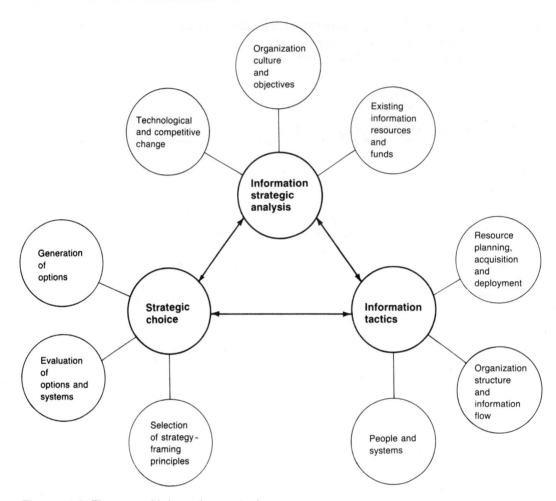

Figure 11.2 Elements of information strategic management.

The information strategy will derive directly from the business strategy which itself comprises the strategies of the other subsystems or business activities. For instance, part of the business strategy may be to improve customer relations, as in the illustrative example below. The way chosen to achieve this objective may be to set up a customer telephone information service line. A major part of the information strategy would, therefore, consist of formulating a plan to set up this service. The specific details of how this will be achieved is information technology tactics (discussed in the next chapter). In addition, the marketing strategy will change as a result of the new business strategy, and new marketing strategies and tactics will also have to be set.

Sometimes the strategy of one of the business activities will have a major influence on, and determine a major part of, the overall business strategy. This is particularly true of information systems — American Airlines (discussed in section 7.14) is a good example. Its initial communication system with travel agents developed, influenced the nature of the organization and led to the president's remark that he would rather be in the information business than the airline business.

11.8   Illustrative example: strategy formulation

In order to clarify the process by which a particular strategy is selected let us assume that a company has carried out a strategic analysis and one of the factors that it has discovered is that customers perceive that the company's goods are unreliable. There are many strategic choices open to the company to remedy this, but the three basic choices are:

- Improve reliability by better manufacturing methods or quality control.
- Provide better service or information to the customer about the product.
- Pick a new area in which to compete with competitors so that the customer does not perceive unreliability but perceives a superior product in some particular area. This could mean, for instance, redesigning the product or providing a faster service.

If the company feels that its products are no more unreliable than its competitors' but that the organization simply has an image problem, it will most likely choose the second option. Let us assume that this is so. The next step will be to decide on the precise method of achieving this. The company may decide to set up a telephone service and information centre, just as General Electric did some years ago (see section 8.15).

The next stage will be to work out a tactical plan for setting up the telephone centre. This will include planning such matters as where it should be located, what size it needs to be, what type of equipment is required and what qualifications and training staff will need.

11.9   The information strategy

Important though it is to consider the links between the subsystems or business activities when formulating the business strategy, the information strategy must also be considered on its own and in its own right. If this is not done there is a danger of overlooking the potential impact that new types of information system might have on the business. The information director should be permanently on the look-out for new techniques and advances in technology which could benefit the organization. Any changes or potential changes in the environment must be spotted so that the organization has time to act positively rather than reacting in haste at a later date. Any information or technological changes that competitors are making which may change the nature of the industry must also be spotted quickly so that the organization has plenty of time to react. One such may be, for instance, the formation of links by means of networks between a competitor and its suppliers or customers within the industry. The potential danger in this case is that if the organization does not respond by developing similar links it could find its position seriously undermined.

The existing information resources of the organization (its communication systems, computing equipment and staff skills) must be compared with those of competitors to determine their adequacy, potential for standardization and future development.

Martin suggests that there are three different aspects to strategic planning for information technology and systems:[6]

- **Strategic business planning**: this considers the implications of new technology on the future of the business.
- **Strategic information technology planning**: this is the evolution and development of the organization's information infrastructure.
- **Strategic data planning**: this involves creating stable **data models** which are *independent* of changes in technology.

This breakdown of strategic planning helps to emphasize the importance of separating the two activities of planning and maintaining good data models in the midst of the possible chaos created by constantly changing technology. The information requirements of managers may change quite rapidly but the data necessary to build them do not usually change and remain fairly stable over time. However, as organizations group and regroup both internally and externally, by forming value added partnerships, for instance, these data models must be maintained and improved.

11.10   An information strategy matrix

The strategic analysis of the information system will provide the basis for deciding on a future strategy. The initial step is to generate ideas and options. Most reasonably innovative organizations will have no difficulty in generating a number of options. The difficulty will be in the selection of the options to be adopted.

For those organizations which may need to be stimulated to generate ideas and which may need assistance in the evaluation and selection process, there are various formal approaches. One systematic approach for doing this is to use a matrix (shown in Figure 11.3) which is based to some extent on the well known Boston matrix. The idea is to consider each of the four categories to determine that satisfactory systems are being developed.

		High	Strategically important	Future potential
Future impact			45%	10%
		Low	Crucial today	Taken for granted
			30%	15%
			High	Low
			Input required	

Figure 11.3 The information strategy matrix.

Future potential

This box contains applications or systems which it is thought will, or may be, of importance in the future. At present they are not of importance or use to the organization but they have potential for future benefit. At this stage the plan should be to develop and test these systems on a small scale prior to possible major investment in future years. An example of this type of system would be the American Airlines's Sabre system when it was being developed during the 1950s and early 1960s. At this point the president had conceived the idea of a future information system which was not really technically possible at the time but appeared to have potential. By getting a foothold into a new technology which is thought will be of strategic importance in future years, any organization puts itself into a powerful position. The aim is to get several potential systems which will be tested quite quickly. Some will be rejected for one reason or another and, therefore, discarded, while others will be developed further. Potential systems which fall into this category will usually be initiated by individuals who have ideas or think they see business opportunities. These individuals may be computer or telecommunication experts but are more likely to be far-sighted managers from other disciplines who can see a potential benefit in one of their business areas.

Strategically important

This box contains those applications or systems in which a major investment of money or time is required *now* because they are believed to be critical in the achievement of a particular aspect of the *future* business strategy. One of the main aims of using the matrix will be to make sure that the company has identified the systems that are going to be strategically important so as to ensure that they are developed and in place by the time they are needed.

Crucial today

The applications or systems which the organization *currently* depends on for success are contained in this box. Investment in these systems will have been quite heavy in the past and they should now be generating major financial benefits. The pay-off may be a major saving in costs or, quite possibly, benefits which are more difficult to ascertain, but are nevertheless substantial, such as better decision making, greater sales volume or happier customers.

Taken for granted

This box contains the systems which were set up some time ago and have become part of the fabric of the organization. They are scarcely noticed and are taken for granted. In most organizations today the systems which fall into this category are likely to be transaction processing systems which process orders, issue invoices, etc. The organization's telephone system may also fall into this category. These systems are not noticed until they malfunction in some way. However, development and improvement of these systems is usually possible and should not be overlooked. Indeed, it may be possible to improve an old system so that it becomes strategically important for the future, thus reclassifying the system in the matrix. All systems should be maintained and improved over the years to avoid the crises caused by their breakdown or the need for replacement. Some of the older systems will not be required much longer as technology advances. For instance, EDI (electronic data interchange) will render order receiving systems and invoicing systems unnecessary, and automatic funds transfer will alter payment systems. This type of change must be allowed for in future planning.

The purpose of the matrix is to make the company aware of the different types of system and to ensure that it has systems which fit into every category. An organization which does not invest some money in the development of systems which may have potential will not remain in business in the long term. The organization which overlooks strategically important systems will not even be in business that long. A rough percentage breakdown of the funds which may be required for each category is also shown in Figure 11.3.

11.11 Education and culture

The organizational culture must be examined to ensure that the correct type of information strategy is developed. The information system together with the organization structure is part of the cultural web of the organization. It groups people together and gives some individuals more power than others. If a decentralized culture is required, the information system must be a decentralized one. If a central information system were to exist in an otherwise decentralized organization, conflict would always abound and the system would not be successful nor achieve all its aims.

A knowledge of technology is a very important aspect in the formation of an information strategy. Education about new technologies has been overlooked, especially for top management, and this has caused problems in the recent past. Information technology specialists have felt that they were not adequately involved in strategy formation and there has been a break-down in communication between the specialists and top management. Top managers themselves lacking the education, have not adequately considered the strategic implications of information provision because they are unaware of developments and of the potential of systems. What needs to be built into any information strategy is an education programme — education *not* training. Training, that is learning how to use particular pieces of equipment and different systems, is for technical people. Nowadays most equipment and systems are used by non-specialist staff and, therefore, they should be easy to use and not require a hefty manual to be read beforehand. Education, on the other hand, is vital, especially for top managers who must be shown and be aware of the potential of systems before their competitors show them. This is a broad brush and corporate-wide education and does not involve, for example, sitting managers in front of a PC and showing them how to use Lotus 123.

11.12 Cost–benefit analysis

Two crucial questions which management will usually ask when formulating an information strategy are:

How much should we be spending on information systems?
How do you assess the benefit of an information system?

The answer to the first question cannot be a specific sum. It will depend on the type of industry, the management style and the organization's particular circumstances. Different styles of management will require the flow of more or less information and the provision of that information in different ways. Different industries will need to spend more or less on information systems at different stages of their development. It was mentioned previously that British Airways is planning to spend 5 per cent of turnover on information systems. This is very high: most industries will spend far less, but an industry norm can be developed as a guide for management.

The second question is no easier to answer than the first. Before the final choice between different information options and strategies is made, there must be some attempt to quantify the cost and assess the benefit of each of them. Once the strategy to be followed has been agreed then the detailed selection of systems will involve a more detailed cost–benefit analysis. Any assessment of the cost and benefit of an information system is not at all easy. A recent survey of sixty UK companies found that 84 per cent of them had no satisfactory method of calculating the costs or benefits.

Too often a straight financial approach is made which may simply assess the cost saving from a reduction in clerical workers caused by installing the new system against the cost of purchasing and operating the new system. This type of financial analysis is usually based on discounted cash flow or return on investment, and often finds in favour of *not* installing any new technology because it fails to consider the main benefits of information systems, such as improved quality, improved customer relations and improved speed at meeting customer requirements. These benefits cannot easily be measured in financial terms and so are often ignored. Other benefits may not be properly envisaged at the time of implementation and, therefore, cannot be brought into the calculation. See, for instance, the American Airlines example in section 7.14. When American Airlines started upon its information system in the 1950s it could not possibly have foreseen where it would lead and how it would develop, or, for that matter, how much it would cost. If it had not been supported from the top of the organization it is unlikely that the system would ever have got off the ground because the measurable benefit would have been small in proportion to the early development costs.

However, the points made in the previous paragraph must not be taken to mean that no cost–benefit analysis should be undertaken. Sometimes managers have said that they have to take on trust that there will be a benefit — not every project does succeed and produce benefits: plenty fail and some failures are very costly. On other occasions managers say that if they do not get into a particular type of information technology they will lose out to their competitors. There must be some benefit that is measurable in this latter case — if they do not invest they will go out of business sooner or later.

The problems of justifying expenditure on new systems to the finance department are well illustrated by the following quotation in reply to just such a question concerning the installation of CIM (computer integrated manufacturing) by the chief executive officer of Allen–Bradley.

> But the old financial models have failed manufacturing companies. Return on investment, internal rate of return — such abstractions focus on the time value of money and give little consideration to the strategic opportunities and threats presented by technological advance. They make no sense when applied to manufacturing systems that aren't junked when the product lines are. Besides,

some of CIM's most valued benefits are simply not quantifiable. How do you put a price on corporate learning?

Anyway, the old investment models were developed to compare one project with another. They were not developed to aid strategic thinking. If I have five guys who are equally honest, and the revenue line is honest, and the cost line is honest, and the capital is honest — and I have to choose two projects out of five — then I just put all the data into the computer and out squirts the numbers that show which project to choose. Zap.

But what if the projects are not all of the same strategic importance? What if one project is crucial to the long-term qualifications of your personnel? We begin to get lazy about such hard decisions — 'risk averse', as the academics say.[7]

There are many, far too many tales of cost overruns on computer projects. It is not unusual over a period of years for costs to rise four-fold. See, for instance, the DSS database in section 9.11. If a project is scheduled to take ten years to become operative, as in the case of the DSS project, costs cannot possibly be estimated with any degree of accuracy and neither can the benefits. Cost overruns usually occur when the project takes considerably longer than the original plan because not all of the technical problems were originally envisaged. It is much better to test and develop the system on a small scale initially, as was suggested when testing new technology in the matrix. Alternatively, a new system can be introduced into small areas of the business on a step-by-step basis so that faults can be picked up and amended as the project develops. This allows for the possibility of shelving the project if costs start to escalate or it proves to be less effective than planned. This is much the best way to introduce systems and is happening more and more often as technology and times change, making possible the introduction of small discrete projects.

However, in some instances a decision has to be made about whether to invest in a large project. This was the case recently at AMR Corporation, of which American Airlines is a subsidiary. AMR is investing $150m in a project called InterAAct which will take about five years to complete. (See also section 12.6.) Max Hopper, a senior vice-president of American Airlines said that endorsing it was partly a matter of faith.[8] Studies were carried out on the work of three hundred employees and from this it was estimated that a 10 per cent return on investment would be achieved. However, as AMR has an investment hurdle rate of 15 per cent the project did not meet the normal financial criterion. The remaining 5 per cent is faith. It is faith that the 'soft' benefits which are so difficult to quantify, such as better customer service and better decision making, will provide at least a 5 per cent return. However, all of the funds are not being committed on the basis of an initial decision. The project is divided into stages and its impact and success will be judged at these stages over the five years. This is in case the 10 per cent 'hard' return on investment does not materialize — which is just as likely, if not more likely, than the non-materialization of the 'soft' returns.

The art of good strategic planning is, therefore, to subdivide the organization's requirements into small modular projects, each as autonomous as possible and yet within the overall plan. Each project should require the work of only a small team and take only a short time to complete. This approach will avoid the worst excesses of cost and time overruns that have troubled so many organizations in the past.

The decision to acquire and install a particular telecommunications or computing system is no different from any other type of investment decision. Most decisions tend both to be difficult to isolate and to result in some benefits which cannot easily be measured and are therefore termed 'soft'. For instance, BP (British Petroleum) recently spent £171m on redesigning and replacing its logo. It was a change which to many appeared almost imperceptible. The benefits from this kind of investment are impossible to measure and much more difficult to isolate than those that arise when assessing the average information system. Yet those who made the decision clearly felt that it would provide a good return and assist in achieving the company's new strategy in the coming years.

Generally, most cost–benefit assessments are made and approved centrally. A different approach to the problem of assessing cost–benefit is to leave the decision with the business unit which initiates the project and will become the main beneficiary. This is done by charging the cost of the project to the beneficiary rather than charging it to the organization as a whole. British Airways does this. Its purpose is to emphasize that information systems and technology are not so much a corporate facility but are part of a particular business strategy developed by a business unit. It also has the effect of placing the responsibility for the cost–benefit decision with the business unit managers and should, therefore, mean that both costs and benefits are estimated as realistically as possible. However, business units are not altruistic, and if the project will benefit other units this is unlikely to be taken into account unless the initiator can recoup some costs from the other units. There are also some investments, such as the provision of an organization-wide information infrastructure (discussed in section 12.6), which must be taken centrally if adequate facilities are to exist.

11.13 A strategic framework in which to make information decisions

The reader may have felt that the previous section on cost–benefit analysis could apply to tactical decisions as well as to strategic ones. The division between the two is not always easy to make and, in any case, tactical decisions do have a major impact on future strategy. The problem with any tactical decision is that it is made by an individual or a small number of managers and yet it has the potential to influence the whole of the organization's future strategy. For instance, the type of advertising campaign which is selected and run by the marketing department presents the organization and its products in a particular light. If a campaign is run which extols the 'cheap and cheerful' virtues of the organization's products, the top management cannot then very easily decide to follow a strategy of quality niche marketing.

The same comments apply with equal force to a tactical decision on information provision. If a manager buys a particular piece of equipment or installs a specific system, unless it can be instantly scrapped, all future equipment and systems which connect with it must be compatible both technically and conceptually. Thus a tactical decision made now may form future strategy; therefore it is important that tactical decisions are formulated carefully. It is vital that the person making the tactical decision has full knowledge of what the existing strategy is. Unfortunately this is not always the case; top managers tend to be secretive about their strategic plans for the organization. One possible reason for this is that if they do not disclose them to lower managers or other employees but instead keep them locked away, their competitors cannot discover them. This is dreadful. According to the dictionary definition quoted at the start of this chapter, strategy is the art of *directing* movements so as to secure the most advantageous position. It is impossible to direct movements if the direction, at least, is not disclosed to those who are supposed to move.

To make certain that the information strategy is known, a strategic framework should be set out within which all tactical decisions can be made. Thus all who make tactical decisions will be certain that they conform to and follow the direction of the overall strategy. The next chapter starts with further consideration of this topic.

NOTES

1. From R.I. Tricker, 'The management accountant as strategist', *Management Accounting*, Dec. 1989.
2. From *Cassell's English Dictionary*.
3. Report by McCallum Layton Associates.
4. James Quinn, *Strategies for Change: Logical incrementation* (Irwin, 1980).
5. Gerry Johnson and Kevan Scholes, *Exploring Corporate Strategy: Text and cases* (Prentice Hall International, 1989).
6. James Martin, *An Information Systems Manifesto* (Prentice Hall, Inc., 1985).
7. 'A CEO's commonsense of CIM: an interview with J. Tracy O'Rourke', *Harvard Business Review*, Jan./Feb. 1989.
8. Max Hopper, 'Rattling Sabre: new ways to compete on information', *Harvard Business Review*, May/June 1990.

FURTHER READING

Johnson, Gerry and Kevan Scholes, *Exploring Corporate Strategy: Text and cases* (Prentice Hall International, 1989). A comprehensive text which gives an up to date view of business strategy, together with many illustrative cases.

Remenyi, D.S.J., *Increasing Profits with Strategic Information Systems* (NCC, 1988).

EXERCISES

1. A large national bookshop/newsagent chain has been outperformed by a rival group in recent years. In order to improve the volume of sales, and thus to increase profit, top management is reconsidering its present strategy. The managers have some idea that an information system may be of use. Advise them as to the type(s) of information system that could help improve the company's performance stating why they could expect an improved performance from your chosen system(s).

2. What factors will an organization need to consider in developing its information strategy?

3. Imagine your university or college has unlimited funds to invest in information systems to aid students in their work. Outline what equipment, systems, applications, etc. you would recommend and what the expected benefits would be. Draw up a brief three year plan for implementation.

12 Information technology tactics

SCOPE AND CONTENTS

A: Tactical decisions. Firstly, tactical decisions are defined. The necessity for tactical decisions to be made within the framework of strategic decisions and how strategy should be communicated to those who make tactical decisions are outlined. The need for technical standards to guide decisions on acquisition of information equipment and software is examined. The change in the type of information decisions being made today is considered as a prelude to looking in detail at making decisions about the information infrastructure, the acquisition and restructuring of software and the purchase of equipment.

B: Implementing technology tactics. The purpose and need for a feasibility study is examined. The traditional life cycle methodology is compared with prototyping and both are examined in detail. The need for documentation and maintenance is outlined. Finally the importance of training and education is discussed.

A: TACTICAL DECISIONS

12.1 What are tactical decisions?

Tactics are the visible side of strategy. A tactical plan is a short-term plan which helps to realize a particular long-term strategy. In the previous chapter, information tactics were shown in Figure 11.2 to consist of three different elements. One of the three elements comprises analyzing and implementing any required changes in the information infrastructure and aligning it with the organization structure. Another comprises planning, acquiring and deploying resources. The final one is concerned with adapting systems and helping people to adjust to changes in policy. A more specific list of some of the more likely tactical decisions is as follows:

- Setting general technical standards for the communications and computer network.
- Shaping the information systems to the organization structure and improving the data and information flow.
- Deciding on the specific nature and structure of the network — that is, the information infrastructure.
- Deciding on the type of systems, equipment, and application packages to be acquired.
- Acquiring and deploying systems, equipment, and application packages.
- Restructuring and rejuvenating existing systems.
- Educating and training all levels of employees as follows:
  (a) In technology so that more advanced systems may be used.
  (b) In how to use the new information made available by more advanced systems.
  (c) In how to discover new uses for the information generated.

12.2   The need for a strategic framework within which tactical decisions are made

Too often top managers are ignorant of the techniques and technologies used in modern information systems. Similarly, technical and middle managers are unlikely to be fully aware of the strategy which top management is currently pursuing. This ignorance or lack of communication may create the types of problem described below.

It is difficult to design the majority of systems without a clear knowledge of the planned strategy for the whole organization. Without this knowledge the designer may consider options which are incompatible with the strategy set by top management. Alternatively, top managers may be continually requested for their views on proposed systems, thus wasting valuable executive time and causing delay. At worst, systems may be installed which have to be modified later when they prove to be incompatible with the organization's strategic aims. This will not only prove exceedingly costly but may create friction between managers.

The selection of the wrong type of information system can have other major implications. For instance, some systems, if selected and installed, will almost certainly restrict future changes in the organization's structure. This will make the divestment or acquisition of subsidiary companies difficult. Phillips Polygram's problems with acquisitions and information systems were discussed in section

8.2 and the problems which STC and ICL faced when trying to combine two quite different systems were discussed in section 4.9. Little can be done to make future acquisitions easier except to keep information systems as standard and as flexible as possible. If the possibility of a particular acquisition is known or considered some years ahead, as it sometimes is, then obviously the system should be designed, if possible, with this in mind.

The possibility of divestment of parts of the organization is much easier to cope with. Information systems should not be set up in such a way that one company or business unit within the group becomes vital to the information chain because that unit cannot then be sold without much upheaval to the whole organization. Dependence may occur, for instance, if databases are built up on a cross-unit basis with one company or unit playing a pivotal role in processing and combining data. It is obviously best to have either a central database within the core business, a business which will never be disposed of, or to have a distributed system such that no one unit is crucial.

To avoid these problems it is necessary that the strategy formulated by top or central management be communicated to those making tactical decisions. This should be done by the formulation of a strategic framework within which tactical decisions can be made. This strategic framework should then be clearly communicated to all concerned.

12.3   Strategic 'information principles'

The strategic framework will take the form of guidelines, or 'information principles' as they have been named by Davenport *et al.*, which will govern the formulation of tactical plans.[1] The guidelines or principles aim to bridge the communication gap between top management and technical or middle management, thus ensuring that the business strategy and the information strategy guide all tactical plans and decisions.

The information principles should be simple statements of the organization's basic beliefs about how it wishes its information systems to develop in the long term. For instance, the statement that, 'all systems will be designed in such a way that the closure of any location will not affect their effectiveness' creates a principle to follow. If followed, it would allow a site or business unit to be closed or sold without major disruption to the rest of the organization's information system. It may, however, be considered rather a foolhardy statement and might lead to speculation by employees as to which business unit will be the first to go, on the basis that there is rarely smoke without a fire! So a statement saying that, 'all business unit systems must be capable of communicating with those in other units and yet be capable of standing alone', may prove to be more politic. It also has the benefit of expressing the view in terms that technical managers will instantly understand.

Suppose, for example, that the management of a bank has identified one of its critical success factors to be the ability to respond at any time to a customer request. The information strategy to achieve this might give rise to the principle that 'sufficient duplication of equipment should exist to allow customer records to be always on-line'. A manufacturing company may have identified efficient control of production as a critical success factor. This could lead to the principle that, 'production control software will be constantly monitored, reviewed and updated'. Alternatively, the managers of a manufacturing company may wish to move towards forming strong relationships with suppliers for JIT, design or supply reasons. At this stage, they may simply state the principle that, 'all data on products and stock requirements should be made available via a single system'. This will ensure that when the time comes to connect with suppliers the information system is in a suitable form.

12.4 Setting technical standards

At a lower organizational level, restructuring or amalgamating departments or divisions will also be difficult if their systems and equipment are incompatible. Complete freedom cannot be given to departments or divisions to decide upon the design and type of their information systems and associated equipment if incompatibility is to be avoided. Nevertheless, as much freedom as possible in selection must be given in order that the systems are fully used and appreciated. Some overall guidelines and standards have to be laid down in order to establish an information network that is properly integrated and, therefore, really meets organization-wide needs. This may, unfortunately, result in rules stating that all equipment must be purchased from a particular manufacturer or be totally compatible with a particular manufacturer's equipment. It would be preferable for all concerned to be able to state that, 'any system using Unix or conforming to OSI is acceptable', but this is not practical at present. However, within a few years this problem should have largely disappeared as equipment which can operate with a variety of operating systems is introduced.

In the mean time, to avoid incompatible systems preventing the amalgamation of departments or divisions, the following types of standard may be set:

- All information systems applications will use equipment supplied by . . . .
- Systems design will adhere to the standards laid down by . . . .
- The same software will be used for all accounting or order-processing systems throughout the company.

Detailed standards should never be set just for the sake of doing so; there must be a compelling reason to impose them. Many applications and systems today are instigated by the user departments and the freedom to choose the system that suits the individuals and their circumstances is of paramount importance. It is often the user departments that generate ideas for new information and systems, and anything which restricts this flow of innovation must be avoided. If a clash does arise over technical specifications, it may be found on close examination to have nothing to do with technical standards but much more to do with power struggles within the organization. It is most important when planning the infrastructure of the information system that it is done to allow as much freedom as possible locally with middle management, and that where standards are imposed their reasons should be made clear to all.

12.5 The changing nature of systems planning

A major change is taking place in the type of information system being installed as compared with those of just a few years ago. This, in turn, affects the type and style of tactical planning. Traditionally, that is for the past thirty years, information provision was synonymous with large scale systems which were designed in-house. This is hardly the case today and certainly will not be in the future. Standardization, as it arrives, will allow almost all hardware and software to be purchased rather than being created in-house. The development of large-scale, in-house systems is becoming too expensive. They are also inflexible and likely to be less reliable than purchased ones. Instead, large projects should be broken down into small, flexible, semi-independent units which can be installed quickly and updated or changed as required. The importance of this approach was also mentioned when considering cost—benefit analysis in the previous chapter.

The change to purchasing systems has major implications for tactical planning. The planning and updating of the organization's infrastructure will become the most important consideration. As most systems and applications will be purchased, little in-house systems design will be required. This means that the full traditional 'systems life cycle' (discussed in general terms later in this chapter) will no longer be relevant; in any case, it has been found wanting in the past. The decision to acquire and install a particular telecommunication or computing system is no different from any other type of investment decision that an organization may face. Most decisions tend to be very difficult to consider in isolation and usually result in some benefits which cannot easily be measured and are therefore termed 'soft'.

Tactical decisions involve selecting the correct infrastructure, equipment and software. These are considered below.

12.6 The infrastructure

The information network or infrastructure is the central nervous system of the organization. Virtually all communication passes through it in one form or another.

Therefore, the primary plans or decisions for the provision of information must concern the infrastructure. The infrastructure consists of a number of hierarchical layers and must be closely allied to the organization structure. It may even change an organization's structure. This is because new systems and networks developed from new technology make relationships possible within the organization which were not so previously. Thus the chain of events may be that shown in Figure 12.1.

STRATEGY ➡️ INFORMATION INFRASTRUCTURE ➡️ ORGANIZATION STRUCTURE

Figure 12.1 The influence of the information infrastructure.

Decisions about the type of infrastructure to employ and the number of hierarchical layers are necessarily long-term in nature and are strategic information decisions. More detailed decisions on the technical side are tactical ones, even though on occasions they may have long-term implications. The following illustration will help to clarify this.

Nordisk SparData is a joint Scandinavian banking group.[2] The banks arrived at the following business strategy for the 1990s:

- To reduce transaction costs by increasing automation and self-service.
- To offer new services.
- To improve the quality of service.
- To grow in size.
- To offer a twenty-four hour service.
- To segment their markets differently.

In order to achieve this, a new infrastructure had to be designed. The information strategy they decided on split the overall system into four levels: central, regional, branch and workstation. The information infrastructure was also split into four: front-end (the connections with the outside world), application front-end (which performs the initial banking functions), application back-end (does all complicated processing), and database interface.

Having devised this strategy the tactical decisions — such as what type of equipment or system to provide — must be made. Let us consider some of the decisions relating to the front-end which Nordisk may have faced:

- What type of ATM (automatic teller machines) to employ?
- How many ATMs to install and where they should be situated?
- What type of customer identification should be required?
- What type and number of services should the customer be able to use from the ATM?

Planning the infrastructure of an organization's information system is becoming more and more important. As standards and open systems gradually become a reality organizations are switching away from a collection of specific applications which do not cohere and therefore do not form a rational organization-wide system. What organizations require instead are information infrastructures, independent of proprietary technology, which will cope with future, and as yet unspecified, demands. This may sound impossible to achieve, and there are dangers. The main one is that the cost of providing a flexible, all-encompassing system will be very high and in reality the chosen structure may prove to be totally wrong and have to be replaced fairly quickly.

AMR Corp., of which American Airlines is a part, started a major investment programme in 1987 to create just such a flexible infrastructure.[3] (See also section 11.12.) The project is called InterAAct and will take some years to complete. It will eventually support a vast number of systems and applications — many of which are as yet unknown, and may possibly not even have been invented yet. Its aim is to help people to do their jobs better, more quickly and creatively, by removing barriers and therefore allowing more time to be spent on productive work. It will connect every employee to all other employees and provide every type of communication via an easy-to-use terminal. In addition to all of this, or because of it, the aim is that the infrastructure generates funds rather than consuming them.

American Airlines has been very successful with information systems in the past and it will be interesting to see how successful this large scale project will prove. It is probably safe to assume that it will not generate as much in the way of funds as SABRE (see 7.14), but who knows, it could lead to a new business activity!

12.7 Systems: acquisition of new software

Ideally, software should be capable of operating on any make and type of computer equipment, but this is not always the case. The organization will find itself vulnerable if, by purchasing one system, it ties itself to one supplier for all its future needs. The supplier may make changes, such as increasing maintenance charges, which the organization is forced to pay. If the supplier is taken over or goes out of business, the organization may well find that the maintenance of equipment becomes a problem which may only be solved by a third party at a greater cost. Also, being reliant on one supplier removes the ability to migrate to more advanced equipment developed by other companies.

Originally, all commercial computerized information systems were for transaction processing, in particular accounting, payroll and stock control. Every application was developed from scratch by the user organization, either by employing its own staff or contractors. During the early 1970s there was a large increase in the number of computer installations. It was obvious that many of these installations were virtually identical. This led to the creation of a new market: off-the-shelf programs. This in turn reduced the cost of systems and as a result the market continued to grow rapidly as did the variety of packages available.

Before an organization spends time and money developing its software in-house it is wise to consider the suitability of off-the-shelf packages. It may well be necessary to call in professional help, although this involves the risk of bias as the consultant may specialize in a limited number of systems or vendors. Once possible suppliers have been found, it may prove possible to contact existing users for their view of the effectiveness of the software, or to test it using the organization's own data. On the other hand, if a suitable package does not exist, the organization will have to develop its own programs. Having done this it may consider that a market exists for the application and either sell it itself or license it to a specialist software supplier. (See the American Airlines case in section 7.14.)

It is probably true to say that nowadays 90 per cent of all software should be bought rather than be developed in-house. The benefits of bought software are:

- It is invariably quicker and cheaper than software developed in-house. There is also no danger of the major time and cost overruns which often occur with in-house projects.
- It is generally more reliable as it will have been tried and tested on many potential users and any initial faults will have been ironed out.
- It is often more user-friendly, both as regards the manuals and screen presentations. This is because a particular skill and much time are needed to produce clear manuals and easily understandable screens for the user. (This is a subject in its own right and some educational establishments offer postgraduate diplomas in interface design.)

Many software packages on the market now can be tailored to the users' needs. The packages contain a number of options which can be switched on or off by the purchaser thus giving a degree of customization. This trend looks set to continue. However, there are two dangers. One is that, with a multitude of options the purchaser will not know precisely what is being bought and what the software is capable of doing. The second is that the initial adaptations of the system could become very complicated, as could the accompanying manual.

12.8   Systems: restructuring old software

Although many systems are bought off-the-shelf today, there are still a large number of systems in use which were originally developed in-house. Too often these systems are taken for granted. (See Figure 11.3 in the previous chapter which illustrated the four different types of information system.) Once taken for granted there is the danger that the system will not be maintained and updated properly. Thus it may become inefficient and unamenable to major change. Sometimes, of course, old information systems should be left to 'die' and replaced by different and superior new ones. On other occasions it is possible to restructure or rejuvenate the existing software. Software products are available which can help to correct the above problems. For instance it is possible to run a restructuring program which will:

1. Evaluate the present structure: that is trace the control logic.
2. Check that the existing program is working properly: this is obviously necessary before further steps are taken.

3. Restructure the program's code following structured programming concepts. The logic is not changed. Code which is no longer used is removed, loops are removed where possible, etc.
4. Reformat the listing of the code so that technicians can understand it.
5. Compare the new version with the original to check that the result or output is the same.

Rejuvenating a system may mean adding new equipment as well as updating and improving the software. For instance, an old database could be given on-line query facilities or the data could be organized so that they are capable of being used in different ways. Sometimes the change can be so dramatic that the updated system becomes of strategic importance to the future of the business. For instance, a data collection system might be changed into a full information system showing such things as items ordered, stock held and stock used in manufacturing.

12.9 Systems: equipment

One of the major decisions to be made when acquiring equipment is whether to purchase or lease it. The choice will depend on the availability of finance and whether the equipment is to be regularly replaced. If it is planned to replace it regularly, as better products become available, it will probably be advisable to lease rather than buy. If this is done it is wise not to enter into a long-term agreement which may incur penalty payments if the equipment is returned before the expiry of the lease. This is for two reasons. Firstly, because technology is developing at such a speed it may be impossible to predict the equipment that the organization will require for more than a couple of years ahead. Secondly, small businesses may be tempted to lease in order to be able to afford the equipment, but the survival of small businesses is somewhat precarious and their fortunes can easily change within a year. If the business is not a limited company the last thing that the owners will want on top of winding up an ailing business is a hefty penalty payment for terminating the lease of equipment early.

Any piece of equipment which is installed must be reliable, foolproof and robust. If the equipment lets the user down there is a danger that it will not be used at all, and it certainly will not be used as frequently as it should. To guarantee frequent use the equipment must also be user-friendly, that is to say that it must be easy, comfortable and quick to use. Many PCs in the early days had their 'on' and 'off' buttons hidden away at the back of the machine. This was done so as to prevent someone accidently turning off the machine while using it and thereby losing hours of work. A switch at the back forced users to grope over the computer in order to switch it on or off, getting their hands mixed up with the wiring and accumulated dirt in the process. This was just poor design — a better switch was required rather than hiding it.

Keyboards should always be tested by those who will use them. Typists who have used electric typewriters have been used to a keyboard with a light touch.

If the typist switches to a heavy computer keyboard regularly for several years the result may be a permanent loss of feeling in the fingers. The consequence of this could be the organization being sued for compensation or prosecuted under the Health and Safety at Work Act 1974. Another keyboard-related illness is tenosynovitis which is a permanent wrist injury caused by work involving extremely rapid wrist movements such as high-speed typing. It is a prescribed industrial disease which attracts compensatory state benefit in the UK. In March 1990, three Inland Revenue data processing clerks were awarded £107,500 between them for traumatic and extremely painful inflammation of the wrists. They had been loading tax details into the Inland Revenue's system and this entailed entering up to fifteen thousand characters per hour. There is also concern about emissions from screens and some colours are supposedly easier on the eye than others. Shields can be bought and attached to most screens if this is a problem. Wise purchasing should avoid most injuries and sickness. Some organizations are changing their old office equipment and work practices to alleviate these types of problem. In any case, it is exceedingly unwise to expect employees to use a keyboard or look at a computer screen all day long. Staff absenteeism and turnover will increase and so will inaccuracies in the data entered.

The problems of connecting different manufacturers' equipment, or even connecting different systems made by the same manufacturer, have been mentioned in earlier chapters. These must be borne in mind when purchasing equipment. It is also important to purchase equipment that has adequate spare capacity as it invariably seems to be the case that more capacity than was originally anticipated is required after the system has been in use for a year or so. On the other hand, the organization should avoid being persuaded by a keen salesperson to buy a more advanced system than required at present on the grounds that it will be needed in, say, two years' time. In two years' time systems will have improved and the advanced system of today may well have been superseded. *Flexibility* is the keyword in any purchase.

The first part of this chapter has explored the nature and type of tactical decisions relating to information systems. The next part will deal with the different methodologies available which provide a formal framework within which tactical decisions may be made and implemented.

B: IMPLEMENTING TECHNOLOGY TACTICS

12.10 Feasibility study

Tactical decisions are initiated in one of two ways. The first is for a functional manager to request a system to solve a particular problem or remove a bottleneck. Alternatively, tactical decisions may flow from the formulation of a particular strategy such as, 'we must improve our customer response time'. After consideration of how to achieve this strategy, one or two options will appear to be suitable for closer examination. One may be to speed up the flow of information at the ordering stage, another may be to speed up the production process. One option will be picked as seeming to be the best at this stage, probably because it is more in keeping with the aims of the organization. This option will then be examined in more depth and consideration will be given to the type of system required in order to put it into practice.

The proposed option must be fully considered to make sure that it will provide the most suitable answer to the problem. If the option involves the acquisition of a new information system, and that system contains new technology or ideas, it will be necessary to carry out a feasibility study first.

A feasibility study should be carried out by a small team or committee in as short a time as possible but it should not take longer than a couple of months. The team should consist of a chairman, a technical expert, a financial expert if major expenditure is likely to be involved and the functional manager who initiated the proposal and who will be mainly involved with the system. The topics which must be considered by the group include:

- An analysis of the problem to make sure that the suggested proposal will solve it.
- Whether the necessary technology is currently available.
- The reliability or otherwise of any new technology.
- How long it will take for the system to become operational.
- The likely cost of the whole system including staff training and its running and maintenance costs.
- Whether the skills and the employees are available or can be made available to operate the system.
- Any likely adverse reaction by employees, trade unions or staff associations.
- Whether it is possible to purchase all or part of the system: for example using a third party EDI network rather than developing one in-house.
- An assessment of the expected benefits of the system.

This is only a feasibility study and so the findings will not be precise. Its purpose is to decide whether to take the project further and, if so, how to proceed.

12.11 Life cycle versus prototyping

It is not our intention in this book to go into detail on how a computer system is designed. That is a matter for specialists. In any case a vast weight of literature has been written on this subject. A great number of methodologies and approaches are available. There are, however, two basic approaches. The first is to use a methodology based on the traditional life cycle model, and the other is to use an iterative process known as 'prototyping'. Each is appropriate in particular circumstances although attempts are sometimes made to combine the two. The traditional life cycle model was developed in the 1960s and is based on the use of **3GLs (third generation languages)**. It was useful for developing the data processing systems of the early 1970s but is less successful in meeting current needs. The development of **4GLs** (fourth generation languages) in the early 1980s has made the alternative of prototyping possible. The prototyping approach attempts to replace the life cycle approach with a paradigm that responds well to complexity and uncertainty.

The traditional process requires a full analysis prior to designing the system and the whole process can take years to complete if the system is a complicated or large one. (See the example of the DSS system in section 9.11.) Rockart and Crescenzi give a vivid portrayal of this in the installation of a system in the early 1980s for Southwestern Ohio Steel.[4] The company wished to review and improve its data processing system to enable it to cope with rapid growth and JIT principles. The company had approached its accountancy firm and after an initial study the firm proposed a solution which would cost $2.4m and take four or more years to complete. This was rejected on the grounds of its high cost, risk and the time required. The steel company then approached Index Group, a consultancy firm, and a three-phase plan or methodology which would lead to a new system was proposed. This would cost much less and be completed within a year. This proposal was accepted and the resulting system proved a success and met the requirements. The three phases were:

1. **Linking the information system to the needs of management by using critical success factors**. This was done by holding two workshops for the management. The forty critical success factors which arose from the first workshop were whittled down to just four, the four that were of paramount importance to the system.
2. **Creating a priority base for developing individual systems**. In this case three new systems were required: a purchasing and stock system, a marketing system and a production scheduling system. The technique used at this stage was the development of decision scenarios. This is not discussed further in this book but it is a technique which helps managers to obtain an insight into what a new information system could achieve for them.
3. **Creating prototype systems**. This has become such a well accepted technique that it is discussed in detail below.

12.12 Prototyping

A software prototype is a first attempt at building a system. It is built using either a 4GL or an applications generator tool. A real system is built which can be tried by the user and modified as required. It may not be a full system; for instance, it may cover only 15 per cent to 20 per cent of all items of data or perform just a few functions. The prototype should be capable of being developed within, say, two months. It should then be used and tested for a similar period before being redesigned, probably quite significantly. The next version may be a full or fuller system and will probably be used for, say, six months before being modified again and the final system produced. The advantages of prototyping are:

- A system of some sort is put in place almost immediately, whereas with the traditional life cycle model it may take years before the system becomes operational.
- The users play an active role in developing the system and, therefore, it should eventually perform exactly as required. This is in contrast to the traditional method where after initial interviews with users the whole system is designed by technical computer employees. The result of using the latter method is that the users of the system are rarely 100 per cent satisfied. This is usually because of communication difficulties and misunderstandings between two quite different types of people.
- Because it is quicker, it is normally cheaper and it will improve the productivity of the technical staff.
- It requires less technical skill to create as 4GLs are easier to learn and use than 3GLs.
- The resulting systems tend to require less maintenance. In any case the skills for maintaining and adapting 3GL systems may not be available in the future as more computer staff learn 4GLs.

Nevertheless, despite the formidable list of advantages of 4GL systems, some systems are still written in 3GLs. Why? It is partly due to tradition within the computer department. If an employee invests time in acquiring a particular skill or learning a particular system he or she is usually loath to change to another. This type of reaction can be seen in practice in the simple spreadsheet. There has been an add-on, called Hal, available for Lotus 123 for many years. It turns all commands into English and incorporates other beneficial features such as an 'undo' button, a recall of the previous command and an audit trail. However, those who have learnt the traditional menu-driven system are loath to change because they feel comfortable with their present system and see only the few disadvantages of the new system instead of the many advantages. Change of any kind presents problems and will only be undertaken if the individual is fully convinced of the advantages.

Some say that 4GLs do not produce such neat compact commands and solutions, but what is this in comparison with 'customer' satisfaction? Some argue that 4GLs are not as flexible as the traditional 3GLs and may not be specialized enough for some projects. They are also less efficient in their use of processing time and this increases cost and the required capacity of equipment. As the cost of equipment decreases over time and capacity increases this is less likely to be a problem. It seems probable, therefore, that within a few years prototyping and 4GLs will have almost entirely taken over since the ability of a system to meet the needs of the customer, the user, and to fulfil its strategic role must be paramount. If it is still necessary to use 3GLs, for instance in a large transaction processing application, a system may be built using prototyping in a 4GL. When it has proved to work and to fulfil user requirements it can then be rewritten in a 3GL.

12.13 Life cycle methodology: analysis

The life cycle methodology is a generic one and a host of specific methodologies exist, some of which are more detailed and rigid than others. A step-by-step list of all the activities that may be included in the life cycle methodology is given below. Many of the specific methodologies, however, cover only part of the total life cycle.

- Feasibility study.
- Full analysis leading to a system specification.
- Design and documentation.
- Installation.
- Testing.
- 'Going live' — operating the system.
- Evaluation.
- Maintaining and updating the system.

Two of the better known methodologies are SSADM and information engineering. SSADM (structured systems analysis and design method) is an important methodology in the UK because it was developed by the government's computer agency and is mandatory for civil service systems development. Information engineering is more widely used, particularly in the USA, and is less rigid than SSADM as it is a framework only which allows techniques to change over time. The better methodologies start at the very beginning of the cycle — at the point of forming the information strategy. One of their main benefits (and one reason why SSADM was developed) is that they help to overcome the problems of frequent staff changes. New staff can easily take over if a well-known methodology is used. Documentation is also good and the programs developed are thus easy to maintain. It is beyond the scope of this book to consider the methodologies in detail but they all attempt to cover most of the life cycle which is outlined in general terms in the following paragraphs.

A full analysis is undertaken following the feasibility study discussed in section 12.10. It covers the same areas in more detail, and in addition includes a full analysis of the information required in order that a system specification can be produced. All users will have to be involved and their views sought on what information they specifically require, how often they need it and in what form. It is vital that all the people who are going to use the system are brought in at this stage to specify exactly what they require. If they are not consulted and, as a result, the system lacks some feature or is not particularly user-friendly in their eyes, it will not be taken up with enthusiasm and as a result is unlikely to be used to its full potential. There is no doubt that this is an absolutely vital stage in the development of the system. Finkelstein uses a survey by De Marco to suggest that 56 per cent of all program errors occur in the design stage, and that because of their nature these errors take 82 per cent of computer staff effort to correct.[5]

In the past many of the errors introduced at this stage have been due to misunderstandings or misinterpretations. Functional managers and computer staff are quite different types of people and often communication between them is difficult. This is further exacerbated by the former speaking the language of management and the latter speaking computer jargon. In recent years various attempts have been made to find a common communication medium. One such is data modelling; this is part of the information engineering methodology although it can be used with others.

Wherever possible, the overall project should be broken down into a series of stages or steps and a timetable drawn up for the completion of each stage. Funds should be specifically appropriated to the different stages. The introduction of an information system on a step-by-step basis helps to control costs and keep the overall project running to schedule. It is also much easier for the employees to cope with the installation as it results in less of a cultural shock.

If the feasibility and full analysis stages take too long, either the information system will be out of date before it is installed or its competitive advantage will have been vitiated.

12.14 Life cycle methodology: design and documentation

The specification which has been developed at the full analysis stage will next be turned into a detailed technical design. Then the equipment will be ordered and, possibly, the software. Alternatively, the computer programs will be written in-house. With most systems it is wise to involve the internal audit department in the design so that the resulting information system is acceptable to both internal and external auditors.

There are two different types of documentation required. The first is a fully written description of the system by its designers and the second is a manual of instruction for users. Good documentation is vital for any information system. Up to date documentation and printouts of the latest programs are necessary to maintain and modify the system. Operating instructions and manuals which are well written and easy to use go a long way to making a system effective. One of the most common complaints of users is the poor quality of the operating instructions and manuals: they are frequently incomplete, badly referenced and written in jargon. Furthermore, they are often written on the assumption that the reader is computer literate, when the opposite is usually the case. One of the most important features of good systems documentation is that it is regularly updated and not forgotten after its initial preparation. Nothing is more frustrating than trying to sort out a system fault with outdated documentation.

12.15   Life cycle methodology: installation and testing

If the installation is handled badly the information system may be perceived as a failure by users even though the orginal design was adequate. Disruption to the normal routine must be minimized and the whole programme of installation should take place according to a well drawn up schedule. The technique of critical path analysis will probably be required to plan the installation of a large project.

Apart from physically siting the equipment, installation of a system also involves generating data files and testing the system. The existing information held on record has to be put into the new system and this means creating new data files. If the previous system was a manual one, this will involve creating files from scratch; if not, the files from the old computerized system will have to be processed and made suitable for the new one.

There are two main objectives when testing an information system. The first is to check that all procedures, equipment and software are performing to their specifications, and the second is to check the reliability of the system and of the information it generates. Where practical, comprehensive real data should be used for testing and any simulations should be as realistic as possible. Users must be involved in devising tests and in monitoring their results because they will have a clearer idea of the operations than will technical staff. The draft manuals should also be consumer tested. User involvement at this stage should also increase confidence in the system when it finally goes live — assuming that not too many errors are found.

Only when everyone is satisfied with the reliability of the system should it be put into use. This is vital because once the users have found that a system is unreliable or does not meet their specific needs, all confidence and enthusiasm for it will evaporate. This was nearly the case with DEC's expert system for its sales staff (see section 10.11) and, unfortunately, happens far too often in practice.

12.16   Going live

A smooth change-over to the new system is essential, and much thought should be given to how it should be organized. The risk of being without any information system at some point during the transfer, and the ensuing damage that may occur, has to be considered in reaching a decision on how the change-over should take place. There are three ways of conducting the switch:

- **Instant**: closing down the existing system and switching the complete operation instantly to the new system. If anything goes wrong there will be no system at all in operation until the problem with the new one has been put right.
- **Phased**: step-by-step introduction. This option is not possible with some types of system. Nevertheless it is probably the most desirable method and should be used wherever possible.
- **Parallel running**: running both systems simultaneously for a period. This was the traditional method when transferring from manual to computer systems. The old and new information systems were run in tandem for two or three months to make absolutely sure that nothing was wrong. Running both systems is costly and staff do not become fully committed to the new system until the one they are used to is no longer in operation. Thus the shorter the period of parallel running the better. As projects tend to be broken down and introduced step-by-step more frequently nowadays, this type of testing is becoming either unnecessary or can be done in a much shorter period.

12.17   Evaluating the system

Once the information system has been fully operational for some months its performance should be measured against the original objectives. This evaluation of information systems is in principle no different from the evaluation of any other type of project, but such evaluations rarely take place. Criteria for assessment might include response speed, throughput capacity, ease of use, effects on staffing and productivity, and whether predicted benefits have been realized. The time taken to become operational should be compared with the estimates made at the specification stage. This should also be done for the costs incurred and resources used.

The gains from carrying out an evaluation of the information system are two-fold. Firstly, if staff are aware that an evaluation will take place they are more likely to produce accurate estimates of the costs, benefits and time involved. However, there is little evidence in practice that managers underestimate costs in order to get a project accepted. The second benefit of carrying out the evaluation, or post mortem, is so that the organization can plan similar installations more efficiently in the future.

12.18   Maintaining and updating

The maintenance of a system should start from day one of its operation and carry on throughout its life. Maintenance involves correcting faults, regularly checking equipment and software to prevent faults occurring, and keeping the system up to date. The latter may include asking the following questions:

- Have screen response times deteriorated due to an increased volume of transactions?
- Is reliability affected by increased throughput?
- Are proposed modifications to the system likely to cause problems?
- Have changes taken place in any other systems which may be incorporated or linked with this one — thus improving or extending it?
- Has any change in technology occurred since installation which could be incorporated to improve the system?

Today, in a typical company about 80 per cent of the computer staff's time is spent maintaining current systems and only 20 per cent in developing new ones. Many see this as unsatisfactory. It is only so if the old systems need constant attention to correct faults that arise. If the maintenance involves updating and improving the existing systems in line with new ideas and technology the 80:20 ratio may well be acceptable. But if too much time is spent in maintaining ageing systems, with the consequence that much needed new ones are not developed, then this is highly undesirable.

12.19   Training

The cost of training is often underestimated at the planning stage. This tends to happen because top management lack knowledge of the technology involved and, therefore, underestimate the staff training required. Similarly, functional managers probably underestimate the cost because they have a vested interest in getting the project accepted. Technical staff in turn also underestimate training costs because being experts in the field they do not perceive the needs and difficulties of new users. Normally the best person to do the training is the individual's immediate superior as he or she will know best how long is required and the approach to take when instructing a particular individual.

Training cannot be divorced from changing people's attitudes. The goal should be that not only are staff able to operate or use the new system but they are also *willing* to use it effectively. The easiest way to make staff willing is to involve them from the start in the development of the system so that they help to create it and therefore look upon it as their 'baby'.

In the future, training in this area will become less important as staff become more used to the technology and as computer systems become easier to use. At present there are some staff who have no experience of computer systems and as a consequence need a considerable amount not only of training but also of familiarization with the concept of the new system so that they can use it to its full potential. Education should be a continuous process. It does not only involve technical staff who are capable of teaching keyboard skills, workshops and discussion groups are required for all levels of employees so that both they and the systems develop as the company changes. The information systems department can help to organize these sessions, but their success will depend on the involvement and enthusiasm of functional managers and employees.

12.20 Illustrative case: devising systems for the Community Charge

There are often problems in producing and designing information systems, especially if the systems are large. The introduction of the Community Charge in England and Wales in 1990 provided a clear example of this. The Community Charge is a tax levied by the local authority on all people over the age of eighteen who live within the local authority area. It replaced a tax on householders based on the rateable value of houses. The computer systems required to cope with this change were specified in advance and were developed using the traditional life cycle approach.

During the first year of the new tax many local authorities had considerable difficulties with their new computer systems. Many of the new systems had been delivered late and most of them contained bugs. This delayed sending out bills and reminders, and made it impossible in many cases to keep track of people living in the area. Recovery procedures against defaulters could not be undertaken because the local authorities could not be absolutely sure of the accuracy of their systems. The result of this confusion has been an increase in the size of the Community Charge per person and, in some extreme cases, staff have had to give up using the computerized systems and do the job manually.

What caused these problems? The main cause appears to have been that contracts with companies for the supply and service of the computer systems were entered into during 1988 when the scope of the Community Charge tax system was still imprecise. At that time, the scale of the system was not expected to be as large as it subsequently proved to be. As a result some of the smaller companies found that they could not cope with the real scale of the system required. One of the main problems was caused by the introduction of 'transitional relief' a year after the initial specifications. This required the development of complex mathematical programs. Changes in allowances and rate capping further complicated the requirements. There have been, for example, difficulties linking the Community Charge systems into other systems such as housing benefit so as to ascertain allowances. Rate capping (i.e. the government imposing a limit on the size of the bills after the local authority had set their tax level) also caused problems. This was because some systems were designed so that they could not re-invoice until the whole process of collecting the bill had been completed for the year. In these cases the software had to be substantially rewritten.

> In summary, the main cause of the problems was that the specification changed during the development of the computer systems. It is easy to say that all requirements should have been specified beforehand (this would obviously have suited the companies providing the computer systems). However, in virtually all circumstances requirements change over time and new systems must be capable of being amended both during the development phases and afterwards when the systems are operational.

NOTES

1. Thomas H. Davenport, Michael Hammer and Tauno J. Metsisto, 'How executives can shape their company's information systems', *Harvard Business Review*, Mar./Apr. 1989.
2. Barbara McNurlin and Ralph Sprague, *Information Systems Management in Practice* (Prentice Hall, 1989).
3. Max Hopper, 'Rattling Sabre: new ways to compete on information', *Harvard Business Review*, May/June 1990.
4. J.F. Rockart and A.D. Crescenzi, 'A process for the rapid development of systems in support of management decision making', *Sloane Report*, June 1983.
5. Clive Finkelstein, *An Introduction to Information Engineering* (Addison-Wesley, 1989).

FURTHER READING

Finkelstein, Clive, *An introduction to Information Engineering* (Addison-Wesley, 1989).

EXERCISES

1. A company has decided to create a marketing database. List the different strategic and tactical decisions that it will need to make prior to installation.

2. List the strategic 'information principles' or guidelines that an organization you are familiar with might set down to govern the formulation of tactical plans. Give reasons for the inclusion of each principle on your list.

3. An educational institution is going to install:
   (a) A network of PCs and supporting facilities so that a number of different application packages may be used, and
   (b) Terminals for on-line connection to various external databases.
   Prepare a detailed programme for the necessary education and training of users, stating at what stage the activities should take place and who should attend or receive training.

13 Internal controls and security

A: CONTROLS ON DATA AND INFORMATION

13.1 Preamble

An information system consists of various elements and stages. The elements involved are data, people, equipment and software. The stages are collecting data, entering them into the system, processing data to produce information, storing data and information, extracting information from the system and transmitting it to the user. Each of these must be examined when considering desirable controls and security measures for a system. The three basic characteristics of a good information system, namely accurate, complete and timely data and information must be preserved and enhanced by the controls and security measures introduced. The measures should not hinder or delay the provision of information under any circumstances.

Control and security measures must be incorporated into the system at the design stage as they cannot easily be added later. However, the measures are too important to be left to the designers of the system and top managers must satisfy themselves that appropriate measures are in place. This is because a major failure in the provision of information or a security lapse may be catastrophic: quite a few companies have been bankrupted by fire or fraud. Controls are just as important as security. For instance, if a company is facing insolvency because of a failure to issue invoices to a number of its large customers, it is too late for the chief executive to sack the accountant. Controls should have been in place which made it clear to management that the system was not operating correctly because insufficient cash was being received. Any new system, therefore, should be analyzed by management to identify what could possibly go wrong with it, and the appropriate controls and security procedures put in place. It is also wise to review the procedures on existing systems from time to time.

The cost of control or security measures should always be compared with their benefits. It is not always easy to assess costs let alone assess the benefits accurately. For instance, what is the likelihood of an employee stealing £3m? What is the likelihood of the computer centre being burnt down? If it was burnt down, what would be the cost in terms of lost records and would sales and revenue be lost? On a less drastic note, what is the likelihood of errors occurring when data are entered into the system and how much might this cost the organization? While it is difficult to produce accurate costs, or even approximations, the act of attempting a cost–benefit comparison will at least reduce the possibility of money being spent on unnecessary or poor value controls and security procedures.

13.2 The distinction between controls and security

The purpose of controls is quite different from that of security. Controls aim to prevent *accidental* errors creeping into the system whereas security measures attempt to keep it safe from damage or *deliberate* manipulation. However, good controls do also add to the security of the system by providing constant checks, and some security procedures may supplement controls. Both are needed to protect a system from 'people', whether employees or outsiders. Part of the answer is to instil good practice in employees and to create loyalty to the organization rather than showering the system and organization with checks and locks.

However, some measures will always be necessary.

Controls are designed to:

- Prevent errors occurring when data are entered into the system.
- Check that the data being entered are complete.
- Check that data are received and entered on time.
- Check that the processing and transmission of data and information are speedy and efficient in the use of resources.
- Ensure that the information generated is complete, accurate and delivered to the right people on time.

Security measures, on the other hand, should povide protection against:

- Unauthorized entry of data.
- Unauthorized access to information.
- Interference with the processing, storing or transmission stages of the information system — whether deliberate or accidental.
- Loss of data, information, or equipment — whether through fire, flood, electrical or electronic faults, or any act of vengeance.
- Legal liability such as the provisions of the Data Protection Act 1984.

13.3 The purposes of controls

A useful analogy with the controls which should operate in an information system can be found in those which must be used by a water company:

- **Input** should be as clean as possible and free from interruption.
- **Storage** should be secure and prevent loss or contamination.
- **Processing** should remove any impurities, guard against any impurities being introduced and produce a product of the standard required by the user.
- **Output** should deliver a clean product to the customer, without introducing any impurities on the way, and provide an interruption-free supply.

In a water company these standards are achieved using filters and additives at some stages and by testing at others. In exactly the same way information systems use 'filters', 'additives' and tests to control and preserve the quality of data and information. Their function is to:

- Act as sieves or hurdles which the data or information must pass successfully.
- Force staff to operate and monitor procedures correctly.
- Provide evidence that data or information are correct and complete.

Operating a system with inadequate controls may initially appear to be cheaper but in the end it will usually prove to be more expensive. The eventual result will almost certainly be error and failure rates which are so high as to destroy the credibility of the information provided by the system. On the other hand, excessive controls slow down the provision of information by introducing too many additional routines. Excessive controls may also either aggravate the users or make them so reliant on them that self-discipline and training standards deteriorate. For instance, when holes punched into cards were used to enter data into a computer it was standard practice to enter the data twice. The holes were punched by one operator, and a second pass was made by someone else to test that the card had been punched correctly. This practice might have been necessary when no other means existed to verify accuracy, but often it serves little purpose except to slow down the entry of data. Human nature being what it is, the initial operators become careless if they know that their work is going to be checked and so the error rate increases thus making the check imperative. Checkers also may be tempted to check samples rather than doing the whole batch. Now that data can be keyed in using a screen-based terminal which provides prompts together with visual and other checks, accuracy can easily be verified by the person entering the data. This gives the operator a more responsible job and should reduce the time needed to enter the data.

There are many different methods of checking that data are entered correctly. Whoever designs or selects the controls must have a good understanding of the data, the people entering them and the conditions under which this takes place in order to understand what types of error may occur. The following methods of checking data entry are some of the more common ones in use. Most of these were developed for transaction processing on mainframe computers rather than entry of information via PCs into, say, a distributed database.

13.4 Input control: transaction numbers

It is basic business practice to give each document or transaction a unique number, just as each cheque in a cheque book is serially numbered. Preprinted numbers are usual on almost all documents used by an organization, such as sales invoices and purchase orders. This guards against loss and facilitates tracing documents or transactions. A system can be programmed to produce either lists of missing numbers or an index which highlight the absence of a document or record from a sequence.

Documents received by an organization, such as purchase invoices and cheques, can either be numbered on receipt or at the point of entry into the system. Figure 13.1, illustrating batch controls, shows how transaction numbers can be used to control and check data being entered.

CHURCHFIELD AUDIO LTD — **Cheques banked** — **Batch control sheet**

1	2	3	4	5	6	7	8
Date	Last ref. no.	No. of cheques	Prev. transaction no.	Last transaction no.	Batch value	Cumul. value	System value
12/3	400	7	32681	32688	587	12657	12657
13/3	412	12	32845	32857	732	13389	13389
14/3	436	24	32962	32986	1258	14647	14647

Figure 13.1 A batch control example.

13.5 Input control: batch controls

Until the early 1970s almost all data were 'prepared' off-line: that is, they were entered on punch cards, paper or magnetic tape away from the computer system. The prepared data were then entered into the computer in batches. Appropriate totals were produced in advance and compared with those obtained at the data preparation and entry stages. If the batch control totals did not agree with those from the previous stage, the batch would be rejected until the reasons for the difference had been found and the necessary corrections made. The same approach is used today whenever data are loaded into the system in batches.

Where on-line data entry takes place, that is when transaction data are entered directly into the system the moment they are generated or received, batch controls as outlined above are inapplicable. However, daily batch totals for each terminal can be produced by the computer system itself, and these can then be compared with totals prepared by each terminal operator. Here control takes place *after* the data have been entered into the system, rather than prior to it.

Typical batch controls involve totalling and comparing the following:

- The number of documents or transactions.
- The total value of the batch, or the totals for each category of value contained in the batch, for instance sales values and sales tax values.
- The totals for data such as dates, account codes or invoice reference numbers. These produce artificial totals known as 'hash totals'. For example, assume that a small batch consisting of just three purchase orders is to be entered. Order number 321 is dated 06/03, number 304 is dated 28/02 and 337 is dated 11/03. The total of the order numbers comes to 962 and the dates can be added together to produce 4508. Both these hash totals are keyed in as part of the batch. Before accepting the data the program will check that the totals agree with those produced by the program.

The following example, illustrated in Figure 13.1, considers how batch controls may be used to assist in recording cheques received. In this particular system, as the batch is being made up prior to entry into the computer, a reference number is written on the back of each cheque. Subtracting the last reference number of the previous batch (see column 2) from the last reference number of the current batch should give the total number of cheques in the batch. If there is a difference between this figure and the actual number of cheques (column 3) an error must have been made either in the cheque count or in the numbering of the cheques. A computerized accounting system will automatically assign a transaction number. Thus the same comparison is possible (see columns 4 and 5).

In addition, the values of the cheques to be entered are added together to provide a total value for the batch (shown in column 6). This batch total is added to the cumulative value of cheques which have previously been entered into the computer, to give a new cumulative value (column 7). As the cheque values are entered into the computer a control total within the system is automatically updated (column 8). As soon as the batch has been entered into the computer this control total is called up and compared with the current cumulative value of cheques processed in column 7. If the two do not agree then either the batch has been incorrectly totalled or a cheque value has been entered incorrectly into the computer system.

13.6 Input control: check digits

A check digit is an extra figure or character added to a code or reference number which can be used to validate the number. Only one error in a thousand will escape a good check digit system: in which case if the error rate was one per hundred entries made only one entry in a hundred thousand would be incorrect if a check digit was used. Check digits are particularly useful at picking up errors when code numbers are used in place of lengthy descriptions such as '1093527' in place of 'size 8, 2″ countersunk steel screws'. This is because the code number may have no significance for the person entering the data and thus keyboard errors are likely to occur.

One of the simplest and most common check digit systems for numeric codes is to add together the figures in the code and use the last digit of the sum as the check. Code number 1093527 has a total of 27 so the check digit would be 7. The code could then be written as 1093527/7. Such a system will trap about 80 per cent of errors, but it cannot spot transpositions, such as 132 instead of 123, which account for about 8 per cent of errors. Other, more complex systems exist which can provide higher accuracy checks for both numeric and alphabetic codes or references.

13.7 Input control: redundant data checks

Redundant data checks are of two types. In the first type, data being entered into the system are matched against data already in it. For example, the first four letters of a customer's name are entered in addition to the customer's reference number — both the reference number and the first four letters of the name should correspond to the information contained on the appropriate file. The name 'redundancy check' is derived from the entry of the second, or redundant, piece of data.

In the second type of redundancy check, two different pieces of data contained in an entry can be compared, and each is able to confirm the accuracy of the other. For instance, forms often ask for a person's date of birth and their age, when clearly the latter can be deduced from the former and could be described as redundant information.

13.8 Input control: data credibility checks

Data being entered can be compared with sets of credibility parameters or lists of information already in the computer. For instance, employee ages below sixteen and over, say, sixty-eight might result in entries to personnel records being rejected. Alternatively attempts to enter a number in the payroll record in excess of three hundred hours for the hours worked by any employee in a month could be rejected and only entered successfully if a special authorization code is used. The street and town in an address can be matched with the post code, using an index contained within the system, to confirm that both are correct. Codes or reference numbers having the wrong length or structure may be rejected by the system.

Customer names, part numbers, accounts codes, contained in an entry may be checked against lists already existing in the system. Only those entries which match a record on the relevant list would be automatically accepted. Entries containing a new name, reference or code number would have to be confirmed in some way before being allowed into the system.

13.9 Input control: computer terminal checks

There are several ways in which a computer terminal can be used to assist in correct entry of data. They include:

- The data can be displayed on screen as they are typed in and only entered into the system when the operator confirms them as correct by pressing the 'enter' key.
- When a reference number is entered into the system the name that the number represents may be displayed on the screen as a check. For instance, when the code 435892 is keyed into a cell on a predesigned screen (template) the name ROBINSON might appear above the code, which gives the operator the chance to confirm that the correct file or record is being used.
- Most computer programs designed for entering transaction data provide the facility to repeat, automatically or deliberately, data from the previous entry. This is useful, for instance, for repeating the date and part number on stores requisitions or the date and flight number of an airline booking. This reduces the number of key strokes and so helps to reduce errors.
- The screen template may allow only a limited number of choices, such as boxes for yes or no, or M or F. This not only helps accuracy but also ensures that the data entered are complete by refusing to allow the operator to move to the next screen until all choices have been made.

13.10 Processing controls

Checks and controls should be planned and incorporated into the system when it is first written. However, programs are often modified during their life and it is very important to check and thoroughly test such modifications. Control on the accuracy and completeness of the processing of data, as opposed to the operating program itself, depends primarily on the agreement between totals for data fed into the system and totals for information generated by the system. In addition, checks must be made to ensure that data brought forward from a previous processing cycle have been correctly transferred to the current processing cycle.

A transaction log, combined with an operator log, will provide a record of what has actually happened. A transaction log is automatically produced by the computer and is simply a list of the details of every piece of data which has been entered into the system together with a transaction number. This number facilitates tracing data from source to destination through the system and makes possible the creation of usable audit trail listings. An audit trail allows the detailed data supporting the information produced by a system to be traced and verified. It consists of a description of the stages that data go through from source to final report, and specifies the readable evidence required to demonstrate that each stage has been carried out correctly. The transaction numbers attached to each item of data entered into the computer system are used to identify the data contained in any control listings used to support output reports or any intermediate processing stages.

An operator log is simply a record of who used the system, when, and what they did. Every operator is normally given a password which has to be entered into the system before work can take place, thus an individual user can be identified. (Passwords are discussed in section 13.15.) It should, therefore, be impossible to use the system without some record of use being created. Knowledge of the user may be needed for either on-line monitoring for security reasons or to make checks on who used the system and for what purpose at a later date.

Transmission errors (either within the system or between the system and a user) can be detected using parity or cyclic redundancy checks — these use a similar approach to the check digit idea, discussed in section 13.6, but are applied to the actual electronic content of the material transmitted. Parity checks involve adding up all the bits (binary digits) in a character and, depending on whether the result is odd or even, adding a binary 0 or 1 to make the total odd or even depending on which standard the system is using. If the standard is that all characters should have even parity then any having odd parity will be rejected and a parity error message produced by the system.

Controls should also be put in place to ensure that the information downloaded from the central information system to PCs remains complete and accurate. Where, for example, information is taken from financial accounting records and used in spreadsheets, care should be taken to check that it is not accidentally changed or overwritten. This is difficult to achieve in practice because the flexibility inherent in end-user applications, such as spreadsheets, may make the use of the formal control totals, etc. which apply to stable routines inapplicable. Hence it is important for the user to devise his or her own checks on the accuracy of information created from their personal system. Similarly, any recipients of information created on end-user systems should not assume that the same standards of control which are used in the organization's formal information system have been applied.

Many systems contain a facility for 'locking' data or information. For instance, once monthly figures have been prepared, the system is locked so that accidental overwriting or altering of figures cannot take place. This also ensures that any alteration has to be made at a set time and is thus brought to management's attention rather than being 'slipped through' as an adjustment to a prior period's results. Locking figures is only suitable for old-fashioned, static systems. Obviously the system cannot be locked where data are continually being entered and current information is permanently required.

13.11 Output controls

Output controls are designed to ensure that processing has been accurate, that information is reliable, up to date and delivered to those who need it.

Wherever possible, regular comparisons should be made with externally produced information in order to verify the accuracy of key figures and other information produced by the system. This type of check is made as a matter of course in the internal accounts by reconciling the figures with bank statements or suppliers' statements. An advantage of some checks against external information is that the suppliers of the verification details (for instance, the bank) also have their figures checked by the reconciliation process. External verification details are less easy to come by in non-financial areas, but where possible every effort should be made to obtain such information. A typical example of this type of verification is the annual routine carried out by professional bodies and similar organizations. Members are sent a copy of their details in the society's records — together with an easy means of indicating any errors or necessary corrections, such as change of address.

Another important control activity is the visual and/or automatic scanning of output in order to check that it is complete and is consistent with previously produced information. This type of check is also useful for picking up unusual items or activities which should be investigated. For instance, the system can have instructions built in specifying that outputs which exceed preset parameters or deviate by more than a set percentage from previous values should be highlighted or listed separately. A typical example of this approach is the checking routine now followed by some credit card companies whereby transactions which differ radically from previous patterns, in respect of amount, location and type, result in the card-holder being contacted to confirm that their card has not been stolen.

All printouts of information should contain the date of issue, as should all manually produced information. This highlights any delay in the user receiving the information and also ensures that the user is referring to current information. Similarly, any screen-based information should indicate when it was last updated. Controls may also be instigated to ensure that the reports generated go to their designated users. This can be achieved by flagging the availability of a particular report on the recipients' screens or by printing their names on hard-copy reports.

13.12 Input controls: recent developments

Computer systems, and thus information systems, are continually changing as technology advances. The development of EDI (electronic data interchange) is having a major impact on the accuracy of data. Because the same piece of data no longer needs to be entered several times into several different systems, accuracy will improve considerably. The single entry may not even be made by a human but by a computer monitoring data entry points such as incoming orders or a production process. While computers do not make mistakes, programs sometimes contain errors. The software must be carefully checked initially, and checks must be installed to make sure that the system continues to function correctly. If errors do occur in computer systems, they can be repeated many times before they are noticed.

The other major change in recent years has been the move away from mainframe computers to a network of PCs and minicomputers. These networks pose quite a problem for control, in particular audit trail conditions must be met and access must be restricted to authorized employees via passwords. Employees may be able to download information from a database, amend it and then write the amended version back to the database. It is much safer to make the database 'read only', but, if this cannot be done, controls must be applied to make sure that errors do not creep into the system.

The quality of software on all PCs which enter data into the central system must be checked regardless of whether it is bought or is in-house software. Stories of poor software causing major damage appear to be increasing rather than declining over the years. A recent disaster with software at AT&T stopped 20 million telephone calls over a period of nine hours. The well known database dBASE IV was found to contain, in the words of the *Wall Street Journal*, 'thousands of bugs'. Word Perfect, a word processing system, received an appalling review in *Practical Computing* largely because the reviewer lost a ten-page document she had written the previous day and found instead an additional forty-eight pages of garbage. Even operating system software is not immune, the first version of DOS 4 by Microsoft was described as totally unpredictable and had the added ability to corrupt the hard disk. Mistakes of this size are relatively few and are quickly put right by the supplier and a revised version brought out. However, it is never possible to guarantee that a program is totally correct and it is conceivable that an organization could suffer a major loss as a result. Therefore, all software must be adequately tested on an isolated computer before it is used to enter data into the organization's central system.

B: INTERNAL SECURITY

13.13 Security measures

Good security measures should aim to keep all data and system software safe and free from contamination, and to keep all equipment and facilities safe and in good working condition. Back-up copies of software and alternative or back-up equipment and facilities should also be provided. This is to ensure that data are not lost and that systems are always available.

There are five categories of risk from which the information system should be protected:

- Fraud.
- Theft of software, equipment, data or information.
- Wilful damage to software, processing equipment or transmission facilities.

- Loss of equipment, facilities, software or data due to fire, flood, loss of power or other disaster.
- Failure to comply with the law.

The next chapter concentrates on the risk and prevention of fraud, theft and sabotage from external sources. This chapter is concerned as much with physical security as with combating crime. The threat to computer systems from criminals attracts a great deal of media attention, but the damage from the less 'glamorous' risks of fire, flood and system failure can be just as devastating for an organization. Studies of UK computer problems in recent years have revealed the following pattern:[1]

Disasters, including arson and software malfunction	34%
Fraud	40%
Crime, including hacking	26%

A more detailed breakdown of disasters reveals:

Explosion, arson, fire	35%
Software malfunction	23%
Lighting and power failures	21%
Other disasters	21%

It is thought that UK companies lose about £1.5 billion a year from such causes and that one company in every thousand suffers a major failure in its computer systems each year. One major computer crash cost a bank £22 million in lost interest because it was unable to place customers' money in interest-bearing overnight accounts. Most companies who are dependent on computer-based information systems will go under if they suffer a major system failure and have neglected to arrange for adequate back-up. Figures from the USA indicate that 90 per cent of companies which suffer a major computer disaster have gone out of business within eighteen months.[2] It is this type of statistic which, according to a survey carried out in 1990, has led UK chief executives to rate computer insecurity higher on their list of concerns than the threat of a hostile takeover.[2]

Good security requires considerable amounts of money and management effort. How much of either will be invested depends on the level of risk perceived and on the consequences of a failure in security. For instance, it *is* possible to guard against the risk of an equipment breakdown by running duplicate systems. This is known as 'redundancy'. However, such duplication is usually impractical because of the high cost involved; instead, alternative back-up arrangements have to be made. In areas where human safety is concerned, duplicate or back-up systems are essential. For example, passenger aircraft have duplicate and frequently triplicate systems.

Security measures should not be so stringent that they upset the user, whether he be employee or customer. For instance, it is perfectly feasible for cash dispenser systems to request not only a user's PIN but also his address and maternal grandmother's date of birth as further identity checks. The effect of this on the length of time spent in the queue is easy to imagine. Controls in an executive information system which permit access only via a user's own terminal and then only between 9 a.m. and 5 p.m. may both appear reasonable means of preventing unauthorized access. The effect of these controls on users who habitually work late or away from their own office would soon deter them from using the system.

13.14 Protection against fraud

The largest category of computer problem is fraud: its prevention should therefore be the organization's first priority. The largest class of fraud is payroll fraud, whereby an extra person's name is added to the payroll. In fact, three-quarters of all frauds involve altering input data and so controls designed to stop this (as discussed in the previous part of this chapter) and security measures to prohibit access to systems are very important. Good business practice for security should incorporate the following procedures:

- *All new customer, supplier and employee records must be authorized by a responsible member of staff*. This will prevent other employees from creating 'dummies' which they can use to defraud the organization. Similarly, it is important to check that people who leave the organization are deleted from the payroll, as it is easy for a dishonest person simply to change the account to which their salary is being paid.
- *All changes to systems or programs, whether manual or computerized, must be authorized by a responsible member of staff.*
- *All new systems, whether bought or written in-house should be reviewed by the internal audit department*. If an internal audit department does not exist the external auditors should be employed to do the job. One interesting opportunity for fraud which had been left in an accounting package designed to handle credit purchases involved typing in BALSUP in place of the invoice number. This caused the transaction to vanish the next time the system was updated. It was only discovered by accident because the accountant used the same set of letters as an abbreviation for 'Balance set up' when transferring accounts from the existing manual system.
- *All payments must be authorized*. In particular, careful control should be exercised over automatic payments such as computer produced cheques or electronic transfers.
- *No one person should handle a complete process*. For example, the same person should not prepare the payroll figures and write the employees' pay cheques. A clear separation of duties should exist together with built-in checks carried out by other staff. Unfortunately, computerization, by streamlining procedures and reducing the number of staff required, has made it more difficult to achieve this in smaller organizations where often only one clerk may remain.

- *All assets should be regularly checked to confirm that the organization still possesses them.* This applies both to physical assets and to securities such as deeds or bonds.
- *Access to computer rooms and terminals should be limited to authorized persons at authorized times only.* Photo-identity cards and magnetic keys, which can easily be withdrawn or changed, are ideal for entry into restricted areas in larger organizations. In smaller businesses, or where equipment is often left unattended, keyboard locks provide some protection against unauthorized use.
- *Individuals should not be left to work alone in computer rooms or at terminals.* This is especially relevant in the evenings when the majority of employees have gone home. Again this is more difficult to arrange in a small organization or department.

13.15 Passwords

Passwords are normally used to control access to a system. Allied with a magnetic stripe card key, passwords can make unauthorized access virtually impossible. If this were not the case then every cash-card holder would be wide open to robbery. Password control must be scrupulous to be truly effective. Each person should have a separate password and each part of the system should have a distinct access code. Passwords should be changed frequently, but this should not be done in a regular pattern which a crook may be able to predict. Neither should all passwords be changed at the same time.

If each part of the system has a separate access code it is relatively easy to stop one person from preparing the payroll and issuing the cheques. More usually, however, the different access codes to systems are used in a hierarchical way within the organization. Only the directors have access to the whole system, the next layer of management has access to most of it but the clerks have access only to their section of the transaction system. The greater the number of passwords, the more difficult it is going to be for a fraudster to move around the system. Unfortunately, this applies to employees and managers as well, and there have been cases where decisions have been based upon incomplete information because access was not allowed to the total information. The individual making the decision was probably totally unaware that he did not have the full information.

Users who are allowed to create their own passwords should be encouraged to use truly random collections of letters or numbers to prevent others from guessing the passwords. Too often passwords consist of standard words such as Fred or love or an anagram of an individual's own name or a birth date written backwards. Employees will probably need some instruction on selecting passwords and this type of instruction should be part of any induction session for new staff. They should also be told never under any circumstances to reveal either their, or anyone else's, password, however plausible the reason. Too often employees have unwittingly aided fraudsters by disclosing passwords over the telephone. The type and length of password to be used should be considered carefully. For instance, a four-figure password has ten thousand different combinations, whereas a six-letter password has nearly 309 million. Long or complicated passwords do have their disadvantages. For instance, a counter clerk in a bank or building society may not be able to attend to customers until his password has been accepted. If for some reason, such as forgetfulness, it is not accepted, a queue of disgruntled customers will quickly build up.

Where PCs are connected via a network to a database, the number of entry points is multiplied and thus security becomes much more difficult. Auto dialling **modems** are sometimes used to dial up the database. Often, a lazy user will extend this so that their password is automatically sent. This is remarkably stupid as anyone using the terminal will be connected straightaway to the database and the security intended by using a system of passwords will have been bypassed. It is wise to include call-back verification on most networks. This involves attaching a device to the computer which intercepts all incoming calls and runs a check on the user's identity against authorized telephone numbers and terminal ports. Then a call is made back to the user to confirm that they are a bona fide user.

13.16   Other data security measures

If the controls on input, processing, and output covered in earlier parts of this chapter are in place, they not only provide the necessary control over system operation and the quality of information provided but they also form an important part of the system's security. In fact, they are an essential prerequisite to any effective security strategy directed against fraud or the abuse of the information system.

One such control is an automatic access logging system which records who used the system (based on the password used), at what time they used it and what they did. This will not only act as a deterrent but will also help in providing evidence should fraud be discovered or suspected. One of the great problems with computer crime is securing convictions because no trace may be left of the actions involved. A log can do a great deal to discourage insiders from committing a crime. It is, of course, essential that there should be no way around the access log: this is not always an easy requirement to fulfil as some programmers (and hackers) delight in finding ways around such obstacles.

Whatever efforts are made, no system can be made totally secure and it is wise, therefore, to take out fidelity bond insurance. This is an insurance policy which can be taken out on all staff who are in a position to commit theft or fraud. Its use not only provides some compensation in the event of a crime but also helps to concentrate attention on the opportunity for it. This is because the organization is required to produce a list of all those employees who have the opportunity to commit fraud and to calculate the sums that could be lost. Fidelity bond insurance may possibly have the opposite effect on some companies, though: making them lax because they have insurance cover.

13.17 Safeguarding equipment

The risk from fire or flood is minimized by *not* locating equipment, data storage facilities and records in the basement. This applies to traditional paper files as much as to computer equipment. If a fire occurs it is much more likely that damage to electronic equipment will be caused by water from hoses and sprinklers than by the blaze itself. Since water will end up in the basement, whether from flood or fire hoses, it makes sense to site equipment as high in the building as is practical. This is a wise precaution for all easily destructible valuables but is not always followed. For instance, a few years ago a burst water main caused severe damage to collections of old china and maps foolishly stored in a basement at the Victoria and Albert Museum in London. In countries where there is a likelihood of earthquakes or tornadoes, or where there is a risk of bombing, the situation may, of course, be different.

The risk of theft can be considerably reduced by restricting the opportunity to commit crime. If employees are permitted to take PCs home, but are not expected to sign for them, the eventual result is obvious. One large accountancy firm, which should have known better, lost dozens of machines in this way.

A computer centre which contains mainframes and central databases will need stringent protection. This may include guards, alarm systems, closed circuit television, strong boundary fences and floodlighting. In offices, equipment should be kept locked up or bolted down wherever possible. However, these safeguards have to be balanced against the need to keep the layout of the office convenient and flexible to the changing needs of employees and the organization. The stamping of post codes onto all movable items may satisfy both criteria.

Disgruntled members of the public or vandals may try to damage computer equipment. The physical safeguards described above, plus keeping equipment out of public view, will minimize this risk. However, little can be done to stop a disgruntled employee from running amok with a hammer or a fire hose — except the good management practice of keeping staff happy and fulfilled.

Some organizations have extensive security measures in place but totally overlook the possibility of damage being caused by their cleaners. Cleaners may be unaware that a spilt cup of coffee can wreck a computer. They are also left alone in the buildings in the evenings and sometimes even given authority to lock up. There must be a proper system for vetting cleaners, whether they are the organization's employees or ones supplied on contract by a cleaning firm. In addition, if the computing area is left unmanned, all systems should be closed down before the cleaners have access to the area.

13.18   Maintenance and back-up

Maintenance contracts, which contain reliable guarantees of speedy attention, and where necessary replacement equipment are vital. These may be provided by the manufacturer, the supplier of the equipment or by specialist companies. The market today for maintenance and disaster recovery is so lucrative that ICL, Britain's leading computer supplier and until recently a subsidiary of STC, has decided to return to it. A few years ago when STC purchased ICL, ICL sold off its maintenance activity to Granada — currently the leading group in this field.

It would be foolhardy to purchase a system without first ensuring that a maintenance contract was available. Where items of equipment are purchased individually or purchases of equipment are made by individual user departments, rather than by the central information systems department, there is a danger that the need for a maintenance policy will be overlooked. Because maintenance costs are visible, and the cost of a failed system is not, there may also be a tendency to try to avoid the high visible cost — yet few company executives would be happy to operate the business without adequate insurance. In the past, a breakdown on the production line could normally be sorted out in hours or days and the financial damage in a slower-moving, less competitive environment was sustainable. Today a serious system failure can put a company out of business.

As was mentioned in section 13.13 an extravagant but certain way of providing security against temporary loss of the information system is to run either a duplicate computer system in parallel so that the system is fault tolerant or to have a second system on instant stand-by. To provide complete security, the duplicate system should also be at a different location. Clearly, for most large information systems such a strategy would be both expensive and cumbersome. However, if the organization's product is dependent on the system, such as a company providing an on-line database service, the duplication of some, if not all, of its equipment and systems will be necessary. Duplication of the power supply to computers is routine nowadays. Even PCs often have sufficient battery back-up to at least preserve their files in the event of a break in power supply.

Alternatively, two organizations may enter into an agreement to provide temporary facilities for each other in the event of a breakdown. This type of arrangement provides mutual security and will probably be considerably cheaper than large scale duplication of facilities. It does require, however, that both parties have enough surplus computing capacity to cope with 'doubling up'. This type of reciprocal agreement will be impossible if an organization considers its data too sensitive to be handled by the employees of another organization. If the organization is willing to pay fairly large insurance premiums to obtain back-up facilities and guaranteed security then it should subscribe to a specialist firm. These firms specialize in storing back-up tapes and disks and will provide a full computing suite (mobile or fixed site) for, say, up to three months in the event of a fire or other disaster.

Providing large-scale back-up facilities becomes less important as companies switch from mainframes to networks of PCs and mincomputers as it is relatively easy to replace a single unit if a breakdown occurs. However, the network then becomes crucial and consideration should be given to backing-up the communications system by duplicating such equipment as lines, switches and modems. The seriousness of this problem was illustrated when the Bell Telephone Company had a fire at a switching centre which was the central hub for thirty local exchanges. It took four weeks to get the service back. Any company which had made the provision of being linked to two switching centres would have had no problem coping with this. As it was, most had to switch to satellite, line of sight microwave, or hastily install a temporary network.

At least one back-up copy should be kept of all program and data files, whether on magnetic disk or tape. One back-up copy should be kept at a different location to avoid the risk of fire. If this is not possible, one copy should at least be stored in a fireproof safe. It is often difficult to keep data files which are continually being updated at a different site, but program files together with all relevant documentation certainly can be.

Back-up copies of transaction data files should be prepared at least once a day, or whenever the file changes if it is not in regular use. It is usual to keep at least three 'generations' of back-up files, often referred to as grandfather, father and son. A useful, if not essential, supplement is to keep a hard-copy of the transaction log which lists all data entered.

13.19 Good staff management

Sometimes employees become so disaffected with the organization that they steal or damage the organization's assets. The only way of avoiding this is by good management and careful vetting when employing new staff. This is especially true when selecting employees who will be involved with the information system as they will be in a position to inflict considerable damage if they should ever feel inclined. Disaffection may be minimized by having proper job descriptions which are clear to both the interviewer and the interviewee, as a lack of clarity over an individual's role within the organization is a prime cause of disaffection. However, job descriptions should be prepared with some care, allowing sufficient flexibility so as to permit employee development and avoid frustrating restrictions.

References should always be requested and thoroughly checked, and evidence of qualifications and experience should be obtained. For some peculiar reason, many commercial organizations cannot be bothered to check a new employee's qualifications. Needless to say it is too late when the systems manager is being charged with fraud to find that he did not possess the qualifications entered on his application form or that he had previous convictions. If there is no-one in the organization who has the necessary experience to interview and vet computing or other technical staff then a reliable agency or consultant should be employed to do so.

Setting high standards of work, paying well, and taking a genuine interest in staff connected with the information system all help to improve and preserve morale. It is also important to train staff thoroughly and help them to keep up to date. This should help their career prospects and improve their loyalty to the organization. Trying to trap personnel into remaining in a job by restricting their opportunities inevitably causes resentment and lays the employee more open to the temptation of fraud or sabotage if the opportunity presents itself.

It is wise to rotate staff wherever possible both for career development purposes and in order to minimize the opportunity for fraud. Similarly, management should also insist that all staff connected with the information system take their full annual leave. This will prevent most frauds which rely on regular transfers of funds because the understudy is likely to discover the crime. In addition, insisting that staff take their annual leave also prevents a sense of indispensability building up which can be dangerous both for the employee and the organization. Employees who get obsessively involved with their organization can easily become unsettled if they perceive their position as threatened in any way and they may take vengeance on the organization.

Sensible training and instruction given to staff should help to increase security. For instance, employees should be told of the dangers in storing floppy disks near terminals. A floppy disk is extremely portable and easy to take from the premises and yet it may contain important company information. Therefore, all floppy disks should be stored well away from the equipment and should be securely locked away when not in use. Similarly, equipment should not be left switched on when unattended as it takes just a few moments to copy information onto a floppy disk.

13.20 Legal considerations

Data protection legislation is concerned with the privacy, accuracy and misuse of information held on outsiders and members of an organization. The UK Data Protection Act 1984 is only concerned with personal data which is held on computers: it does not cover data stored traditionally and processed manually. Two of its aims are to protect individuals and to comply with aspects of the Council of Europe's convention on data protection (mentioned in section 7.4).

The Act provides that:

- All those using or processing personal data (that is data containing names or personal reference numbers) must register with the Data Protection Registrar, and state the purpose for which the data are used and for whom they are intended.

All data must be:[3]

- Obtained and processed fairly and lawfully.

- Held only for the stated purpose and disclosed only to registered recipients.
- Adequate, relevant and not excessive in relation to the purposes for which they are held.
- Accurate and, where necessary, kept up to date.
- Held no longer than is necessary for the registered purpose.
- Made available on request to the individual to whom it relates. The individual has the power to insist that it is altered or erased if it is incorrect.
- Kept securely to prevent unauthorized people gaining access to it.

The Data Protection Act deals only with computerized records, but Section 722 of the UK Companies Act 1985 deals with all types of record. The Section was first enacted in the last century and re-enacted in the 1985 Act. It states that if permanent records are not kept in a bound ledger then adequate precautions for guarding against falsification and facilitating its discovery must be taken. Thus a company keeping computer records, a loose-leaf ledger or recording in pencil may not be taking adequate precautions. This should be overcome on a computer system by operating an effective audit trail (see section 13.10). However, audit trails are not always easy to operate on the more modern networked systems and complete security is also difficult to achieve when there are so many ways of entering a networked system.

Information law is complicated and open to various interpretations, so it is wise to seek legal advice as a matter of course. If any action is to be taken in the courts against an individual or group of individuals for theft or fraud it is likely that the legality of the organization's information system will be considered by the court. This happened in the 'Prestel' case (also referred to in section 14.10) in which British Telecom tried, unsucessfully, to prosecute two hackers. It was clear from British Telecom's evidence that their Prestel billing system was in breach of the Companies Act. Needless to say, the system has since been rewritten. In any large or medium-sized company a senior member of staff should be familiar with the law and have the power and responsibility to ensure that the organization complies with its requirements.

13.21 Control and security as part of the organization's philosophy

The controls and security arrangements provided for an information system should, ideally, form part of a set of procedures which cover the whole organization. If the same high standards do not prevail throughout the organization, the controls and protection provided for the information system will become diluted or be more difficult to enforce.

Control is not just about check digits and batch totals — to be fully effective it requires the right organizational philosophy and attitude. The aim should be that controls are potentially, though not actually, redundant. High quality operating standards rather than controls themselves should produce the correct information at the correct destination at the right time.

Security arrangements and procedures should not be an end in themselves such that employees concentrate on carrying out the procedures without any conviction. This can result in staff 'going through the motions' and an 'I'm only covering my back' or 'it's more than my job's worth' type of bureaucratic abdication. What is needed is the sort of atmosphere where all staff are acutely, but realistically, aware of risk and take a personal responsibility for using their judgement in applying any rules and regulations designed to protect the information system. This situation can best be achieved through good training and clear management guidance and leadership.

NOTES

1. From surveys by BIS Applied Systems Ltd reproduced in *A Handbook of Computer Security*, Keith Hearnden (ed.) (Kogan Page, 1990).
2. Phillip Virgo of Winsafe, *Daily Telegraph*, 30 July 1990.
3. Parts of the description of the 1984 Data Processing Act are reproduced from the Guidelines published by the Data Protection Registrar, Second Series, Feb. 1989.

FURTHER READING

Information technology statement No.1, *Security and Confidentiality of Data* (Institute of Chartered Accountants in England & Wales, 1985).
Information technology statement No.3, *Control and Management of Information* (Institute of Chartered Accountants in England & Wales, 1987).
Beddie, Lesley and Scott Raeburn, *Introduction to Computer Integrated Business* (Prentice Hall International, 1989). Expecially chapter 9.
Moscove Stephen and Mark Simpkin, *Accounting Information Systems* (Wiley, 1989).

EXERCISES

1. Relying on memory, observation and your imagination list the controls, and their purposes, which are (a) visible to the user and (b) invisible to the user of ATMs ('hole in the wall' cash dispensers).

2. Design a short questionnaire concerning people's voting habits. Assume the results will be processed by computer. Consider the input, storage, processing and output controls which would be appropriate. What security and legal considerations are there?

3. The Marcus Group has a chain of hotels which operate a centralized room reservation system. What are the likely consequences and costs of poor system controls?

4. What are the dangers from unauthorized access to information systems? What steps should be taken to protect the system from these dangers?

14 Crime: fraud, theft and sabotage

SCOPE AND CONTENTS

The chapter starts by considering a broad range of lapses in security by using a case which highlights many shortcomings. Then the extent of computer crime is discussed followed by a brief look at several different types of crime: hacking, large-scale theft and sabotage. Different types of virus, together with examples of recent occurrences, are dealt with, followed by vaccines and security measures which can be taken to prevent them. Espionage is briefly mentioned. The state of the law regarding computer crime is reviewed. Finally the coin is reversed and there is a brief discussion on how information systems may prevent theft and fraud.

14.1 General security

Nowadays any mention of the words fraud or theft in connection with business information almost automatically produces an image of computer crime. This is largely because these crimes have received, quite justifiably, much publicity in recent years. However, even now, much information used in crimes of fraud or theft is taken from systems other than computer ones. The careless storage of, and degree of access allowed to, paper documents makes crime very easy. The following case which took place in the USA in the early 1970s is a good example of lax security in a range of different areas which almost invited crime. As you read through the case make a list of the different points of weakness in the company's systems which Jerry exploited, and consider what could have been done to make the organization more secure.

14.2 Illustrative case: Jerry Schneider and the Pacific Telephone Company[1]

The story begins in 1968 when Jerry Schneider was at high school in Los Angeles. His walk to and from school took him past the offices of the Pacific Telephone Company. The company's rubbish bins often contained manuals, pamphlets and memos about the business — and on at least one occasion contained unopened sets of stock procurement and storage instructions. Jerry helped himself to this information and by 1971 he knew more about the stock systems of the Pacific Telephone Company and its supplier Western Electric than most of their employees.

When Jerry left school he decided to put the information he had gained to use. He formed a company called Creative Systems Enterprises and rented a warehouse in Los Angeles. He then persuaded a friend who worked for Pacific Telephone to sell him a key to the gates of their warehouse. Next he went to an auction of telephone company goods and bought a second-hand Pacific Telephone truck which still had the company's name emblazoned on its sides. He also bought a touch-tone telephone so he could order telephone equipment by dialling into Pacific's on-line equipment ordering system. Finally Jerry got identification numbers and account numbers of the sites likely to order goods from an employee of Pacific Telephone. He did this by posing as a supply/delivery agent who was an employee of the company.

Jerry placed his first order in June 1971 for $30,000 of equipment. By 2 a.m. the following morning the goods he ordered had been transferred from the main warehouse to the local warehouse to await collection by a site employee. At 5 a.m. Jerry drove his Pacific Telephone truck into the warehouse and used the key he had acquired to let himself in. He loaded the equipment, signed the relevant documents and drove off. He repeated this procedure almost every day for the next six months or so. Three times during this period the computer passwords were changed by sending a notice of the change to the individuals concerned via their terminals.

On arrival at Jerry's warehouse some of the goods would be repackaged and others would just be labelled 'released for resale'. He soon had ten employees working for him and his customers were amazed at his speedy service. He said later that quite a large portion of his business was legitimate and that he only used dishonest methods to get equipment for rush orders. As time went on he grew more cocky and got Pacific Telephone to deliver to the sites he was supplying. The manuals he had obtained years before had given him knowledge of the stock reorder points: he used this to purposely run down lines by placing large orders. Then he would offer to sell the same stock back to the company to save them the trouble of reordering in haste from the normal supplier.

The pressure eventually got too much for Jerry. He was going to night school to please his parents, making early morning trips to Pacific's warehouse to collect goods and supervising his employees during the day. Eventually he confided in a particular employee so that he could make the early morning pick-ups in place of Jerry. After a time the employee asked for a $40 a week pay rise which Jerry refused. After the disagreement over pay the employee threatened to tell all to the telephone company. So Jerry sacked him. Not surprisingly the ex-employee did inform the Pacific Telephone Company of the fraud.

Jerry was caught with $8,000 worth of stock on his premises but the extent of the fraud could not be determined because Jerry had been careful not to keep records and had seen to it that wherever possible the telephone company had no records of their transactions also. The goods had passed backwards and forwards so many times it was impossible to sort the situation out but the total loss was probably around $850,000. Jerry was sent to prison for two months. The newspaper coverage he received had made him quite famous and on his release he became a management consultant in computer security.

The case of Jerry Schneider highlights a number of security weaknesses which together allowed the crime to be perpetrated. They are:

1. **Rubbish bins**. Nothing, however innocent it may appear, should be thrown out without being put through a shredding machine. A piece of paper may appear to yield little worthwhile information in isolation but when viewed in conjunction with others valuable information may be pieced together. Certainly complete manuals should never be thrown away at any one time unless their contents have been shredded or otherwise destroyed.

2. **Locks and keys**. Locks should be changed regularly wherever practical. If possible, keys should be collected in before the employee leaves the premises at the end of the day in order to make it more difficult to get duplicate keys cut. A second key should not be issued automatically if the employee reports the first as being lost. However, in this instance staff loyalty is probably the best protection and should be actively cultivated.

3. **Identification and account numbers**. These should not be common knowledge and should not be disclosed without some form of identification. If the request is made over the telephone the employee should always telephone back or check with the department involved to verify the status of the person requesting the information.

4. **System checks**. A good information, accounting or physical flow system should incorporate checks at various points. Employees should also be encouraged to think and to check any unusual occurrences. In this case the following questions should have been asked at some stage during the seven

months. Who was this person who was signing the documents? What was he doing with the goods? Why did he always collect so early in the morning?

5. **Changing computer passwords**. There is very little point in changing passwords if all people using the system are automatically notified through the system itself. The idea of a change of password is to make sure that anyone who has gained knowledge of a previous one is barred from the system after the change. Changing passwords only three times in seven months is not adequate. They should be changed irregularly but approximately once a month.

14.3 Computer crime

Figures on computer crime are not easy to obtain as organizations do not have to disclose them in the UK. Banks, in particular, have not been keen to disclose details of computer crimes because of a possible loss of face and customer confidence. In the USA, where computer crimes over a certain size have to be disclosed, they cost between $3 and $5 billion in 1988. An estimate, by the police, of the cost of computer crime or attempted crime in the UK for 1989 was £477m, an alarming increase of 25 per cent over their estimate for the previous year. The situation may be much worse, however, as estimates by financial organizations put the figure much higher — at £1 billion or more.

The crimes may be large or small in scale. One person in the UK once obtained £6m through credit card fraud, but the average loss is much smaller — approximately £390,000 in 1989. Nearly half of all computer crime in the UK is fraud, and three out of four fraud crimes involve altering or adding to the data being entered into the system. The remaining categories of crime are sabotage, hacking and theft, with theft of equipment being more prevalent than theft of information. However, the latter category may be seriously underestimated because it is exceedingly difficult to establish whether information has been taken even if the organization is aware that someone has entered the system and been examining files. Often the company becomes aware from the audit trail that someone has entered the system, but unless something appears to be wrong it will not be investigated in detail because of the cost.

14.4 Hacking

Hacking is the cracking of codes and passwords and entering into a computer system without authority in order to browse through information. It is considered by hackers to be both a sport and an intellectual excercise, and is not usually done with criminal intent. The sport will not be stopped by laws but by good security systems which involve layers of passwords. Just as locks and bolts do much to deter all but the most ardent burglars, so good security in a computer network will deter most casual hackers. In answer to a survey carried out in July 1989, fifty-six out of the sixty-two companies taking part said that they had been the victims of hacking. More than half said that no damage had been done, but nine admitted sabotage. Hackers' clubs abound throughout the world. One well known club, the Chaos Club of Hamburg, hacked into the videotex system and acquired the password of the Hamburger Sparkasse, a large savings bank. The bank's pages were normally accessed at a cost of DM 10 per page. The twenty-five members of the club accessed more than thirteen thousand pages over one weekend in 1984 to deliberately run up a bill of DM 135,000 payable by the bank to the bank.

The impression should not be given that hackers are just pranksters. Some are, and they have caused considerable disruption and havoc on occasions; but other hackers are criminals, and, in rare instances, dangerous criminals. Fictional stories exist of hackers, who are in effect murderers, entering hospital systems and altering patients' prescriptions or drip solutions. A crime that may appear almost negligible in comparision, but still of major concern to the company involved, was the theft of information from Herbert and Sons Ltd of Suffolk. Herbert's had developed an individual program which controlled its weighing scales. It had cost £160,000 and had taken over three years to develop. It was important because it helped give the company a competitive edge in a cut-throat market. A supermarket assistant hacked into their system and copied the software which was later used by a rival company that were unaware of its origin. There was little that Herbert's could do as the knowledge was now no longer theirs alone and their advantage had been lost.

14.5 Large scale fraud

It is perhaps unsurprising that European crime syndicates have become involved in computer fraud. Three crimes that were attempted but foiled, all of them against financial institutions, involved sums of £15m, £31m and £32m. These are not isolated cases. It is normal for the money to be diverted to Swiss banks in several packets via a variety of routes and through a variety of accounts. One rather strange case involved a European underworld figure known as Kim, who made contact with a roofer and tiler called John Felinski in a public house in London. Felinski then made contact with his old friend Angelo Lamberti who worked at the London base of an American securities house. Angelo knew some of the passwords which the pair used to hack into the system of the securities house. They operated from John's home with a personal computer and sent £8m through four countries to a Swiss bank. As they were not greatly skilled in the art it is hardly surprising that they were caught. Felinski was sentenced to eighteen months imprisonment and Lamberti to three years.

14.6 Sabotage

Most computer crimes, especially sabotage, are inside jobs. The perpetrator could be a computer programmer but more normally has only a relatively low level of computer skill. The typical person committing such a crime is a disgruntled male clerk who knows a few passwords and who has, by using the system, spotted a weakness or two in it and, when so minded, can exploit this knowledge to cause havoc. It is quite possible for an organization to prevent many of these crimes, by good company practice. This would include the following:

- Make sure all staff are treated fairly and are happy in their work.
- Employ women — 80 per cent of the computer crimes are carried out by men.
- Check references of all new staff who will work with important data and codes.
- Change passwords regularly.
- Examine all systems regularly for weak points and immediately correct any that are spotted.

The first three suggestions need no further explanation and the fourth was discussed in section 13.15. The last is very important and quite a few organizations are now aware of this and have instigated appropriate monitoring procedures. For instance, IBM has a team of 'penetration testers' whose job is to regularly test the security of their networked computer mainframe systems. If they succeed in breaking the security of the systems, severe action is taken against those who have been lax. Barclay's Bank spends £20m a year on systems security and has specialist teams to deal with hacking and virus crimes. One of the teams' jobs is to write anti-virus programs; at present they have programs to deal with more than two hundred different viruses, but, of course, they are always one step behind the virus creator.

14.7 Viruses and worms

A virus infection in an organization's computer network has become a real possibility in recent years. This is shown by the results of a recent survey carried out by the Information Technology Promotion Agency. Five hundred computer manufacturers and users in Japan were questioned and it was found that 13 per cent of their computers had been infected by viruses.[2]

A virus is a bug which attaches itself to a program or file in such a way that it cannot be detected. It is a rogue bit of programming capable of performing some mischievous action: normally replicating itself. When triggered by some specific occurrence the virus will copy itself onto the next piece of software and so it spreads through the system, onto other disks and into other networked computers. Viruses may be categorized as being either benign or malicious. A benign virus is just a nuisance but causes no real damage. The 'cookie monster' which originated at the Massachusetts Institute of Technology in the 1970s was an example of a benign virus.[3] As an idividual worked at a computer the word 'cookie' appeared on the screen and the user's work would begin to disappear from the screen. The work disappeared slowly at first but at an increasing rate until the computer flashed 'cookie, cookie, give me a cookie'. If the user typed in the word 'cookie' the words 'thank you' appeared and the monster vanished. If 'cookie' was not typed in, eventually the monster relented and said 'I didn't want a cookie anyway' and disappeared. No real damage was done but the user lost valuable time and may have received quite a fright at the thought of losing hours of work. At the time of writing, the Computer Threat Research Association, an independent organization, is receiving increasing reports of musical viruses. Viruses which play tunes are quite harmless and can be removed fairly easily.

There are two types of malicious virus. The first destroys its orginal host when it has copied itself, and continues in this manner until all the computer's memory disks have been wiped out. The second is in theory harmless as it does not destroy or corrupt but by proliferation uses all the spare capacity of the computer thus making it inoperative. The virus is usually attached to the operating system itself or to the 'bootstrap' (the bit of software which gets the computer going and loads other programs). This has the effect of spreading the virus across the system, and onto other disks and networked computers.

Viruses are triggered into action by some specific occurrence. Those known as time bombs are activated by a particular date, such as Friday 13th, and those called logic bombs by a particular set of circumstances, such as, 'when my name is wiped off the company's payroll'. Worms are similar to viruses in their effect and in the way they replicate but are normally on separate pieces of software rather than being attached to another program.

One of the earliest viruses was the Christmas tree. A West German student wrote a computer Christmas card to his friends at university not realizing that the university was connected to a world network. The receiver of the card was asked to run the program which resulted in the card being sent to all his friends too. The card spread across Europe to the USA and back again. It found its way into private businesses one of which was IBM, Portsmouth. This highlights one of the additional problems of security created by networks: that a virus can rapidily spread from one organization to another if preventative measures are inadequate.

The October 13th virus called 'Data Crime' is particularly destructive and has spread extensively through many countries. It attaches itself to programs run after that date with the result that the hard disk eventually becomes inaccessible. Two hundred and sixty computers in the Danish post office had this virus and were disinfected just in time to stop major damage occurring. It was the biggest virus infection to date in Denmark. The virus spread across many countries; in Holland the police issued their own anti-virus to help deal with it. The October 13th virus should not be confused with the Friday 13th virus, sometimes called the 1813 virus, which is another time bomb that has caused wide-scale havoc. It wakes up whenever the 13th is a Friday and starts to copy itself and attach itself to other programs. It adds 1813 bytes to every program it attacks, hence its name. Gradually the computer memory is used up and the computer slows down.

Another example of the same type of virus was that left by an aggrieved computer programmer as a gift to the organization which had just given him the sack. It was called 'creeper'and it occupied just 400 bytes of memory. It had just one function — to copy itself. Twenty-four hours after he left it woke up, duplicated itself and went dormant again. As the computer had a 300 million byte memory no harm had been done as only 800 bytes of memory had been lost. Two days later it became active again and the two copies duplicated themselves and 1,600 bytes of memory were gone. After a fortnight there were delays and odd occurrences in the peripheral computer functions. After twenty days the system packed up altogether. The company's experts created emergency memory space and also an antidote, a program called 'reaper', whose job it was to destroy all creepers. As the reapers reaped their harvest so the creepers crept stealthily on but eventually after a long battle the reapers were victorious.

14.8   Vaccines and security measures

Electronic programs called vaccines are available to deal with most of the known viruses, but, of course, the problem is never solved as new viruses are created all the time. Vaccines search a suspect program for known viruses looking for the unique programming code of the particular virus. Alternatively, a suspect program can be compared with a clean, original version and any differences drawn to the attention of the user. This is called a cyclic redundancy check. The virus creators have hit back by producing 'protest' viruses which are created to show that particular anti-virus programs are ineffective. Fortunately, these viruses are harmless and exist solely to prove the superiority of the virus creator.

However, the real answer to the problem is good computer 'hygiene'. For instance, a computer which is not connected to a network can only become infected if a disk is used which contains a virus. Therefore, free or cheap disks should be checked on an isolated computer before they are run on the main system.

All editing commands should be displayed and checked for hidden viruses. It is, of course, good practice to check all disks in this way but the likelihood of infection from disks which arrive in their original wrappers from well known software houses is slight.

Two common ways a virus can enter a system are through **bulletin boards** and, more likely, via the computer games software which technicians run during their lunch hour. Banning games would be unpopular and difficult to enforce, but employees must be strongly encouraged to check all software before use. Individuals who have done work on their home computers should also have their programs checked for viruses. This procedure is vital and every computer terminal should have a warning of the penalty for loading unauthorized programs or using unauthorized networks.

As viruses usually attach themselves to the operating system, operating systems which have their own software code write-protected, on disk and storage, are protected against them. Most viruses have occurred on workstations running the DOS operating system. Only a few viruses have been noted on the Unix systems, but perhaps they will increase as Unix becomes more widely used. A virus can only harm a computer system if it gets into the computer in an executable form, that is as a program rather than data. Thus systems should only import data wherever possible and not receive executable programs via the network. The segmentation of program storage from data storage can also help, as viruses cannot replicate themselves if programs only update data files rather than program files.

That security is very lax in far too many organizations was all too apparent with the scare created by the 'Aids' disks. This was a 'Trojan horse' which, as its name implies, appears innocent but hiding inside it is something rather nasty, in this particular case a logic bomb. The disk was manufactured in Panama and some twenty thousand disks were posted in the UK in 1989 to unsuspecting recipients. The disks were labelled 'Aids information' from 'PC Cyborg Corporation'. They were accompanied by a leaflet which encouraged the payment of $378 to a box in Panama for a lifetime licence. There was also a slip with the disk warning that the program contained mechanisms which 'will adversely affect other program applications on microcomputers' and further on it said, 'your microcomputer will stop functioning normally if the licence fee is not paid'. Many recipients quite happily put the unsolicitated disk into their computer without bothering to even read the leaflet let alone check the disk for unwanted bugs. When the computer had been switched on thirty times after the initial running of the program, the rogue software scrambled information on the hard disk and the computer became unusable and data were destroyed. Is it a criminal offence to send out disks like this with a warning attached to them? Was this blackmail? Whatever else it was, it was a salutary lesson to those organizations foolish enough to run the program and get caught by this Trojan horse. Many of the organizations who were sent copies either suspected them or were careful and checked them first. Others, alas, did not and their stupidity was summed up rather well by Alan Solomon, chairman of the IBM PC Users' Group: 'it is like finding an open beer bottle by the side of the road and drinking from it on the assumption that it contained good beer'. Preventative measures are absolutely vital, especially as disinfecting costs can be high. One large organization which has learnt the hard way once had to check ten thousand disks after an infection: a procedure which took several months and cost a considerable amount of money.

14.9 Espionage

Espionage is not a threat which should be taken lightly. The Bath School of Management estimates that there are more than 100,000 listening devices sold in the UK each year and that 2,500 companies spy on their competitors each year.[4]

Many managers would seem to be unaware that someone sitting in a van parked outside their premises could be snooping on them. All word-processors and computers leak radiation. An individual in a van can, with the right equipment, use the radiation to obtain a picture on a screen inside the van. The image can be recorded onto video tape and stored for analysis at a later date. New car designs, legal and confidential letters and the organization's current strategy analysis can all be spied upon in this way. At present, it is perfectly legal to do this, and the equipment — a programmable scanner — is cheap and available for purchase in the high street. An organization can protect itself by purchasing special metal cases for computers together with metal meshes for their screens.

Management should also be aware of the possibility of a bug being placed in a conference room and have offices swept for bugs regularly, say once a month or even more frequently during particularly sensitive times. There have been quite a few instances of devices being found during takeover battles in the UK recently.

Software engineers could deliberately place a virus in a new system which they are installing in order to ensure that they will be recalled to rectify the situation at a later date after the virus has become active. They can then read all the company's information, which by that time will be in the system, with a view to selling or using it to their advantage.

Special enciphering or encryption equipment may be purchased and located at both ends of a data transmission link to convert data into a coded format. Any tappers on the network, or inadvertent listeners who pick up a radio-based message, hear only the encoded message which is relatively hard to break. The situation is being made more difficult for tappers as fibre optic cables replace copper ones because they are more resistant to undetectable line tapping. However, crime in this area should not be overlooked on the grounds that it is unlikely as the following case illustrates. The chief technical engineer of Nippon Telephone and Telegraph Company used wire tapping to withdraw 130 million yen.[5] He was responsible for testing and maintaining the lines leased to a bank by NTT on the ATM (automatic teller machine) network. As there was no encryption of the data being transmitted from the cash dispensers to the central system he was able to copy the account data and PINs onto cassette tapes. At home he transferred this onto magnetic stripe cards which the company had given him for testing purposes. The crime was discovered when customers queried the mysterious withdrawals from their accounts.

In order to scramble and unscramble data the equipment and message formats used must be standard. The Data Encryption Standard, first introduced in the USA in the mid 1970s, ensures this and is based on the technique of multiplying the digitally coded message by some factor. This, and the development in the late 1970s of a two key system which was much better than previous systems, made encryption more popular. With this system one key, the scrambling key, is made public by the receiver via a directory and it can then be used by anyone wishing to send a secret message to the receiver. The other key, the unscrambling key, is kept secret and is used by the receiver to decode any message received.

Cellular and cordless telephones are the most vulnerable type of telephone because a radio or television set can be used to pick up a conversation taking place several hundred feet away. Radio communication systems are similarly vulnerable, and some national police forces use encryption to prevent eavesdroppers and criminals from hearing their conversations. Telephone scramblers can be used but rarely are by business organizations. Most telephone companies leave it up to the user to install scramblers, but Deutsche Bundespost Telecom provides an automatic service to customers by scrambling all the telephone traffic it carries over microwave links and the cellular network and cordless telephone conversations are also scrambled.

14.10 The law

If money is stolen or equipment or information files damaged or destroyed, a charge can be brought under the Criminal Damage Act 1971. Hacking, however, presents a problem because there is no damage, and theft of information, if it does occur, might be hard to prove. Steve Gold and Robert Schifreen who hacked into the Prestel mailboxes of various people, including the Duke of Edinburgh, were charged under the Forgery and Counterfeiting Act 1981 for forging Prestel IDs and passwords. This was because they had caused no damage apart from leaving one or two humorous messages and altering the spelling of some words. They were acquitted on a point of law following a House of Lords decision. The decision was that 'forgery' requires an instrument to be forged, merely inputting numbers into a system was not creating an instrument and therefore not forgery. The Telecommunications Act 1984 could be used to prosecute for the theft of electricity. Other than that, there was little that could be done in the UK until the Computer Misuse Act 1990 was passed. It is based on a report issued in 1989 by the Law Commission which recommended the introduction of three new offences which are now law. The Act states that:

- Any unauthorized access to programs or data is punishable with a maximum of six months imprisonment, a fine of up to £2,000, or both.
- Unauthorized access to a computer with the intent to commit or facilitate the commission of a serious crime is punishable with a maximum penalty of imprisonment of five years or an unlimited fine.
- Any unauthorized modification of computer material (such as the introduction of a virus) is punishable with a maximum penalty of up to five years imprisonment or an unlimited fine.

Hugh Cornwall, lawyer and author of the *Hacker's Handbook*, has criticized the Act as being too draconian. This is because a literal interpretation of its provisions would mean that anyone typing a letter to a friend on an office word-processor would lay themselves open to prosecution on the grounds of unauthorized access to the computer system. This could not occur if a typewriter was used. However, it could occur if a telephone call was made to a friend from the office and the telephone was part of a computerized telecommunication system.

A new law was also passed in the USA called the Computer Fraud and Abuse Act 1986. It was used in 1989 for the first time to convict Robert Morris, a Cornell graduate and son of a computer security expert. He paralyzed six thousand computers with a worm which, he said, he intended should make only a single copy in each computer and, therefore, cause no harm. It was, he said, an academic exercise to see how far a worm could spread through networks, which had gone badly wrong due to a programming error. The worm did not actually destroy data but caused so much confusion that many computers were closed down for several days. It reproduced itself with incredible speed and instructed the computer to send it to all other users on the network. The worm copied files and sent them to all subscribers and thus rapidly filled the computers' memory. It was inserted into the US defence network called Arpanet. From there it squirmed its way through some of the most secure establishments in the USA — the National Security Agency, the Strategic Air Command, the space agency NASA, SRI the leading computer security company in California, and the Lawrence Livermore Laboratory where nuclear weapons were being developed.

A further legal problem may occur in the instance of international hacking, namely, the difficulty that could arise in deciding in which country the offence was committed.

14.11 Using information systems to prevent theft

Thus far in this chapter the vulnerability of computerized information systems to a wide range of crimes has been discussed. It should not be thought, however, that computerized information is necessarily only a vehicle for fraud. Rather it may be used to prevent it.

For example, theft at the point of sale can be minimized by requiring all cashiers to enter their personal number into the information system when they come on duty. Till discrepancies can, therefore, be traced to individual cashiers. This can also be done, less efficiently, on a manual system by initialling the till roll. Similarly, in any information system, if passwords are recorded when an individual starts work, all entries and alterations to data can be traced to that person (see section 13.15). This should help to prevent crimes such as payroll and invoice frauds. The evolution of smart cards, such as those used in the French banking industry (see section 6.7), also helps to prevent fraud by checking that the customer has the funds to meet the cost of the transaction.

A comprehensive computerized information system can be a valuable aid in protecting the assets of banks and building societies, as well as their customers. For example, if an individual has his wallet and cheque book stolen, the thief will try to use the credit cards and cheques fraudulently. He will, however, be unable to draw cash from any bank or building society which has an up to date computerized information system, such as is used by many leading UK building societies. When the thief goes to the cash desk the account number will be entered into the terminal and, provided the bank has been notified, a message refusing payment will be relayed to the cashier. Unfortunately, at present, many UK banks do not have such a system. If, for instance, a cheque book and guarantee card are stolen, the thief can draw cash daily until the cheque book runs out. Under these circumstances the cashier has no way of knowing that the cheque book has been stolen because the information cannot be relayed to the branch. This could cost the bank £5,000 for a single lost cheque book: surely a computerized system would pay for itself very quickly! In theory, a paper list of account numbers could be produced and sent to branches daily, but, due to the volume of theft nowadays, this is considered impractical by most banks.

Fully computerized systems deter thieves. Even though the victim may not report the theft immediately, the wise thief will not dare to attempt to gain funds from a bank or building society which uses a fully computerized information system. This is because, at the very least, a description of the villain will be given to the police, or more likely a closed circuit television in the branch will capture his identity. This is of great benefit to the negligent customer who may not immediately notice or report the theft: his funds will still remain intact.

NOTES

1. Stephen A. Moscove and Mark G. Simkin, *Accounting Information Systems*,4th edn (Wiley, 1989).
2. *Daily Telegraph*, 23 July 1990.
3. Hugh Cornwall, *Hackers Handbook III* (Century Hutchinson, 1988).
4. 'White collar crime: fact or fiction?' *Management Accounting*, Mar. 1990.

5. Ken Wong, 'Computer fraud and retail banking: what are the risks?' in *A Handbook of Computer Security*, Keith Hearnden (ed.) 1990.

FURTHER READING

Cornwall, Hugh, *Hackers Handbook IV* (Century Hutchinson, 1989). A must for all those interested in the techniques involved in hacking.

Heardean, Keith (ed.), *A Handbook of Computer Security* (Kogan Page, 1990). Contains chapters by various experts on a wide range of security measures.

Moscove, Stephen and Mark Simkin, *Accounting Information Systems* (Wiley, 1989). Has a good chapter on computer crime and another on security controls.

EXERCISES

1. Networks bring with them many benefits but they also create many problems not the least of which is security. Discuss the security problems created by networks and consider whether they could ever be so great that management might decide not to link up with other organizations via industry networks.

2. Briefly outline a computer fraud/crime that has taken place recently. State clearly the security weaknesses that made the fraud/crime possible and suggest ways in which the organization could rectify, or has rectified, these weaknesses.

15 Influences and behaviour

SCOPE AND CONTENTS

This chapter looks initially at the problems that individuals have in coping with change and new technology. The actions that management can take to overcome these problems are examined. Whether new technology and systems are always better and improve the quality of work is discussed. The need for different types of information in different business cultures is examined. The influence of government on information and information systems, in particular the telecommunicatons industry, is discussed. The various governmental 5th and 6th generation initiatives to develop more advanced computer systems are considered. Finally the action of Singapore's government to improve the information infrastructure is outlined.

> Under the surface of flux and of fear there is an underground movement,
> Under the crust of bureaucracy, quiet behind the posters,
> Unconscious but palpably there — the Kingdom of individuals.
> from *The Kingdom* by Louis MacNiece

15.1 The individual

Underneath there is always the individual. It is the individual who must be influenced by the organization or state and who in turn influences them. Thus it is the behaviour of individuals which is paramount. This chapter begins by looking at the behaviour and fears of individuals in relation to new technology and changes in information systems and procedures. On occasions, both governments and organizations attempt to influence or direct the behaviour of individuals to achieve specific ends. Governments attempt to stimulate or direct research into new technology by providing funds and setting up agencies and organizations. They also influence the nature and number of organizations which provide the information infrastructure. They do this by granting licences for operating particular services, such as satellite or EDI, and by controlling the entrants into particular industries. The emphasis, or lack of it, given to information technology by the education system is largely a function of governmental pressure and resource provision. The various governmental initiatives in France are a good example of how a government seeks to influence the behaviour of *individuals* with regard to information technology.

Organizations can also direct events and procedures by installing particular types of system which encourage a particular behaviour pattern. For instance, the extent and willingness with which banks and credit card companies switch from credit cards to smart cards influence customer and employee behaviour. The ways in which an organization can attempt to satisfy customer requirements have been considered in previous chapters and will not be discussed again here. Despite the influence of the organization and state, ultimately it is the behaviour of the individual which dictates events. The chapter starts, therefore, with the attitudes and behaviour of individual employees and their reaction to new systems and change.

15.2 Coping with change

Most people are frightened of the unknown, and one of the major unknowns in the workplace is new technology. To some individuals, grasping how a keyboard works is much more difficult than learning to drive a car. They in fact suffer from technophobia. Added to this is the problem that change upsets a steady routine and some employees feel that it must be resisted. Far too frequently clerical workers have been allowed to 'make the job their own' in the worst sense of the phrase. They have probably performed the same job for years; it would take most people seven hours a day to do it but they have learnt it and adapted it to their style so well that it can be done in, say, four hours. The trouble is that nothing constructive is done in the remaining three hours. The time is spent getting bored, thinking how tedious work is, doing the crossword or in visits to the cloakroom or another office. To these people any new system which threatens the one they have created is a major disaster and must be resisted. Little can be done once this situation has been allowed to arise. The answer is to prevent it occurring in the first place by rotating staff in order to expand their knowledge and the scope of the job that they perform. Thus their horizons are being continually extended and they cease to look on change as a threat.

Harmon and Peterson cite the influence of a high-level manager making a bet that a popular new technology would not work in his plant.[1] He actively worked to hinder and minimize the benefits of the project by resisting change wherever possible. As a result, the installation proved much less satisfactory in his plant than in similar companies. The reasons for this type of behaviour, which is not uncommon in a manager, may be because he is:

- Unable to accept that other people can have good ideas.
- Incapable of discarding old concepts.
- Unsure of himself and feels that his lack of management ability will be shown up by the new system.

The only way to overcome this problem is to try to convert the manager to the new technology before introducing it, and if this fails, move him to a different position within the company. The removal of active and passive resisters should be management's first concern before any change is introduced. As a good company should be changing continually, this should be a permanent consideration. Having done that, they should consider introducing changes to systems in stages; small frequent stages are more easily absorbed by individuals and are perceived as less of a threat.

Before Kwik-Fit introduced its POS (MAT) in the early 1980s an aggressive campaign was instigated to sell the system to its branch managers. The campaign focused on the problems that MAT could solve and the time it would save. As a result, the managers were desperate to receive the new system rather than being worried by the change to new technology.

15.3 Keeping employees informed of change

The planning and installation stages are critical to the success of a system. If these have been handled badly and, as a consequence, employees have turned against the system, it is very difficult to overcome their resistance. There are several tactics which can be used to make sure that implementation goes well as far as employees are concerned, and which should give them a positive attitude to change. None of the tactics are unusual: they simply amount to a common-sense management approach to any type of organizational innovation.

As many employees as possible should be involved at the planning stage of a new information system. This gives individuals time in which to get used to the idea of a new system, gives them some knowledge of what it will do, and should make them enthusiastic about its success. Involving employees in the planning stage gives them the chance to incorporate their ideas into the system. It also helps management to produce the best possible system by drawing on a spectrum of views.

During implementation, all employees, and particularly those who are directly involved, should be kept fully informed. This means telling them about timetable schedules, what events will happen and why. The employee's immediate superior should impart this information rather than a member of the information systems department or an outside consultant. This does not preclude the information department organizing large meetings from time to time in order to keep everyone up to date. But this will not be enough. Every individual will want to know how their particular job will be affected, and the only person who can discuss this properly will be the employee's immediate superior. Therefore, the first stage in any implementation is to keep middle managers fully informed of what is occurring so that they, in turn, can pass this information on to their staff. Too often top management intends to keep all employees fully informed about new systems but, for one reason or another, a break in the communication link occurs at middle management level. Unfortunately, the sole cause for this is often poor quality middle management.

Employees should not only be told what is happening, they should also be given the opportunity to react and comment on progress. This will allow them to explain their fears, lack of understanding, or ideas for improvement. If middle management does its job properly then this should happen automatically, but this is not always the case. To try to overcome this, a project suggestion and query box can be set up in which any employee can raise any relevant point. This is unlikely to be a success unless top managers actively respond to the suggestions and queries. A better method could be to enlarge the concept of the suggestion box, thus giving it more importance. This can be done by management offering large pay bonuses or rewards to those who put forward good suggestions for modification of, or improvement to, the system. This should ensure that everyone thinks about the system thoroughly and that, when completed, it is as good as it could be. Passive systems, like suggestion boxes, are not a substitute for good middle management. They may, however, help to bridge the gap between top management and low level employees where middle management is not as dynamic as it should be. Any rewards given must be substantial enough to encourage employees to respond.

Another tactic is for each new system introduced to have a 'champion'. The champion is usually the manager who initiated the project. He should enthusiastically support it and give strong and clear leadership during the planning and implementation stages. This person acts as a figurehead and is also available to hear personal grouses and worries about the new system. The champion must have genuine enthusiasm for the proposal but still be sufficiently open-minded to act on valid suggestions and criticisms. An appointed champion without such enthusiasm will obviously not be so effective. However, even that is better than a 'faceless' approach under which the employees are merely informed that central office is imposing this system. In this case the only contact the employees are likely to have is with the technicians who install it and who are unaware of its concept and purpose. This 'faceless' approach will make any change seem more threatenening than it really is.

15.4 Training and assistance for technophobia

Those who suffer from technophobia will not be helped by simply being kept informed of progress during the installation. They can only be helped by patient and steady teaching and assistance over a relatively long period of time. In most cases the individual simply needs the chance to build up confidence in using new systems and technology. This is not achieved instantly. A two-day course on how to use a word-processor or a spreadsheet will not give adequate help to people who suffer in this way. Instead they need steady and regular help. The aim should be for these people to learn a small amount, and then to use that new knowledge until they are sufficiently confident to move onto the next stage. Thus technical knowledge is gained slowly initially but the pace will quicken as confidence is gained. If the individual's confidence is shattered again, progress will stop and the mental barrier to learning about new technology will be re-erected.

The type of person who offers the training is very important. It is unlikely that staff from the information systems department will prove successful when teaching people who suffer from technophobia. Information systems staff will not themselves have had first-hand experience of the problem and, therefore, will not be naturally sympathetic. On the contrary, they probably embrace new technology cheerfully and enjoy the challenge it presents. Neither are information systems staff, on the whole, very outward going people who need to communicate with others constantly: instead they tend to have a low social need. This is perfect if they are simply programmers, but it is not so good if they are systems analysts and are supposed to be communicating with managers and users when developing systems. It is even worse if they are attempting to help and train people who are frightened of new systems and technology.

Large organizations should have their own training manager who is a good communicator and who can understand people's fears and cope with them. Such a person may be found more naturally in the personnel department rather than among the ranks of technical staff. In smaller businesses it may be possible for an individual to combine personnel functions with those of training and assisting staff to assimilate new technolgy. It is important that this role is filled by *someone* within the organization if proper use of new systems is to be made by all.

Quite a few organizations have found that adding a diary facility to a new information system proves advantageous. Apart from saving time and making planning meetings much easier, it also encourages all but the most technophobic to use the system. If every manager, and possibly every employee, logs appointments into the diary then their movements are known. The diary systems usually include a facility for keeping details of confidential meetings secret from others, but, if they are not confidential, the nature of the meeting will be disclosed. If a meeting between a large number of busy executives is to be arranged the system might be asked to arrange the first possible meeting date between the managers. It will do this and then notify those involved of the date and time via electronic mail. Immediately prior to the meeting photographs of those taking part may be shown on screen to avoid any problem of recognition. Most managers will enjoy using the diary facility and soon realize its benefits. Once they have become familiar with computers and programs through the diary they will probably feel bold enough to try other applications.

There is always a learning effect with any new method or technology. Management should not be impatient for improved results as it may take quite some time before a higher performance level is reached. This has nothing to do with employees' resistance to technology but to the normal pattern of events with new methods. This phenomenon is known as the learning curve. For instance, when employees begin to make a new product it may take them three or even six months to reach their full productivity level. A similar pattern occurs when new information systems are installed.

15.5   The influence of poor design

Equipment and systems are rarely designed with the technically unsophisticated user in mind. Even loading a program is not always as straightforward as it ought to be: it often requires some knowledge to pass through the operating system into the application package. If the user has no knowledge of the procedures, a string of strange characters and commands will have to be memorized. Screen displays, help facilities and keyboards often leave much to be desired in the way of design.

For example, consider Libertas, the library information system that many UK educational establishments have installed at great expense. It is not a totally bad system but it could have been designed to be much more user-friendly. In the first place, a full computer keyboard is used, which is unnecessary. It might be excusable if there were such a thing as a standard keyboard; but in the absence of such an item why should the user be presented with a complicated keyboard which contains twice as many keys as are required. Neither does the use of particular keys to perform tasks appear to be well thought out. For instance, to move to the next page of information the shift key and the plus sign must be pressed. This is an awkward action which requires two hands quite apart from being difficult for someone with no knowledge of a keyboard as the instruction at the bottom of the screen merely says ' + '. The letter 'N' for next might have been easier. Most users of Libertas will wish to use the system to locate a book on the shelves. The page containing the information on the book, which first appears on the screen, contains virtually everything else one could want to know about the book except where it may be found in the library. The instruction at the bottom implies that one must type LOCATION to find this important piece of information. This is a remarkably long word to have to type in when so much of the keyboard is unused. Actually, one needs only to type in LOC, but the uninitiated are not told this by the computer. In any case, why does the system not simply use 'L'?

Libertas, the new user is told, is much better than a card index or microfiche because it will search for books on a particular topic for you. Try typing in 'information systems' and see how many books Libertas replies with. It will probably be more than 2,000. On doing this in one library, the system's display said that there were over 1,000 books on information, more than 4,000 on systems and that 805 matched the request closely. On examining the first item in the list of 805 it was found to be a book on social accounting! After the user has attempted that type of search a few times it is doubtful whether that facility will be considered sufficiently user-friendly to be used again.

Libertas has been selected for consideration because it is a system which will be familiar to many readers. It is also a system which has a simple purpose and should, therefore, be straightforward and simple to use. However, Libertas is not alone, there are many other systems which suffer from similar drawbacks.

15.6 Is new technology always for the better?

Before introducing any new system the question should be asked: 'is it an improvement?' Sometimes perfectly good systems are ripped out for technology's sake and the new systems which replace them are slower, less reliable and not so well liked by the staff. Alternatively, the level of improvement achieved is too small to justify the disruption and cost involved. It should be borne in mind that some managers who are devoid of innovatory ideas actively seek promotion by changing systems. This gives them the appearance of being dynamic. Unfortunately, the change achieves little, as it was not needed, and, once the manager is promoted, the staff and his successor have to pick up the pieces and make the new system work. The following example shows how a system and an office which might appear old-fashioned at first sight still functions efficiently.

About ten years ago one of the authors in her role as area organiser for CAMRA (the Campaign for Real Ale) visited a rural brewery in order to pick up some beer for a beer exhibition. This is not the usual procedure: a brewery normally receives few direct sales customers. She walked into the sales office which was a relic from Dickensian times. It had lots of polished wood and there was a high stool behind the sloping desk for the clerk to sit on. The clerk, himself, was obviously an ex-colonial type as he was dressed in khaki shorts which appeared somewhat incongruous in the British summer. After she stated the order, the clerk opened a door at the back which led to the loading bay and boomed, 'two kils of bitter and a firkin of mild for the office, Bill'. On his return he sat down on the high stool and leisurely opened a leather bound ledger and began to write. She was amazed to note that he was using a fountain and not a quill pen. She wondered whether he thought it was very daring to adopt such modern technology. When the entry was complete the receipt was written in perfect copper-plate writing, by which time, judging by the sounds outside, the beer had been rolled to the front door of the office.

The system seemed perfect: so simple and quite quick. If the recording took slightly longer than it needed, it did not matter because the overall time was governed by the time it took to fetch the casks. But, above all it was a thoroughly pleasant experience and gave one customer satisfaction! Change, unfortunately, comes to everyone and everything in due course, and eventually the old clerk left and was succeeded by a young man. The system was then changed. Whether the company had waited till the old clerk retired before changing it, knowing that he would not cope with the modern technology, is not known. Perhaps, as seems more likely, the new clerk could not cope with the old system: he may not have had a loud enough voice to shout the order or, perhaps he did not know how to fill a fountain pen, let alone keep a ledger!

15.7 Does new technology improve the quality of the job?

Generally, more advanced information systems are considered better as they provide more information which helps employees to make more and better decisions. They also remove some of the more tedious elements of a job and as a result allow employees to widen the scope of their work. The latter is important because there have been many instances where employees became bored or frustrated by just doing a single task. Sometimes they have had no idea of the purpose of their particular job and do not even know which product they are helping to make. There is an apocryphal story of the president of an American manufacturing organization going onto the factory floor and talking with one employee. The employee had no idea what purpose the particular operation had, but worse, thought that the company produced quite different products from those which it actually did. Imagine working in a car company and thinking you were producing washing machines! Lack of job satisfaction under these circumstances is inevitable. Improved technology can lead to more job satisfaction because the job can be expanded and thus an employee gets a broader view of the organization and of his role within it.

However, more information does not necessarily mean less stress and strain. A manager today may feel under great pressure because he is permanently required to make decisions. He has no excuse if the decision is poor. He has had nearly all the information he could possibly require. Twenty years ago the job may have been easier because part of it entailed obtaining the information, an activity which generates little stress by comparison.

A good information system should relieve stress and not add to it. But what is a good information system? The answer may not be that manifest. Quicker information is not always advantageous. For example, research into two data systems used by the US Social Security Administration produced the following findings.[2] In the original system staff used teletypewriters to gain access to information stored on a central computer. Requests for information about claimants were stacked in a queue and as a result it could take up to eight hours to receive a reply. The replacement system used on-line video terminals and response was immediate. The systems were in operation concurrently, sometimes the two systems operated in the same office. It was found that mental strain and absenteeism *increased* with the newer on-line system and as a result job satisfaction decreased. The reason for this incredible result could not be properly explained, but it was noted that the new system allowed the employees to deal with more claimants a day and that this was probably the cause of the increase in stress. Dealing with frustrated claimants was considered a worse problem than dealing with a frustrating system. Perhaps the frustration of the claimants was worse because the answer was given immediately after consulting an 'impersonal' machine. If it took a day to give the answer the claimant might feel that someone was at least looking at his individual circumstances. In addition, a day later the claimant's temper may have calmed or another officer might take over the case.

An alternative reason for the result could be that a faster system requires staff to make more decisions in a shorter time. Too many decisions made in a short space of time without adequate breaks in between are a cause of stress. Whatever the reason, it is interesting to note that a technically better system does not always benefit those who operate it.

15.8 New technology can change behaviour

An information system may be used to encourage or require particular behaviour from individuals. It is standard management practice to use the environment to affect the way in which employees behave. For example, open-plan office layouts are sometimes adopted in an attempt to improve communication. Similarly, a good telephone system permitting three-way communication, a fax machine or an on-line information system may also improve communication thus allowing for greater exchange of information and better decision making.

Providing too much technology may not always change behaviour for the better. For instance, it is often said that one of the reasons for the success of Japanese production managers is their frequent visits to the factory floor in order to see and assess progress. Details of operator performance, output during the last week and such like are written up in large writing for all the employees concerned to see. Instead of receiving weekly or daily reports, as is traditional in the West, Japanese managers can only get the current figures by going and looking at these charts and statistics on the factory floor. This makes them much more aware of what is happening there and helps the employees to realize that the manager is part of the team and takes an interest in their work. If the western manager's weekly or daily reports are replaced by an on-line information system which will give him up to date information and tell him everything he wishes to know, what need is there for him to leave his office at all? In twenty years' time, when the modern factory may operate without any workers, that may be quite acceptable, but today it is not. Employees must feel that management is not remote but instead takes an interest in operations and knows and understands their problems. Thus a new information system could prove to be a hindrance to good relations. Perhaps the answer would be to put the information system on the factory floor for all to use. This would have the added benefit of giving the production manager some exercise!

Many company chief executives consider it an essential part of their job to practise MBWA (management by walking about). These include the chief executives of Kwik-Fit, Ratners and Marks & Spencer. No information system can ever replace first-hand experience and personal contact. The executive learns about the problems at the ground level, something which no traditional information system based on figures and statistics can do. From the employees' point of view, it boosts their motivation and morale as they at least know the chief executive by sight, even if they have not talked to him, and realize that he is concerned about their part of the business. Information systems can then be used, very successfully, to back up this personal style of business. For instance, up to date statistics on individual stores or units provide the chief executive with current knowledge before a visit, or a telecommunications system can be used as a supplement to visits.

Of course, the introduction of a system incorporating new technology will not necessarily alter human behaviour. A computer system can use the same forms and procedures as the old manual method. This will not create any changes to the working patterns of the organization. On the whole computer systems which do this are poor because they miss the opportunity to improve procedures and performance. Generally speaking, if computer systems do not change procedures it means that no-one has studied the flow of data and information properly, or considered the different ways in which tasks could be performed as a result of the new technology. Such mistakes were often made in the early days of computer systems when transaction processing systems aped manual systems. The computer staff studied the system and 'put' it on the computer. This was a waste of resources. In consequence, no extra information was obtained and no other uses for the information were found. A simple example of computerizing an existing system is often seen in accounting packages for small businesses where a day-book is compiled *after* the ledger has been entered. The whole purpose of a day-book was to log incoming invoices, etc.to make sure that they did not go astray *before* they were entered into the ledger. There is little point in having a list which is made up from the ledger entry. All such computer systems include an audit trail report which is a list of all entries into the system. This is, in effect, the same as a day-book and should make the inclusion of a day-book a complete waste of time. Rather interestingly though, the 'day-book' which consists of transaction listings has found a new use as it is much quicker to check for errors in invoice entries using the day-book report than the audit trail.

15.9   Information in contrasting business cultures

In the traditional western organization, with its hierarchical structure, management is often viewed as a superior species. This is often reinforced by managers giving themselves privileges and erecting barriers between themselves and the rest of the workforce. This creates the 'them and us' attitude. As a result, managers require detailed, day-to-day information on what the workforce is doing in order to maintain control over employees and processes and to enforce corrective action. In this situation it will be necessary to record and measure individual performance so that employees can be encouraged by a wage structure which incorporates large bonuses. Standard costing and budgetary control systems, which concentrate on the retrospective analysis of variations from plan and the assignment of responsibility for such variations, epitomize this type of organizational mentality. This approach often leads to a basic misunderstanding: that managers consider that they require the information for planning and controlling the *business*, but the workforce are under the impression that this information is needed to control *them*. It is not surprising that behaviourial problems arise under these circumstances.

The type of organization discussed above is an X type of organization as identified in McGregor's X and Y theory. (There are many organizational theories; we mention just the one in this book.) The X theory states that employees are idle and that they only work to get pay, therefore, they will only work if a 'whip' is held over them. The whip will take the form of achieving specific work targets. The Y theory suggests that employees actually enjoy work and take an interest in it, therefore, they will respond without being pushed and are quite willing to take responsibility. McGregor did not advocate one or the other. He said that the first approach led to antagonism and the second to laziness. Instead, management should develop an atmosphere of trust and respect and then integrate the employee goals with the goals of the organization as far as possible. This should make the organization effective, as a Y theory approach can be used because the employees's goals are now the same as those of the organization. A business culture which promotes the ideas of mutuality of interest, co-operation and commitment to the organization at all levels will be doing this. The type of information required in such a culture will be different: instead of an emphasis on control information to enforce compliance with organizational goals it will be necessary to give to employees the information which *they* require to monitor and modify *their own* performance.

It is also necessary to provide the employees with more information than is strictly necessary for them to perform their specific jobs if this type of approach is to work really successfully. The organization may go as far as providing employees with all the information they could possibly require. The information system currently being created by AMR Corpn, called InterAAct (briefly mentioned in section 11.12) aims to get close to achieving this. Various applications are being developed to reduce common sources of delay and frustration among employees. Examples of these are:

- Automating the progress of investment proposals. On-line forms and electronic signature control will help to speed approval of capital expenditure and the suppliant can see the current position at any time.
- All employees will have access to their personal files via a terminal.
- Employees will be able to check, via a terminal, how much overtime they have earned to date during the week and eventually be able to check their own pay particulars.

Lack of information is undoubtedly one of the major factors contributing to poor industrial relations within an organization. In the future, if not quite at present, it will be possible to provide systems to supply any information an employee may wish for. It might even include the lunch menu at a local restaurant!

Businesses in the West tend to concentrate on short-term goals. This is partly caused by reward and promotion schemes for management. In the UK, the reliance on equity finance, largely provided by pension funds, which puts emphasis on good *annual* profits is another influencing factor in the concentration on short-term results. Some people think that the increasing dominance of the pension funds as major shareholders has led to an increase in takeovers as pension fund managers are more likely to sell their shares at a high price during the takeover. Under these circumstances managers need information which will assist them to maintain profits and share price and to spot potential predators. Management's time horizon will be short, all investments must provide quick and visible returns. A business which is able to take a longer-term view of its development will not be so concerned with pursuing short-term advantage and can afford to dispense with much of the information required for this.

15.10 Competition encourages the use of new technology

It is probably true to say that most individuals, organizations and states do not change their ways unless forced to do so. Having found a comfortable and suitable pattern of activity, it will be followed and not reconsidered for suitability unless some external factor forces reconsideration. This can be seen in the behaviour patterns not only of individuals, but also of organizations that have for years been complacent because of the lack of competition. Suddenly something occurs to permit competition and the organization is forced to undergo a rapid metamorphosis in order to stay in business.

Governments and the activities which they control are affected in the same way. As an example, consider the provision of the English Law Reports. In the 1860s, a publication called the *Weekly Reporter* came into being which provided transcripts of the week's cases in a weekly publication which could be sent to any subscriber in the country. The law was reported privately at that time and there were other rival publications though none were as fast.

Later, private reporting was largely replaced by the official English Law Reports. Today it takes eight weeks to obtain a transcript of a case, even direct from the High Court. One might have imagined that a stenographer in court could be typing into equipment which was connected to a printer so that an immediate copy could be obtained, even if one or two typing errors had to be corrected later. Most of the delay is apparently caused because the transcript now has to be approved by the judge first. The delay is not important except to lawyers who are seeking to advise clients on an issue which has recently been decided. As a result of this delay, Lexis, the on-line law database (which has to rely on the official reports) is eight to ten weeks out of date. So much for modern technology!

15.11 Government influence on the information industry

Governments play an important part in influencing behaviour and shaping society. They influence the nature of business, that is whether it is private and profit-orientated or whether it is publicly owned with quite different goals. Governments also play an important part in shaping the information network of the country. Most countries have nationalized telephone networks, few have allowed private business total control of the telecommunications system. Over the past ten years or so there have been moves in a number of countries to limit state influence. For instance, in the USA the single national telecommunications organization AT&T was broken up, and, in the UK, British Telecom was privatized once more, after a hundred years or so, and a limited amount of competition introduced. The extent and direction of government influence in the telecommunications industry is very important as it is this which governs the communications infrastructure of a country. The structure of the industry is especially important during a period of rapid development both in technology and in network-building, as at present. Consider again section 8.8 and the development of the UK telecommunications industry since 1983. Would such rapid progress have been made, or so many new products introduced, if British Telecom was still owned entirely by the state and no competition existed?

One important telecommunications issue, which governments influence either directly or indirectly, is the price structure of calls. A country where charges are high will be at a severe disadvantage in the future in comparison with a country with low charges. This is because the one with low charges, providing it has a good service and network (this is essential), is likely to attract more industry in the future. When it comes to encouraging industry to set up in one country rather than another a good communications infrastructure is just as important as a good transport system of roads and railways. Few governments appear to have realized this, or if they have they have not acted on it. Singapore, discussed in the next section, is one of the few to take positive steps to improve its information infrastructure.

One of Eastern Europe's major problems in building up and attracting new industry is the lack of a good telecommunications infrastructure. Poland, for instance, has only 3.1 million telephones compared with 24.1 million in Britain, and many of those are party lines or lines where the operator works only until 10 p.m. One quick way to build the infrastructure is to install mobile telephone systems. Hungary has already awarded two licences for mobile telephones, both are joint ventures with US organizations. However, mobile telephone systems may not provide an adequate long-term solution, and much investment on trunk and local lines and exchanges may still be necessary.

Another area in which governments have influence is that of international telecommunications and computing standards. Occasionally, politicking affects decisions and governments or international groupings, such as the EC, feel obliged to do their own research and development in order to protect their own industries and prestige. The consequence is that international standards are not always accepted as readily as they ought, and generally everyone is the poorer. This is particularly well illustrated by the two standards for magnetic ink and optical typefaces discussed in Chapter 7. See also the lack of standards in the telecommunications and computer industries discussed in Chapter 8.

15.12 Government investment in new technology

In 1981, Japan started research into fifth generation computer systems. A conference was arranged in Tokyo to which heads of research institutions and government representatives from the West were invited. The Japanese outlined a plan for an ambitious research programme for the next ten years. Their aim was to build computers which had far greater capacity, which were easy to use and would be able to tackle much more complex problems. Japan's stated intention to take the world lead in advanced computer technology startled the West into some sort of national and supranational action. The EC founded a research programme called Esprit (European Strategic Programme for Research in Information Technology). Not to be outdone, the UK government set up its own five-year programme in 1983 named the Alvey Programme after its chairman. This was a mainly state-funded programme.

To an extent, most fifth generation projects — as all the projects of the 1980s became known — may be considered a failure as they did not produce highly visible results. However, much of the research was worthwhile and, besides, the aims were technology development rather than product development. The original fifth generation strategy which Japan espoused was probably successful because it did succeed in raising the international standing of Japan's advanced computer industry.

Japan's MITI (Ministry of International Trade and Industry) is now preparing for the sixth generation project. This will be to develop massive parallel computers with processing systems which operate as much like the brain as is possible. From the 1940s until very recently computers operated with Von Neumann architecture. That meant that only one operation could be done at a time and that the whole process consisted of a sequence of operations. Technology improved over the years and so, therefore, did the speed of processing. But now this architecture is proving a limitation to further development. In the 1980s, parallel processing was introduced which allowed more than one operation to be carried out simultaneously. The new Japanese project will take this much further and try to create a computer which will consist of small microprocessors operating in parallel, much as the human brain might work.

The idea is not to produce applied work which will result in a specific computer so much as to create and develop the mathematical theory behind this type of computer system. On the whole, quite understandably, governments do not like giving money to the development of theory because they wish to see some tangible result for their investment. This is just as true of the Japanese government as of western governments. It is not of much benefit to the government which instigated a particular piece of theoretical research if it is possible to look back only after twenty years in order to see the benefits it generated: it is a generation too late for all but the most altruistic of governments. Under these circumstances it could be argued that the approach taken by the Singapore government, described below, is more successful and beneficial to the country. It is normally the case that the organization which spends its funds on research rarely reaps the rewards. It is normally the second or third company to take up and develop the product that makes the profit. This is sometimes referred to as 'the third bite of the apple being the sweetest'. The reason for this is that the third company to enter the market will be able to produce a superior design or to target the product better. What is true for companies also applies to nations. Therefore it may be better to encourage the use of existing technology in new situations rather than inventing the technology itself.

15.13 Illustrative case: Singapore, the island with IT

Some years ago Singapore faced two main problems which led the government to seek a solution in information technology. The first was that strong competition from ports in other parts of Asia was beginning to threaten Singapore's status as a trading nation which relied on trade flowing through its port. The second was that high growth of around 6 per cent per year was required in the economy. This did not seem possible with a population growth of only 1 or 2 per cent and little room on the island for immigrants. Quicker and better information flow, which would generate competitive advantage at the ports and reduce the ever-increasing need for employees, was chosen as the answer. A government agency — the National Computer Board — was set up to prepare and execute a national plan for information technology. Today the work of this agency has borne fruit, and information technology has penetrated just about every aspect of the Singaporeans' lives. Some of the systems are outlined below.

Shipping was the main area where new ideas and technology were needed to stave off competition. The answer was to use information technology to become fast cycle both in terms of cargo and paper handling. Now an expert system determines the best way to off-load containers destined for various ports. The system receives details, in terms of numbers, weights and position in the hold, of every cargo by fax, telex or datastream. The expert system turns the information into colour-coded diagrams of the contents of the ship's hold and determines the best and quickest plan for using two cranes to unload the ship without unbalancing it. As a result a ship can be unloaded in six hours as opposed to two days, as is normal in other ports in the area.

Dealing with the paperwork involved in shipping is normally complicated and time consuming. This was the case in Singapore as it is in the rest of the world. There were forms for customs and permissions for restricted goods to be obtained from a series of government agencies. The paperwork used to take two or three days to obtain, but today in Singapore it can all be done in fifteen minutes by using a computer terminal. A single application for import/export clearance is made on a system called Tradenet. This is connected to a supercomputer which stores information from all the government agencies involved in trade, and so all the permissions are given in just a few minutes. Tradenet is a very powerful network and provides links between importers and exporters, shipping lines and airlines, container terminals, sea and air agents, banks, and the government departments of census & statistics, trade and customs. Shipowners are now keen to use Singapore for off-loading, as with a quick turnaround their ships are more productive.

Singapore also has other systems, one of which is the underground railway information system (discussed in section 6.3). The others are too numerous to describe in detail, but they include Lawnet (which contains all case law), Medinet (which contains medical records for use by hospitals and doctors), Ecomnet (links all economic development boards), Silas (the library service) and School Link (an administration system for schools). Yet another is Land-data which is a computerized map containing details of every building and information on whether it is mortgaged. It also contains details of all drains, utilities and even pollution levels. It seems likely that no other country has such a comprehensive plan of its land and assets.

Finally all the services are being linked in Teleview. Although still at the trial stage, Teleview is the world's most advanced photo videotex system and is able to transmit colour photographs in a fraction of a second. It is also fully interactive and provides immediate access to a central computer for the retrieval of pages of information.

NOTES

1. Roy Harmon and Leroy Peterson, *Reinventing the Factory* (The Free Press, 1990).
2. J.A. Turner, 'Computer mediated work: the interplay between technology and structured jobs', cited in *Information Systems Management in Practice*, Barbara McNurlin and Ralph Sprague (Prentice Hall, 1989).

FURTHER READING

Arnod, Erik and Ken Guy, *Parallel Convergence: National strategies in information technology* (Frances Pinter, 1986).

EXERCISES

1. 'The design and/or operation of an information system can have a profound effect on organizational behaviour.' Discuss.

2. An organization is renewing the major part of its information systems and wherever appropriate is replacing its manual systems with new technology. Discuss the behaviourial problems that might arise under the circumstances and draw up a step-by-step programme which the organization could implement to avoid any behaviourial difficulties.

Epilogue

Part One   Information and information needs

In this book we have attempted to demonstrate how important information and information systems are to an organization. Information bestows power, and as such is extremely valuable. However, too much unfocused information can result in the business suffering from 'indigestion'. As a manager's mind can absorb only a certain amount, the information that is provided must be carefully selected so as to ensure that it is pertinent for the decision being taken.

Managers should themselves select the information they need because only they know precisely what they require. Each person will set about making their decisions in slightly different ways and will, as a result, require slightly different information. In most circumstances, not only should the managers select the information they require but they should be allowed to obtain it themselves at a time convenient to them. This can be done via a network and a database. Allowing managers to select and obtain their own information will only be satisfactory if they have been well educated in terms of the information available and if they are enthusiastic for the company to succeed. If they are not well educated they may need assistance in selecting the information. If they lack enthusiasm they will not be disposed to obtain the information themselves and thus will require a system which actively 'pushes' information towards them. The remedy is not really with the system, however, but with top managers — they should obtain and train good managers.

The information system itself must be built to meet the specific information needs of the organization and its managers. These needs will change over time as the organization develops. The information needs are also dependent on the type and spread of the business and on the style of management. A key word to remember, therefore, when selecting suitable systems and equipment is *flexibility* so that they can be adjusted to new information needs.

Another key word to remember is *simplicity*. All information flow and provision should be regularly examined to see whether the system could be simplified or streamlined. It should not be thought that, as the organization grows and as technology becomes more complex, the information flows must also become more complex and convoluted. Technology should only be applied to information flows which have been streamlined — and only then when absolutely necessary. Simple systems such as the kanban or passing a baton on a single track railway may be quite adequate. The latter is a satisfactory information system whose purpose is to prevent railway collisions. However, it does not give a monitoring office any information on the position of the trains at a particular time.

It is also wise to remember that an information system is a good servant but a bad master. It is there to serve the information needs of the organization and not to dictate them. The system must be adaptable to an individual's needs and foibles and must not dictate how an individual must behave when obtaining data or information. If the system cannot be adapted to the individual's requirements then it will not be used to its full potential and may even prove valueless.

Part Two   Techniques and technologies

The different techniques and technologies which were considered will undoubtedly change in the next ten years, if not before. The world has been through a period of rapid change and development in information technology products and it seems reasonable to expect a calmer period of rationalization and permeation to follow. However, technological progress will not cease, and all organizations should be aware of new developments so that they can be incorporated where valuable. Needless to say, new technology should not be used for its own sake.

'Solutions in search of problems' is a phrase common in the world of computer experts. A technique or a technology is normally developed to solve a specific problem because funds are only forthcoming on this basis. Sometimes, however, a new technique or technology is developed for its own sake. Without a specific purpose it is likely to become a 'solution in search of a problem'. Sometimes the technology has to wait twenty or thirty years before it finds its problem and is put to practical use. An example of this was the technology used in optical memory cards which was developed in the 1930s, half a century before it was used in optical memory cards in the 1980s.

Part Three   Strategy formulation and implementation

Over the past decade or so many organizations have felt the need to invest considerable sums in information technology. Much of this money has been wasted. In this book we have concentrated on the more positive aspect of the benefits to be gained by using information systems. It takes little imagination, however, to realize that several million pounds spent by an organization (which was not in the best of financial health anyway) will make problems worse rather than better if the system for one reason or another proves to be unsatisfactory. Putting money into information systems is no guarantee that the right information is provided in the right way and that competitive advantage is realized. The money must be spent wisely and managers and employees must be committed to its success. Recently several studies, including one by the Kobler Unit, have been made in this problem area with the intention of providing guidance for management.[1]

It is rather worrying that so many managers have become disillusioned by information technology: this could lead to a lack of commitment and investment. As information is such a powerful aid — the invisible business asset or weapon — we have to hope that this will not occur. On the other hand, managers must guard against pouring money down an ever-deepening pit called 'information technology'. It is not necessary to renew the majority of systems every few years simply because technology has slightly improved. Any decision to invest must be justified on the grounds of cost—benefit but the 'benefits' must be interpreted broadly: they *must* extend beyond the obvious and immediate ones that are commonly assessed by accountants so as to include those which are difficult to put into words, let alone quantify.

Finally, a salutary note to all who have gained the impression that organizations should be supplying more information to their managers and employees and that failures of new systems and technology projects will be a thing of the past once organizations have gained experience in that area.

In 1981 Kwik-Fit (the car exhaust and tyre replacement organization) was in difficulties having just increased its number of centres (branches) from 50 to 185 following acquisitions.[2] The company was suffering from a lack of control and, in the words of their chief executive, Tom Farmer, a 'profit sabbatical'. The company was advised to set up POS terminals at all centres to obtain the necessary information in order to control costs and stock. Not appreciating any of the difficulties involved in being one of the first in the field, the company took the advice without further thought. The project was completed in less than a year and was a great success. So much so that business people from all over the world came to see the system and the company's turnover and profit rose from £43m and £2.6m respectively in 1983 to £102m and £11.1m in 1987.

In 1987 Kwik-Fit decided that it had to replace its mainframe computer which was no longer adequate for the size of the business. (Its POS terminals and the software were still very satisfactory.) It decided to use a different supplier and this necessitated rewriting the programs, which the supplier undertook to do. The whole project was a disaster. The programs had numerous bugs and the computer was the wrong model. How could this have happened after the initial success? The lesson Kwik-Fit learnt was to keep future projects under its own tight control.

Kwik-Fit, which now has five hundred centres, recently decided that the system installed in the 1980s was supplying *too much* information. The situation was becoming dangerous as regional managers no longer communicated with centre managers, instead they looked at the reports supplied by the system. As a consequence, personal contact and communication of problems was gradually reducing. The company wanted the regional managers to pick up the telephone and talk to the centre managers and so it scrapped 90 per cent of all reports, forcing the regional managers to get information by telephone. In Tom Farmer's words 'big businesses need small reports'.

This clearly illustrates that business information is not always conveyed in the printed word or figure. Humans gain much of their information in an informal way by meeting and chatting with others. An individual may come away from a meeting with an intuitive feeling, such as: 'from what he said I feel there may be a problem developing in that area in the next month or two — I must watch that area carefully'. Thus computers cannot, as yet, collect all types of data and information, and in many ways the telephone is still the best business communication/information system.

NOTES

1. B. Hochstrasser and C. Griffiths, *Regaining Control of IT Investment: A handbook for senior UK management* (Kobler Unit, 1990).
2. Tom Farmer, 'Integration through communication' paper, Hoskyns Group plc Oct. 1990.

Glossary

The purpose of this glossary is to offer explanations or definitions of words which appear in the text with which the reader may not be familiar. Words from quite a wide range of disciplines are used in the text, and as a result they may not be familiar to all readers. The glossary also contains explanations of all technical words which are considered in detail in the text. In order to indicate in the text that a particular word is included in the glossary it is printed in **bold** the first time it is used.

Annual budget A predetermined plan of an organization's activities and costs for the coming year. It comprises detailed statements of expenditure, output and staffing levels for all departments. These are split into weekly or monthly sections for control purposes. The budget also includes summary statements such as a profit and loss account for the whole organization.

Application package A piece of software developed to perform specific operations on particular data or information files, e.g. a payroll package or a spreadsheet.

Banks' Automated Clearing Service (BACS) A service for automatically transferring funds from one bank to another, or to and from organizations and individuals, e.g. the transfer of monthly salaries. (See section 7.8.)

Bulletin board An 'electronic notice board' used by hackers and computer buffs to exchange information.

Business unit A section of an organization which produces a discrete product or product range and could, therefore, operate independently of the rest of the organization.

Competitive advantage A company's ability to be better than its competitors at performing particular tasks and meeting customer needs. There are many different ways of achieving competitive advantage but they may be divided into two broad categories: price advantage and product/service differentiation. Achieving competitive advantage forms a major part of an organization's strategy.

Computer aided design (CAD) A system which allows designs and drawings to be modelled and manipulated on a computer. (See section 5.8.)

Computer aided engineering (CAE) A system which verifies the feasibility of a planned design or the technical aspects of product specifications. (See section 5.8.)

Computer aided manufacturing (CAM) A computer system which controls the operation of equipment by (1) determining what products should be made and (2) producing operating instructions for the equipment. (See section 5.8.)

Computer integrated manufacturing (CIM) A totally computerized manufacturing system which consists of a series of linked manufacturing and information systems. It encompasses all the physical production processes (i.e. the acquisition of materials, planning production and controlling manufacturing operations) and all the production information flows of an organization. (See section 5.9.)

Critical path The longest route or pathway through a process or project, such as manufacturing an aircraft or installing an information system. The time taken to complete this route governs the length of time it takes to complete the whole project. If delays occur on the critical path the whole project is held up.

Critical success factors The factors which are crucial to the successful performance of an organization, business unit or manager. (See section 2.4.)

Data dictionary A computer based dictionary which contains definitions of all data held in a database. (See section 9.7.)

Data model In the technical terms of information engineering, it comprises a data entity list and a data map. In layman's terms this means a list of individual data items together with their associated data items and also a diagram which shows these associations schematically.

Database A collection of data stored in a manner which enables information to be drawn from it in a range of different ways and formats in order to answer a range of different management questions. (See section 9.1.)

Database management system (DBMS) Software which organizes the storage and retrieval of data held in a computerized database. It acts as an intermediary between the application package and the data files. (See section 9.8.)

Distributed database A database that is physically split over a number of locations. However, the database operates as a single system so that the user does not need to know where a particular piece of data is stored in order to gain access to it. (See sections 9.3–9.6.)

Distribution resource planning (DRP) A computer system which provides the information necessary to plan the flow of goods through an organization in order to distribute them efficiently to customers.

Downtime Unproductive time due to the resetting or cleaning of equipment between different batches of production.

Electronic data interchange (EDI) The automatic exchange of data between the information systems of two organizations. It is used mainly to transfer data relating to customer orders, despatch notes and invoices.

Electronic funds transfer (EFT) The electronic movement of money between two organizations via a telecommunications network using EDI. Cheques and other paperwork are not required. (See section 7.8.)

Electronic funds transfer at point of sale (EFTPOS) The transfer of money electronically, rather than by cash or cheque, at the cash point in a shop. The identity and account to be debited is identified by a card passed through a terminal at the cash till. (See section 7.8.)

Electronic point of sale (EPOS) An electronic cash register which includes a reading or scanning mechanism and a means of storing or transmitting sales data for future analysis, in addition to preparing a bill.

Expert system A computer program which contains the accumulated knowledge or wisdom of an individual or group of individuals (experts) on a particular topic. The program may be interrogated by the user to find answers to specific questions or problems. (See section 10.1.)

Fast cycle company One which attempts to serve the customer's specific needs in the shortest time possible. This philosophy is reflected in all aspects of the business including its information systems.

Fifth Generation Project A ten year computer research project initiated by the Japanese in 1981. (See section 15.12.)

4GLs (4th generation languages) Computer languages introduced in the early 1980s. They require less skill from the programmer than their predecessors because they are non-procedural languages (i.e. they allow statements to occur in the order that suits the programmer rather than the sequence required by the computer). They also contain many facilities not available with 3GLs, such as report generators, data dictionaries and interactive query facilities.

Hacking Gaining unauthorized access to a computer system. (See section 14.4.)

Heuristic knowledge Knowledge gained by investigating or discovering patterns of behaviour and events, e.g. after seeing a red sky in the evening predicting that the weather will be fine the next day.

Image processing A system which stores documents or other information on laser (CD) disks. A replica of the document can be produced and the documents can be sorted in order to provide specific pieces or sets of information. (See section 9.9.)

Inference engine The part of an expert system which handles the 'reasoning' process. This is done by working through previously set rules or paths. (See section 10.1.)

Infrastructure In the context of this book, the hardware and equipment which forms the networked system of communication and information.

ISDN (Integrated Services Digital Network) A set of standards and recommendations being developed in stages by the CCITT (Consultative Committee for International Telephone and Telegraph). The aim of the standards is to eventually integrate all communication systems into one standard telecommunications network. (See section 8.7.)

Just-in-time A manufacturing philosophy which is based on flexibility and responsiveness to the customer. Thus production is governed by customer orders rather than by a predetermined production schedule. Little or no raw material, work in progress or finished goods stock is held. (See section 5.5.)

Knowledge base Part of an expert system which contains the 'expert' knowledge. (See section 10.1.)

Lead time The time it takes to supply a customer with a product or to obtain a component from a supplier.

Local area network (LAN) A network which links PCs, printers, minicomputers, etc. so that resources can be shared or group writing can take place. The network is normally restricted to one building. (See section 7.3.)

Magnetic tape A storage medium for computer programs and data.

Manufacturing resource planning (MRP II) An information system which provides an integrated decision support system for production planning, scheduling and control. (See section 5.7.)

Material requirements planning (MRP I) An information system which analyzes the production plans of a manufactured product. Given knowledge of lead times and component manufacture times, the system provides a schedule of the necessary delivery dates for all the different components and materials which comprize the final product. (See section 5.6.)

Material turnover rate A measure of the speed at which material is taken from stock and used in production during the course of a year. If stock is held for three months before being used in manufacture the turnover rate is said to be four times (a year). If stock is held for only six weeks the turnover rate is 52 weeks divided by 6, i.e. 8.7 times.

Matrix organization structure One which resembles a grid. For instance, the vertical axis may represent a functional division of the organization and the horizontal axis project or product divisions. Each grid cross-over point represents an individual or group of individuals. As a result, each person is responsible to two managers.

Micro-film A photographic technique which provides miniaturized copies of documents on film which may be examined through a 'reader'. Its main benefit is that it requires much less storage space than paper documents. (See section 9.9.)

Modem (MOdulator–DEModulator). A device which changes the digital signals of computers into analogue signals for transmission over traditional telephone cables.

Networkers People who work at home but are connected via a computer and communication network with their employer and others. (See section 8.9.)

On-line A system in which terminals have permanent and immediate access to databases and/or computer processing power.

Operational information This is information which relates to the day-to-day running of the operations of a organization. It may include, for instance, information on how many items, and of which type, were sold yesterday and how many are expected to be sold today, how many people worked for how many hours yesterday, and how much material was used in production.

OSI reference model (open systems interconnection reference model.) A model put forward by the International Standards Organization for standard computer systems and links, so that systems, wherever they may be in the world, can communicate with one another. The model consists of seven layers, three of which deal with standards for networks, three for computer software and one for transporting the communication. (See section 8.5.)

Overhead absorption The process whereby overheads are related to the products or services produced so that a total cost per unit may be calculated. It involves determining the cause of overhead expenditure and relating that to specific products or services.

PCNs (personal communication networks) Communication systems which are being developed at the time of writing to permit communication between individuals (wherever they may be) rather than between fixed places (where the telephones and cables are sited).

Primary activity One which is directly involved in the generation of a product or service as opposed to a support activity.

Primary data Data collected either by, or under the direct supervision of, the investigator or interpreter for a particular survey. (Secondary data are those which have already been collected by others, possibly for different purposes, and are therefore cheaper to use but are liable to be misinterpreted.)

Punched cards Thin rectangular cards which represent an individual data record. They have holes punched in them at specific points and these represent individual pieces of data which can be read by a mechanical or electronic system.

Real-time information Information which is processed and transmitted to users at the moment the event, to which the information relates, occurs.

Reposition To alter the 'position' of a business unit or group of products in the marketplace, by, for instance, moving 'up market'.

Segment Market segment — a section of the total market for a particular product or service which has been differentiated in terms of potential customer needs, requirements or characteristics.

Specialized satellite services operators Specific organizations licensed by the UK government to operate satellite transmission services to anyone who has a receiving dish. (See section 8.11.)

Strategic alliance An alliance between two or more organizations which is of mutual benefit and long lasting. It does not have a specific aim, unlike a joint venture: instead it is a more general relationship which can develop and change over the years.

Strategic information Information which may be required to make strategic decisions, that is decisions about the long-term and shorter-term strategic position of the organization. It will include information about competitors, the development of new products and changes in markets.

Support activity An activity which is only indirectly involved with the generation of a product or service. Its role is to provide services to support those activities which are directly involved in the provision of a product.

Teleconferencing Communication between more than two individuals or between groups of people at different locations. Teleconferencing may refer to either computer messaging systems or to video/audio communication. (See section 8.16.)

Telemarketing Telephoning potential customers with the aim of selling products or services. (See section 8.15.)

3GLs (3rd generation languages) 'Traditional' procedural computer languages which require a high degree of programming skill. They were used almost exclusively between the 1960s and the early 1980s and are still quite popular. Examples are Cobol, Fortran and Pascal.

Value activity An activity which adds value to the business, e.g. the activity allows the selling price of the good or service to be increased by more than the activity's cost. For example, manufacturing, marketing and after sales service functions.

Value added data services (VADS) Telecommunication network services provided by organizations which have been licensed to carry out this function by the government. The services must add value, e.g. access to an information database, and not simply be the provision of a network. (See section 8.12.)

Value added networks (VANs) Licensed organizations which provide some sort of service, over and above the simple transmission of data, to subscribers. (See section 8.12.)

Value added partnership (VAP) A close partnership between two companies in order to manage the flow of goods or services. It is based on the value chain and usually results in an informal type of vertical integration.

Value chain A series of value activities which link to form a value chain for a specific business. (See section 5.4.)

Value system A series of suppliers' and customers' value chains which are linked together to provide a complete value system for a particular company or industry.

Virus An additional piece of programming on a computer program or file which is triggered by some event into replicating itself repeatedly, thus clogging the computer memory. Alternatively it may destroy its host after replication thus wiping out the computer memory. (See section 14.7.)

VSATs (very small aperture terminals) small satellite dishes suitable for voice communication. (See section 8.11.)

Wide area network (WAN) a network which consists of a series of local area networks which are linked via the national telecommunications network or specifically dedicated lines. A WAN may be created for an individual company or for an industry. (See section 7.4.)

Index